CONTENTS

CHAPTER

3

The Interactive Piece   41

CHAPTER

4

Case Studies   53

PART II A Guide for the New Developer 101

CHAPTER 5 The Multimedia Production Team 103

CHAPTER 6 From the Idea to the Content Outline 109

CHAPTER 7 World Building and Metaphors 119

PART III   Nonlinear Script Writing   127

CHAPTER
8   Story, Character, and Structure   129

CHAPTER
9   Script Formatting and Prototypes   143

FOREWORD

Have we become intoxicated by technology? As citizens in this modern world, don't we believe that technology will do about anything, if not now, eventually? I have to admit that I am one who thrills with the technology push—a sort of "technojunkie." But all of us should know by now that gadgetry by itself is short lived—look at all those Commodore 64's that ended up in our closets. The most important thing about any medium is the message, not the technology that conveys it.

We can take some lessons from history. Did TV or radio take off immediately? The answer is no. Both were just curiosities at the beginning. Only after programming became interesting, engaging, and entertaining did TV and radio come alive.

Television has made the most significant technological impact on our culture during this century. But I fear that TV, among other things, has made us brain dead. The sensory barrage of TV is like mind candy; once addicted, we forget how to think and imagine. Pure experience without reflection destroys imagination.

Radio had allowed some room for the imagination. My favorite childhood radio program was *Sergeant Preston of the Yukon.* I still have vivid memories of the worlds I created in my mind as Sgt. Preston and his dog, King, tracked down the bad guys. When my folks brought in the TV, there was no more radio for me—I was hooked on *Captain Midnight.* But try as I might, I don't remember much about my TV-viewing experiences. Tellingly, my favorite and most vivid memories are the ones that my mind created while being stimulated by reading.

But I do remember some of the movies. My favorites were Rodgers and Hammerstein musicals and some epic sci-fi adventures, starting with *Forbidden Planet.* Maybe there is something to seeing a really big picture on the screen. Unfortunately, one of my favorite worlds was destroyed when I saw the cartoon version of *Lord of the Rings*—a real mistake. I had built this marvelous imaginary world with Frodo and Bilbo Baggins and had a delicious mental model of Gollum. The movie destroyed all that. My imaginary world didn't match that of the screenwriter, though mine was better.

Now, digital media have entered the world with their confluence of computation, film, video, audio CD, music, and electronic distribution. These new media bring interactivity—an opportunity to participate again! Indeed, interactive media replace something we have lost in television. We can experience a story but also change it by our actions. The prospects are thrilling!

For example, I have been changed forever by *Myst,* a standard in multimedia entertainment. It's a story, but it's also a world to be explored. Through the freeze-frame tours of the world of *Myst* and its intrigues and problem-solving mysteriousness, I gained a renewed appreciation for what good art and storytelling can be in multimedia.

There is further power in multimedia when networked, as in the World Wide Web. Again, I find myself captivated by the prospect of this information space. I feel like an adventurer probing new kinds of worlds and trailing along some flypaper to collect bits and pieces of the experience.

Perhaps the most intriguing thing about the Web is its novelty. However, it will push the boundaries of nonlinear storytelling as written text is concatenated with animated video and interactive VRML content. Otherwise, Web exploration will be unrewarding. After a session on the Web, I often find myself empty. Electronics cannot make up for the lack of quality content.

Perhaps the ultimate in multimedia may be virtual reality. I have been fascinated by the power of the 3D immersive medium of virtual reality (VR), which my colleagues and I have been developing at the Human Interface Technology Laboratory at the University of Washington. In spite of the initial excitement about an immersive experience, VR also becomes a boring and even lonely place without intelligence in it (either in the design of the world or the entities that inhabit it). By default, most of our worlds are built by hackers, the tool builders. It's like hiring the guy who designed and manufactured the hammer, nails, and saws to build your house. Creating the message in the medium requires a different set of skills. We really do need architects, artists, and storytellers to build these worlds.

So the real challenge is creating content for multimedia. This requires a new level of storytelling that anticipates the thought processes and imagination of the participant and the various paths one can take in nonlinear story lines. Unfortunately, because of its complexity, creating good multimedia titles requires a new mind-set and set of skills beyond just storytelling. It also takes a long time to create these titles, perhaps longer than writing a novel.

How then does one create multimedia content? Michael Korolenko has answered this question. I admire Mike for this work—it's fun. I love his conversational style and the depth and breadth of his understanding about this subject. You will find his book well researched and important for people who will write for multimedia. I also find it a refreshing respite from the pedantic and self-serving pomposity of scholarly publications written by authors who talk about this new world of media but who have not actually done it. Mike Korolenko *has* done it, and now in this volume he has gone the extra mile to help others to do it.

It seems that after the birth of each new medium comes a fear that the new will replace the old. Again history shows that this displacement has not happened. TV didn't kill movies and radio, but it did change them. Similarly we can predict that multimedia will not replace TV, radio, the movies, or even newspapers, but it will make them different. Even now I have to temper my techno-enthusiasm lest I forget that the library is still full of worlds to be explored.

In the end, content is king and always will be. The demand for content is exploding, far exceeding the supply. Creators, designers, and writers are needed—sign up now! Oh, and by the way, don't stop reading books.

Thomas A. Furness, III
Seattle, Washington

PREFACE

"Like a Hollywood film, multimedia narrative includes such specific representations that less and less is left to the mind's eye. By contrast, the written word sparks images and evokes metaphors that get much of their meaning from the reader's imagination."
— Nicholas Negroponte
Being Digital, 1995

"Too many software companies are still too wowed by the technology—and not wowed enough by the stories the technology allows one to tell. A strong narrative presented in an interesting way is far more intriguing than just a lot of video or pictures."
— Frank Catalano
"ByteMe" column, *Eastsideweek,* 3/15/95

THE PURPOSE OF THE TEXT

Until recently, little information has been available for anyone wanting to write for interactive digital media. Even instructors are often confused about the difference between writing multimedia and multimedia **authoring**. The latter consists of a team, particularly the programmer, who utilizes several tools, such as Illustrator, Photoshop, Premiere, Director, and Toolbook. The authoring team can also include a project manager, a graphic designer, an instructional designer, editors, and a subject matter expert (SME).

Most people wouldn't try to shoot a video or program a computer if they didn't have at least some background in these respective areas. Unfortunately, everyone seems to think they're a writer. This attitude has changed somewhat in the film industry, where writers can receive over five million dollars for a screenplay (sometimes in advance of writing it). Even so, a variety of directors, producers, actors, and agents still tend to give input that can radically affect the final screenplay. For example, the screenplay for the "feel-good" film *Pretty Woman* originally included the use of drugs as well as an unhappy ending.

Until very recently, interactive multimedia producers often didn't even consider writers for programs. Since multimedia takes a lot more than just a writer to create it, some writers found themselves hired by multimedia production companies not for their writing skills but primarily for other skills, such as producing and editing.

In autumn 1981, I was hired by a New York firm working with MIT to create an early interactive presentation for the U.S. Pavilion at the 1982 Knoxville World's Fair. Given the fair's theme, "Energy Turns the World," the developers tried to present "energy screens" that allowed the fairgoers control over what type of energy they wanted to learn about. Thus, if a visitor decided to learn about coal, he touched the coal symbol on the screen to bring up a short film about coal. At certain points, the viewer could stop the film and find out more specific things about coal, such as how it's mined or how it's converted into energy. Touching another symbol allowed the viewer to see different individuals speaking on the energy crisis and various forms of energy. For instance, one expert proclaimed how terrific nuclear energy is while another spoke about the dangers of nuclear waste.

This project wasn't so much written as it was cobbled together. Because all of us at the firm were novices, we had to make up the rules as we went along. For organizational reasons, I began to create a guide for myself and others entering this new realm of writing for nonlinear education and entertainment. In the past fifteen years, this guide has grown and changed considerably along with the technology and the variety of multimedia projects and the people involved in their creation.

Writing for Multimedia covers the field of writing for all interactive media, including kiosks, computer and CD-ROM products, interactive movies, and online services. This book will serve as a comprehensive text for the student, detailing writing for the various multimedia markets—from edutainment to interactive games and science-fiction thrillers to documentaries and instructional programs.

The textbook will serve as both guide and sourcebook for the writer of multimedia. It will also allow multimedia producers to understand what processes the writer must go through to achieve the goal of each stage of a program. For the novice, it will define multimedia and give a clear understanding of the technological, cognitive, and creative tools that the writer must use.

Specific programs will be discussed in detail and serve as templates for writers of interactive multimedia. A number of in-depth interviews with both multimedia producers and writers will be presented to give the student some idea of both the background of those involved in new digital media and the various processes these people use in creating their programs. Though one can employ a variety of processes in creating multimedia, most interactive games use a screenplay-for-film format, while many instructional programs use a video teleplay format (both discussed later in the book). All those involved in multimedia, however, agree on the following:

- The writer should know his or her audience.
- The writer must work as part of a team.

Many writers like to go off à la Thomas Pynchon and write for weeks at a time with no feedback except perhaps from one editor. This way of writing has obviously produced many great novels, essays, and short stories. However, it does not produce good multimedia. Along with writing skills, multimedia writers need both communication and social skills. This may prove difficult for some writers, especially those who become attached to their characters and dialog. However, developing a multimedia project offers writers a way to socialize with small groups of people interested in the same things they are.

Finally, I hope that this text will teach students to develop their nonlinear writing skills, instruct them in a variety of useful techniques (from the use of metaphors to the plotting of pathways), and describe a variety of tools and methods (such as storyboards, flip-books, and computer prototypes) for approaching this new and limitless creative horizon.

ACKNOWLEDGMENTS

My heartfelt thanks to the following people:

- All those who graciously allowed me to interview them, many times in spite of their own heavy schedules: Andrew Anker, Theolene Bakken, Tony Bove, Emma Bull, Frank Catalano, Neil Gaiman, Al Lowe, Janis Machala, Drew Miller, Susan Palwick, Paul Saffo, Rob Schmults, Lorelei Shannon, Alex Shapiro, Delia Sherman, William Shetterly, Terry Weston, Terri Windling, and Ruth Zaslow.
- The people at Sierra On-Line, Inc., particularly Eddie Ranchigoda, Kathy Gilmore, and Rebecca Buxton.
- Robin Worley.
- Mary Francis Feider and Tracy Van Hoof for the images from Microsoft.
- Jim Gallant and Bradley J. Watson at CORBIS.
- Charles Platt for the use of his wonderful article from *Wired*. J. Dianne Brinson and Mark F. Radcliffe for the use of their *Intellectual Property Law Primer for Multimedia Developers*.
- Anthony J. Margherita, M.D., and Lynn Gottlieb of Harborview Medical Center.
- Leslie Johnson-Evers, Tim Hulley, Ursula Acosta, Helayne Waldman and Amanda Moore for their support and help with this text; Jim Benton for his terrific CBT material; Steven Conrad of MediaPro; Tim Rohrer for his excellent material on the use of Metaphor; and that guy with the shorts at Egghead Software who kept mumbling "plastics" one hot summer day.
- My friends and colleagues at Bellevue Community College, one of the most supportive environments I've ever worked in: Dr. Michael L. Talbott, Dr. James L. Bennett, Rhonda Davis, Jim Shuman (who was instrumental in bringing Wadsworth and me together), Christopher James, Suzanne Marks, Genevieve Tremblay, Peggy Benz, Tim Kennedy, Mark M. Elliott, College President Jean B. Floten, and the folks in Technology Services including Gary Mahn, Tom O'Rourke, and Mike Dunn.
- Special thanks to Bruce Wolcott, Clay Sherman, Reilly Jensen, and Matt Robkin—past students who did research for this text and who are now in the position to teach the teacher, and to Dr. Tom Furness of the Human Interface Technology Lab at the University of Washington, for his continuing support, advice, and eloquence.

- I thank the following manuscript reviewers for their constructive criticism and helpful comments: Jeff M. Gold, Tennessee Technological University; John J. Hirschbuhl, The University of Akron; Greg Sherman, Emporia State University; and Judith E. Wakefield, University of Central Oklahoma.
- Thanks to Molly Roth, manuscript editor, and to Greg Hubit of Bookworks. And, to my editor and publisher at Wadsworth, Kathy Shields, as well as to Tamara Huggins.

And of course, thanks to my parents, for their constant support and for being tactful yet important noodges to "get the thing done already."

Michael Korolenko
Bellevue, Washington

Background

1

Multimedia—
What It Is, Where
It Comes From

"A multimedia CD-ROM works best when there's a compelling approach, perspective, or narrative that the media and interactive aspects support and help propel, not just when there's enough room to fill a CD-ROM disc to overflowing. As multimedia moves out of the Talkies stage, customers won't be satisfied just to hear someone speak. They'll actually want them to have something to say."
— Frank Catalano, "ByteMe" column, *Eastsideweek* 3/15/95

"The future isn't what it used to be."
That quote is attributed to both the writer Arthur C. Clarke and the poet Paul Valery. Whoever said it first, the statement is undeniably true. Not only is the future not what it used to be, but the present itself seems like some science fiction novel, perhaps one part *Brave New World,* one part *Neuromancer,* and one part *Do Androids Dream of Electric Sheep?*

More than just a buzzword in this digital present, *multimedia* has become the key to a kind of Holy Grail—a world where interactive technology, combined with the untapped power of the **Net,** will give everyone the opportunity to be entertained, educated, and enlightened by the best the world has to offer. Many people also feel that it offers everyone the opportunity to become completely addicted to their telecomputer or virtuphone or whatever the ultimate multimedia device will be called.

The Components of Multimedia

Before writing for any medium, be it books, films, television, or multimedia, one must first understand the technology of that medium. In the excellent text *Multimedia: Gateway to the Next Millennium,* Robert Aston and Stanley Klein state that, by definition, "multimedia must contain interactivity whereby a user becomes a participant in the communications, even a director or creator."[1]

They continue, "The content in new media must have an entertainment quality or intellectual level that compels a user into an interactive environment."[2] In other words, **multimedia** must engage its audience and cause them to *want* to be interactive.

The merging of many technologies has produced what people today call *interactive multimedia.* Because it is still so new, this development is not easily defined. Michael J. Miller, in his article "Multimedia," writes, "Trying to describe multimedia brings to mind the words of Supreme Court Justice Potter Stewart: 'I can't define it, but I know it when I see it.' "[3]

The best definition of interactive multimedia I've found comes from the Extended Education Multimedia Studies Program at San Francisco State University. Professor Robert Bell wrote that "multimedia is the convergence of computers with video, film, sound, graphics, and text. It is described as a 'technological loom'* that weaves media together."[4] The program guide goes on to state that "multimedia promises to give people of all kinds and classes the power to seek, learn, create and present information. It is an emerging technological force creating new industries, new jobs, new art."[5] In *How Multimedia Works,* Erik Holsinger similarly writes, "Multimedia has the potential to be one of the most powerful forms of communicating ideas, searching for information, and experiencing new concepts of any communication media ever developed. This is simply because multimedia *incorporates* every type of media ever developed."[6]

Here is a description of the components that make up multimedia: sound, video, and digital storage.

SOUND

Sound components include CD or digital audio, waveform audio, and MIDI. True CD or **digital audio** can almost duplicate reality. Sound is read directly off a disc. **Waveform audio** lets you create sound by **digitizing** an analog audio waveform and then storing the digital sample on a disc or hard drive.

MIDI, or Musical Instrument Digital Interface, has no intrinsic sound of its own. Through MIDI, electronic musical instruments can communicate both with the computer and with each other. MIDI will receive a string of computer commands and then create a sound from a group of preset sounds and play it through speakers.

VIDEO

Video components necessary for interactive multimedia include a **graphics adapter,** which is either a card installed in a slot on your computer or a chip on the **motherboard.** It lets you display computer-generated text and graphics,

---

* Originally stated by Christopher Evans in his book *The Micro Millennium* published by Viking Press in 1980.

scanned images, and animation. Basically, the graphics adapter links your computer to your monitor.

There are also **video adapters,** which accept input from a variety of video sources that use NTSC (National Television Standard Committee) standards. In recent years, developers have produced video adapter boards that convert analog to **digital** video images that you can display on your computer monitor. **Video capture boards** or *frame grabbers* let you digitize a single frame from your NTSC source and store it on your hard disc. **Full-motion video boards** digitize and then compress multiple frames and store them in your computer. This allows you to create special effects as well as **nonlinear editing,** in which you manipulate images stored digitally on your hard drive. This is much easier than linear editing, where you might have any number of videotapes you have to go through to find the takes you want to use. All nonlinear editing systems, from D-Vision to the Avid, make use of this digital conversion of analog video.

DIGITAL STORAGE

Last, you must have sufficient *digital storage* capacity for using interactive multimedia. Of course, your computer has a **hard disc,** which retrieves information quickly. Today's hard drives can hold as much as 1 to 4 gigabytes of information, but drives that hold that much information cost more than a **CD-ROM.**

When CD-ROMs first entered the marketplace, most computers had very limited disc space on them. Even today's much bigger hard drives often do not provide enough storage for audio and video files. Most multimedia today utilizes the CD-ROM, which generally stores a little over 600 megabytes of data. Many argue that the industry has, for the time being, made the CD-ROM the storage standard mainly because it does the job at a relatively low price. Under ideal conditions, a CD or compact disc should theoretically last a very long time. However, CDs are not indestructible. Air can get under the plastic cover and onto the metal disc where the information is encoded and the metal could rust. However, compared with long-playing records that can warp and scratch or videotape that can tear, crease, or exhibit dropout (video information lost for various reasons), CDs seem positively invulnerable.

The Recent Growth of Multimedia

Already, multimedia capabilities are becoming part of the standard personal computer (PC) platform. Because most PC users now usually have multimedia capabilities that run faster than predicted a few years ago, a burgeoning industry has grown, encompassing both independents and major corporations. Now, Hollywood is getting into the act, as agents and agencies, now as powerful as the studio moguls of the recent past, seek out independent multimedia producers. As the L.A. Times writer Amy Harmon puts it, "Ten percent of the deal—the agent's traditional fee—seems rather costly to many start-ups working out of their kitchens."[7]

To put it bluntly, though many in Hollywood are interested in multimedia, most people in the film industry have no idea what multimedia is, let alone what its current capabilities and limitations are. Even people integrally involved in multimedia still grope at making engaging, interesting, and salable products.

Multimedia also presents special challenges and opportunities to those who make their living as writers. "For adults, the term *multimedia literature* may seem an oxymoron, but talking, moving, responsive books and magazines are distinctly in our future."[8] Or, perhaps, our present: Already "users can hear the dinosaurs roar in Jurassic Park or watch Huckleberry Finn float downstream on his raft."[9]

There were over 500 CD-ROM books as of fall 1994,[10] and that figure will likely more than double in the late 1990s. Many magazines, including *Newsweek* and *Time,* are now both online and interactive. The idea of an electronic newspaper or electronic magazine makes a lot of sense to those in the publishing industry: "Letters" to the editor might be answered almost instantaneously; a user who wants more information on an article might easily find it; users might even interact directly with people in the news and journalists. In fact, the newspaper or magazine might become the main source of news and information in the next five years, supplanting television for the first time since the early 1960s.

In the spring of 1995, *American Heritage* went online. In his editorial for the July–August 1995 issue, Richard F. Snow writes somewhat facetiously of how he once felt the "newspeak" of our era—words such as *interface, modem,* and *Internet*—were corrupting the language. However, to his surprise, he soon discovered that interactive multimedia, especially on the **Internet,** could make history come alive: "I found, for instance, a debate about which was the *worst* fighter-bomber of World War II. ... Elsewhere in the ether (or whatever it is) I came upon a dense and very high-level discussion about what sort of compromises in the decade before the Civil War might have averted the test of arms."[11] Now, the "American Heritage Picture Gallery" is on Prodigy. Within the year, it will present some 500 pictures users can look at and learn about.

Roadblocks and Benefits of Multimedia

Obviously, interactive multimedia has arrived, and many are jumping on the interactive multimedia bandwagon. But exactly what jobs are available for the writer of multimedia, and what jobs will be created in the future? And what of the problems inherent in this new technology?

Wayne Bitterman, the founder of the Bellevue Community College Media Program, has noted that "the job you will get in media probably doesn't exist yet." So, the first problem with interactive multimedia is that the product of 1999 might differ substantially from that of 1996.

Furthermore, there is still no universal standard for interactive multimedia. You can find CD-ROMS, laser discs, game cartridges, computer software, and online communications (possibly the interactive medium of the future).

According to Dataquest Incorporated—a global market research and consulting company that serves the high-technology and financial communities—the number of multimedia CD-ROM titles tripled in 1994, with games, reference books, and education titles the biggest hits with consumers. However, Bruce Ryan, the director of the company's Multimedia Worldwide program, has pointed out that "along with the battle for retail shelf space, the profit margin squeeze is choking developers as the average factory selling price of CD-ROM titles has sunk to an all-time low."[12]

A student of mine, Tim Hulley, has written a concise essay describing both the upside and the downside of multimedia:

> Depending on how it is utilized, multimedia (could easily be) a very useful learning tool that allows individualized interaction and access to enormous amounts of data. Conversely, it would also become a typical form of American entertainment, with excessive amounts of violence and sexual material. At its worst, multimedia could be a deadening, passive pursuit; the computer equivalent (of today's television), prompting an odd blend of hyperactivity and apathy. Currently, the major roadblocks to more effective multimedia are in the technical realm.[13]

Obviously, multimedia presents many potential benefits. It already provides, for example, education for children and adults, informational kiosks, electronic publishing, artistic expression, and entertainment. Flooded with thousands of multimedia products and titles, the market offers subjects ranging from history to ecological preservation, from Stephen Hawkings on the universe to reading lessons from animated characters. "One of the great benefits of multimedia is that it can present large amounts of information in an interesting way. Educational and historical materials, in particular, are conducive to this approach."[14]

A History of Multimedia

At this point, you might ask, "Just when and where did the road towards the "interactive" future begin?"

In *Wired* magazine, Charles Platt maintains that every time a parent tells a child a story, they are engaging in interactivity. He writes that Barbara Hayes-Roth of the Knowledge Systems Laboratory at Stanford pointed out to him that *"Alice in Wonderland* was originally told as a tale to a schoolgirl who asked questions, raised objections, and made requests. In this way, the written version evolved from a process of genuine interactivity."[15]

In fact, one is tempted to say that interactivity really began thousands of years ago when a village shaman told a story to a group of people who then embellished it for the next group of people, and so on. For purposes of time and space, however, I shall focus on technologically based interactivity, beginning with the Chicago World's Fair of 1893.

INVENTIONS AT THE WORLD'S FAIR

The World's Columbian Exposition of 1893 exhibited the marvels of the next century for all to see. Presumably a celebration of the 400th anniversary of Columbus's landing in the New World, this "White City" of the future served as a showpiece for American ingenuity and invention—the apex of an era Mark Twain had dubbed "The Gilded Age." For perhaps the first time, the technology that would eventually evolve into multimedia was shown to vast audiences in a single location.

With demonstrations of long-distance telephone calls, Thomas Edison's kinetoscopes heralding the birth of motion pictures, and live orchestra music transmitted over wires from New York City, the public could view all the marvels the coming century had to offer, including Elisha Gray's wondrous tele-autograph—a device that transmitted facsimile writing and drawings—the first fax machine.[16]

Not long before the fair opened, in the spring of 1893, the inventor Nikola Tesla made the first public demonstration of radio communication in St. Louis. Invited personally by George Westinghouse, Tesla presided over exhibits in the Palace of Electricity at the Chicago Fair.[17]

Neither the purveyors of the fair nor the inventors could foresee, let alone exhibit, how these new technologies would affect the way people viewed "reality." The exhibits showed people how they might have a "home projected kinetoscope" in their houses in thirty years and presented teleautographs or "picturephones," but they never touched on the potential economic, sociological, and political effects of the new technology. Any predictions that were made at this and all the world's fairs of the late nineteenth and twentieth centuries merely projected the morals and etiquette of the times. Few people have realized that new technology not only changes etiquette but by its nature makes it necessary to invent new etiquette. Similarly, interactive multimedia requires a whole new way of writing.

TRAVELING THROUGH TIME: EARLY FILM

Interestingly enough, the same year the Chicago Fair opened, H. G. Wells's *The Time Machine* appeared in *The Strand* magazine. An early film pioneer, Robert Paul, noted the novella and contacted Wells. Initially, Paul was intrigued that Wells used "cinematic" or kinetoscopic techniques in his story, as in this section, when the time traveler first begins his trip: "The Laboratory got hazy and went dark. Mrs. Watchett came in ... and walked toward the garden door. I suppose it took her a minute or so to traverse the place, but to me she seemed to shoot across the room like a rocket."[18]

Later on in the story, the narrator describes Mrs. Watchett going backward, much like a film in reverse.

Of course, Wells wasn't the first to include such scenes in a story—just take a look at Dickens's *A Christmas Carol*: "Scrooge's former self grew larger at the words, and the room became a little darker and more dirty. The panels shrunk, the windows cracked; fragments of plaster fell out of the ceiling, and the naked laths were shown instead."[19]

In Wells's day, one could accomplish such "time traveling" with moving pictures, as this anonymous editorial from the *St. Louis Dispatch* notes: "The kinetoscope, we are told, has recently been made to run backwards, and the effects of this way of running it are truly marvelous. ... The effect is said to be almost miraculous. In the process of eating, food is taken from the mouth and placed on the plate."[20]

Considered a poor person's entertainment, the kinetoscope was usually on display in arcades, as virtual reality games are today, and the first interactive games were some fifteen to twenty years ago. Wells and Paul, however, hoped to improve on linear moving pictures. In 1895, they patented a "novel form of entertainment" they hoped would liberate the spectator from the here and now. Wells and Paul wanted to lead their audience "back and forth along the infinite line of time,"[21] to give spectators the ability to travel from past to future to present in any order they desired. The effect would result from a series of moving platforms, magic lantern slides, projected motion pictures—"successive instantaneous photographs after the manner of the kinetoscope," as Paul called it—and sound effects. Wells and Paul hoped to create nothing less than a Victorian interactive multimedia presentation. Alas, this "time machine" was never built. In this way, Wells and Paul's machine was not unlike "The Difference Engine," a computer conceived by Charles Babbage in 1822. In both cases, neither machine was constructed because the components to make them work could not be fabricated.[22] One might correctly assume from these examples that no idea is really new, just the technology that can make it a reality.

The actual birth of "successive instantaneous photographs after the manner of the kinetoscope" took place in 1908, when D. W. Griffith began to assemble the mechanical and optical properties of the motion picture into a new art form.

"RADIO-PLAYS"

During these same years, Guglielmo Marconi, after having his new invention, a wireless means of communication, rejected by the Italian government, took the invention to England and later to the United States. Interestingly enough, both Marconi and Tesla claimed that they had received radio signals from the planet Mars.[23] In 1904, John Fleming developed the vacuum tube, which would pave the way for actual voice transmission over Marconi's "wireless." Near that time, Reginald Fessenden proposed that radio waves be sent out continuously rather than in bursts as they had been. This way, one could superimpose a voice on the wave.

In 1906, L. Frank Baum decided to present his Oz stories in the form he called "Fairylogue and Radio-Plays." Baum's shows combined a live orchestra, actors on stage, Baum himself as the narrator, magic lantern slides, and hand-colored motion picture film (invented by Michael Radio, whose name appears in the title). Though successful, the show closed in New York City in 1908 because of the expenses involved in producing it.[24] These "fairylogues" might be tagged as the first traveling multimedia shows. Baum's original and inventive technical innovations (such as two strips of film used to show Dorothy being flung about in the open sea) were soon outdone by new technologies.

EXPERIMENTS WITH TELEVISION

In the meantime, experimentation with television broadcasting had been going on for many years. In 1884, Paul Nipkow created a mechanical scanning wheel. The wheel, containing tiny holes, was set in front of a picture. As the wheel turned, each hole scanned one line of the picture. In the 1920s, Ernst Alexanderson used the system to fabricate a missile attack on New York by scanning an aerial photo of the city, moving closer and closer until the picture disappeared in an explosion. Seventy years later, audiences would watch a similar but real image as missiles with tiny cameras rained down on Baghdad during Operation Desert Storm.

During the twenties, the researchers from General Electric, RCA, and Westinghouse worked together to solve problems in the fledgling technology. They increased the number of scanning lines, along with definition, brightness, and image size. In 1928, Felix the Cat became the first televised personality, his image sent from New York City to Kansas City, picked up by sixty-line experimental television sets.

Television had intrigued futurists for years. As Joseph Corn and Brian Horrigan wrote in *Yesterday's Tomorrows,*

> Throughout the 1920's and '30s, the idea of television in our future heated the popular imagination as few technologies ever have. The range of predictions for television technology was broad, and most are outlandish in retrospect, but with the technology so unproved all predictions had more or less equal claim on plausibility. Doctors would diagnose patients in the future via television; civilians would help the military spot enemy planes with television. There might even be *Murder by Television*, a murky and altogether dreadful movie of 1935, in which Bela Lugosi plays a dual role. ...
>
> In much of popular culture, television was seen as a future means of two-way communication, rather than what it truly became, that is, essentially a one-way medium devoted to mass entertainment on the model of broadcast radio. 'Radio finds its eyes,' announced the Saturday Evening Post, in a felicitous phrase of 1929.[25]

Mainstream writers also found the idea of television fascinating. As far back as 1909, E. M. Forster, in *The Machine Stops,* wrote of a future where human beings live in a hivelike environment, completely isolated from each other and the outside world. Their only means of communication was television.

By 1932, experimental broadcasts were transmitted from the Empire State Building. In 1935, David Sarnoff, the president of RCA, announced that the company would invest millions of dollars to develop the new medium. "Television ... will give new wings to the talents of creative and interpretive genius," Sarnoff announced.[26] A *National Geographic* article relects RCA's success in a report on the world's fair: "Odd, futuristic-looking sound trucks you may meet, too, with poles sticking up on top like masts. These are the RCA television trucks. At the World's Fair of 1939, this first baby of radio takes its first step in public. Though on a very small curtain, with reception limited to points within 50 miles of the sending station, RCA will give World's Fair visitors their first taste of television."[27] President Roosevelt, opening the fair "to all mankind," was broadcast by television. And so, RCA and Westinghouse, which had its own television studio in its pavilion, presented the medium of tomorrow as the world stood on the cusp between the Depression and World War II.

In 1941, stations went on the air, some 10,000 sets were sold, and the first commercial television time was bought by the Bulova Watch Company. However, by 1942, except for air-raid-warden training films broadcast by NBC, all broadcasting stopped for the duration of the war. Unfortunately, television, with many other ideas put forth by the 1939 fair, would have to wait until the end of World War II to emerge from its infancy.

In Germany, television had been broadcasting since the 1936 Olympics, and programming continued to air during the war. However, German television was used not for family viewing, but as a group event. Mass viewings took place in special television sitting rooms. Nazi rallies were specifically tailored to the new medium, making them perhaps the first use of television for propaganda.[28]

PROCESSING INFORMATION

Although television in America would not come into its own until the war ended, radio became an extremely powerful and potent medium. Audiences were eerily reminded of Orson Welles's fake 1938 martian invasion broadcast as Edward R. Murrow reported live from London, with bombs literally exploding around him during the blitz.

During this period, reporters used phonograph discs to record radio broadcasts. Towards the end of the war, however, a new system of recording emerged. American soldiers entering German radio stations found them void of people, operated by machines using clear-sounding plastic recording tape. These tape recorders were confiscated and sent to America where they would eventually revolutionize broadcasting.

As the war drew to a close, Vannevar Bush, the director of the Office of Scientific Research and Development, published an article in which he predicted, among other things, microfilm that developed instantly and would be accessed by a MEMEX desk machine, basically a desktop computer. Bush described it as "a device in which an individual stores all his books, records and communications, and which is mechanized so that it may be consulted with exceeding speed and flexibility."[29] In fact, the MEMEX would interactively (and instantly) bring files and materials to the operator's fingertips, using icons and symbols on the bottom of a translucent screen.

In the same article, Bush remarked on the future of computers:

The advanced arithmetical computation machines of the future will be electrical in nature and will perform at 100 times present speeds or more. Moreover, they will be far more versatile than present commercial machines, so that they may readily be adapted for a wide variety of operations. ... They will select their own data and manipulate it in accordance with the instructions. ... They will perform complex arithmetical computations and they will record results in such form as to be readily available for distribution or for later further manipulation.[30]

Of course, the picture of Bush's thinking machine shows it taking up the entire floor of an office building. The point, however, is that Bush's fifty-year-old article shows insight into the way the mind works, how technology that imitates the human mind might expand our horizons, and why something like interactive multimedia is so exciting now that it is a reality.

The same year Bush made his predictions about the MEMEX, Arthur C. Clarke came up with the notion of communication satellites, an idea that would bloom nearly twenty years later.

A VIEWING PUBLIC

With the end of World War II, more and more people began to buy television sets and sat enthralled in front of small, flickering images. By the end of the decade, television was affecting people's lives subtly and not so subtly. For example, on Tuesday nights, attendance at dining establishments, sports events, and motion picture theaters declined to almost nothing as millions tuned in to watch *The Milton Berle Show*.[31]

As television technology improved and literally hundreds of new stations received their licenses, television purchases in the United States exploded. At the end of 1949, there were a million sets in U.S. homes. Three years later, there were sets in some fifteen million U.S. homes.[32]

By 1961, television had become a fact of life in most households. This was the year Newton Minow, appointed the chairman of the FCC by President Kennedy, addressed the National Association of Broadcasters. It was in this address that Minow coined the term "vast wasteland," which became a metaphor for U.S. television programming. Minow went on: "You will see a procession of game shows, violence, audience participation shows, formula comedies about totally unbelievable families, blood and thunder, mayhem, violence, western badmen, western good men, private eyes, gangsters, more violence and cartoons. And endlessly, commercials—many screaming, cajoling, and offending. ... Is there one person in this room who claims that broadcasting can't do better?"[33]

THE SIXTIES

The Future Is Now In 1962, another world's fair once again proposed the future of the media. Seattle's Twenty-First-Century Exposition featured the Bubblelater, a Plexiglas-covered elevator that raised audiences into the next century via pictures, films, and models that flashed in succession: "And how will our descendants learn? The artists' images show schools where television and electronic teaching machines assist human instructors; libraries whose books have been digested by computers and whose readers may order, electronically, sections from any author on a pertinent subject."[34]

According to the exhibits, business offices would use audio-visual communications systems in the next century, and homes would have computers.

The U.S. Science Pavilion boasted two major media exhibits, both using motion picture technology. The first, the Boeing Spacearium, projected 35mm film images onto a dome-surface screen. The second exhibit, designed by Charles Eames, dealt with the history of science. He mechanically synchronized seven 35mm projectors together so that they ran simultaneously, creating one of the first multi-image theater installations.[35]

That same year, AT&T and NASA launched the Telstar I communications satellite. Arthur C. Clarke's 1945 prediction had come true.

The following year, 1963, new ideas about electronic media came from the typewriter of Marshall McLuhan. In his book, *Understanding Media,* McLuhan coined the phrase *Global Village,* stating that the new media were reordering people's senses, weaning them from the habit of collecting information "linearly" from the printed page. With television and the media of the future, an electronic tribal culture without bounds would be created.[36]

During the same period, television began to enter the classroom in earnest. In business and research, people referred more and more to "information retrieval." It seemed to some as if the news, information, and history would soon be coming to them via television or computers. Not coincidentally, the mid-1960s saw the death of myriad newspapers and magazines. Stewart Alsop wrote then of the demise of the *Saturday Evening Post:* "Television threatens to engulf the written word like a blob from outer space. The decay of the written word, of which the *Saturday Evening Post*'s death is a symbol, is surely a tragedy, and maybe not a very small tragedy either."[37]

More World's Fairs   New York's "unofficial" world's fair began in 1964. More a showplace for products and corporations than a display of international unity, the fair did offer some glimpses into new media and how it might eventually affect the world. The Johnson Wax Pavilion used three screens to show the film *To Be Alive,* an eighteen-minute piece depicting, as the fair catalog put it, "the joys of living shared by all people."[38] Scenes of children at play in Africa, North and South America, and a variety of other regions were shown at the same time via split-screen effects. (Such imagery would be used thirty years later by Watts-Silverstein and Associates for their CD-ROM highlighting families and cultures from around the world).[39] Across the Avenue of Commerce, the IBM building housed a 500-seat "people wall" that rose into an egg-shaped theater housing fifteen screens that showed "how computers and the human mind solve problems in much the same way."[40]

Multiscreen films would also prove popular at the Montreal World's Fair, Expo '67. In La Ronde, the Expo's amusement area, people could experience the Laterna Magika, which simultaneously combined movie and transparency projection, sound recording, and live action. Pioneered in Europe, the technique was one of the first well-known "multi-media" extravaganzas.

Bruce Wolcott, a multimedia developer, recalls the expo:

This fair really had some mindboggling experiments with multimedia technology as it existed back then. There are two exhibits that stand out in my mind. The first was a Czechoslovakian exhibit which made use of hundreds of slide projectors in gigantic screen matrixes that were synchronized with sound. The second was "The Labyrinth." In this exhibit, people experienced first-hand a core archetypal symbol from the collective unconscious: the labyrinth, which makes its appearance in cultures and stories from all over the world. You underwent a journey through a maze of corridors that at one point opened up onto a gallery where you could see huge movies projected on three gigantic screens. It depicted old age, birth, the work world ... every person's life magnified. Then people were led into a darkened corridor, which was actually lined with mirrors, so that when they turned on these tiny lights, it looked like you were standing in the midst of an infinity of stars. The finale had you enter a darkened theater, which showed an African native on a terrifying nighttime hunt for a crocodile.

This experience was so bizarre and wonderful I'm not sure whether it really happened or if I am just remembering some kind of delirium I had once when I was sick with the flu.[41]

There was also an "interactive-movie" where the audience, by way of a split screen and two projectors that responded to buttons on the arms of the theater seats, could interact with an on-screen murder mystery: deciding who is the victim, the murderer, etc.

Summer of Love   While people marveled at these new forms of entertainment, on the other side of the continent the counterculture was in full bloom. During the so-called summer of love, a number of "be-ins" and "happenings" took place in and around San Francisco. Luria Castell of The Family Dog described what was going on to the writer Ralph Gleason: "We want to bring in the artistic underground, use light machines, boxes projecting a light pulse from the tonal qualities of the music ... I think that rock 'n' roll people are just starting to know how to use their instruments. They're doing new things in electronics, the generation brought up in the insanity ... Young people today are torn between the insanity and the advances of the electronic age."[42]

One event in particular would influence numerous "hippie" artists who would one day serve on the front lines of digital communication: The Trips Festival, a three-day event held in January 1967 at the Longshore Hall, boasted a multimedia light show: "There were five movie screens up on the wall and projectors for the flicks and other light mixes spread around the balcony. A huge platform in the middle of the room housed the engineers who directed the sound and the lights. Loudspeakers ringed the hall and were set up under the balcony and in the entrance ... Stroboscopic lights set at vantage points beamed down into the crowd and lissome maidens danced under them for hours, whirling jewelry."[43]

The Space Race   As the quagmire of Vietnam, the social and political revolutions, and the growing violence in the streets played themselves out every night in American living rooms, another revolution was taking place—in computer and video technology. In its own way, this quiet, almost unnoticed revolution would have a more profound effect on our way of life than any of the manifestos touted by either college students or politicians of the period. Spurred in part by the space race, technicians developed video cameras small enough to be handled by astronauts on the moon, as well as more compact and faster computers. At universities and colleges, researchers worked on developing interactive computer-based multimedia. At the same time, computer scientists were quietly changing the future of communications as they attempted to build a computer network that would enable researchers around the country to share ideas.[44] By the 1990s, the Internet would be a fact of life, used not only by researchers but also by students, librarians, lawyers, and computer users.

THE SEVENTIES

In November 1970, *Look* magazine put out a special issue on "The Now Hollywood." The articles on the new movie ratings, the new faces of Hollywood, the new moguls, and the "new sex styles" today read as exactly what they are: pieces written twenty-five years ago, separate from the way we are today as if by light years. But, hidden between glossy photographs of the newest stars and Paul Mazursky directing the "now" movie *Alex in Wonderland* are pieces that gave the reader of 1970 a glimpse into the near future.

John Kronenberger wrote a one-page article entitled "Push Button Movies: The Video-Cassette Revolution," in which he projected that eight years into the future consumers would be able to pop a cartridge containing the movie *Butch Cassidy and the Sundance Kid* on video and watch it whenever they wanted to. He mentioned what was already available: expensive but crude video cassette machines and tapes that offered only fifty minutes of black and white or twenty-five minutes of color taping. Kronenberg also mentioned the incompatibility of different "VTR" systems, a problem that would come to a head in the early 1980s, when Sony's higher-quality Betamax system lost out to the more compatible VHS system. But Kronenberg and others knew that another revolution was on the way: "As the costs come down, as the range of items available grows, the video-cassette revolution seems inevitable. And somebody will have to be providing the content for it. Will it be what is still called Hollywood?"[45]

Future Shock At about this time, Alvin Toffler coined the phrase *future shock,* the title of his 1970 book. In it he argued that, once upon a time, any obvious change took centuries to be observed. During the last 150 years, though, change became apparent from decade to decade. According to Toffler, change was continuing to accelerate. One had only to look at the quickly changing technology to realize the truth in Toffler's theory: from vacuum tubes to transistors to integrated circuit chips in less than fifty years.

In 1970, the Museum of Natural History in New York, to honor the first Earth Day, hosted a temporary exhibit called "Can Man Survive?" I remember this exhibit fondly: Audiences walked into a series of enclosed tunnels filled with the sounds and images of industrial society. Looped audio tapes and 16mm films showed everything from garbage dumps to tree-planting ceremonies. I still remember the final image I saw as I exited the place: a piece of scrawled graffiti on the wall that read, "We have met the enemy and he is us—Pogo Possum."

Media Mix and The New York Experience   The early and mid-1970s saw the start-up of many multi-image companies that employed multiple projectors and slide shows for mainly corporate clients. In 1972, Bruce Wolcott had the chance to work on a multimedia programmer, put out by Spindler and Sauppe, called Media Mix. "It involved running a strip of punch tape across a metal head containing switches. When a punch hole traveled over a switch, it sent a signal to a dissolve unit that controlled transitions between slide projectors. Programming and playback was a nightmare because it kept going out of sync."[46]

In 1975, Wolcott was working on an internship at Motiva, Ltd. Motiva's president, Robert Schwartz, had developed an early multimedia programmer in which holes were punched into a wide band of tape. When this tape was run through the programmer, it would travel over a series of sensor lights, with each hole triggering a series of slide projectors. These projectors stood behind a screen display called a "matrix module." The images in these multiple slide projectors were synchronized with music to create composite pictures and graphics. This story-telling medium could hop around in time and show multiple perspectives simultaneously. That year, Motiva had displays at Penn Station, the Museum of Natural History, and the New York City Museum.[47]

"The New York Experience" also opened during the mid-1970s. Billed as a multimedia experience, it was the first of several similar exhibits that opened across the country. It featured everything from a dummy representing the body of the hanged patriot Nathan Hale dropping from the roof to fog rolling into the audience. " 'The New York Experience' used multiple 16mm motion picture projectors, about twenty to thirty slide projectors, smoke, strobe lights, curtains, surround sound ... the whole enchilada. The event was integrated by a media programmer put out by Arion."[48]

A "black box" controlled both audio and visual media for the show. In time, the black box was becoming a new medium unto itself as "the personal computer and other media were added—film, video, live action, music, and props. The integrated output was stored on videotape, optical discs, motion picture film, and other information storage media."[49]

***Pong* and Other Games**   At this time, the first interactive arcade game arrived: *Pong*. Most readers under the age of fifty-five will most likely remember playing this electronic Ping-Pong game in a pub or arcade. The correct term for *Pong* and similar games is **interactive video,** which allows the user to move and control an image on a video screen, television screen, or monitor.

In 1975, Ed Roberts advertised the Altair 8800, a computer kit with 256 bytes of memory. It sold for $397. Hoping to sell a total of four or five hundred of the new machine, Roberts took that many orders in one afternoon. The age of the personal computer had begun.[50]

In 1977, *Zork,* "the first commercially distributed interactive adventure game,"[51] appeared. Written by MIT students using a PDP-10 mainframe computer, the game had users enter commands on a keyboard to find a hidden treasure. "The game could be freely accessed through Arpanet [the forerunner of the Internet]. A year later, it was rewritten in Fortran and became a well-known time waster in computer labs throughout the world."[52]

THE EIGHTIES AND NINETIES

In the late 1970s, the three American television networks hit their peak of popularity, just before television entered a period of massive changes. During the 1980s, a restructuring of U.S. television and radio took place mainly because of economic factors. A series of mergers, acquisitions, and new start-up companies resulted in many new networks, including FOX Television, Turner Broadcasting, Showtime, and MTV. In fact, the average share of the prime-time viewership of the "big three" (NBC, CBS, and ABC) went from 85 percent in 1980 to 67 percent in 1989.[53]

Television had changed from a unified medium geared toward mass appeal to a fractionalized medium appealing to smaller audience groups. With the VCR and the remote control, audiences no longer felt compelled to stay tuned to one channel for the evening. In fact, using the remote control to zip through a variety of channels led to a new phrase: *channel surfing.*

In the meantime, the market for personal computers continued to grow. According to Michael J. Miller, "You can look at much of the history of the computer industry as a series of additions of various kinds of information to the user interface, culminating in this grand design called multimedia."[54] Miller also points out that personal computers in the early 1980s added the ability to work in a graphical mode, "but typically only at a lower resolution that was not sufficient for text."[55]

In 1981, a New York firm and MIT put together one of the first truly interactive exhibits using the cutting edge of laser and computer technology. Designed for the U.S. Pavilion at the 1982 Knoxville World's Fair, the exhibit supported the fair's theme, "Energy Turns the World." This interactive exhibit offered different views on the energy crisis and provided inspiration to writers, filmmakers, videographers, and technicians and scientists at MIT's Media Lab.

Some scientists began talking about a "technological mutation" caused by television and the coming of video games. They point to children who cannot sit still long enough to read more than a few pages of a book unless it is presented on a computer screen. Some today feel that the written word itself will become anachronistic and superfluous over the next fifty to a hundred years.[56]

Big Brother   In 1984 Apple Computers aired an ad during the Super Bowl that asked why 1984 wasn't going to be the 1984 Orwell predicted. With the introduction of graphical interface on the Macintosh, computers had become more "user-friendly."

Orwell had thought that, by 1984, television would become the controlling influence in people's lives. The essayist, Neil Postman, disagreed. In his book, *Amusing Ourselves to Death,* Postman pointed to Aldous Huxley's *Brave New World*. Published in the early 1930s, this novel created a future filled with drugs to make you always feel good, continually blaring advertisements, and "feelie movies." As the title of his own book suggests, Postman felt that we were becoming an audience who could not tell fantasy from reality, entertainment from news. Our worst enemy wasn't an authoritarian Big Brother, but ourselves and our own craving for more and more entertainment: "What Huxley teaches is that in the age of advanced technology, spiritual devastation is more likely to come from an enemy with a smiling face than from one whose countenance exudes suspicion and hate. In the Huxleyan prophecy, Big Brother does not watch us, by his choice. We watch him, by ours."[57]

By the mid-1980s, it seemed as if Huxley's future, though originally considered sharp satire, had all but come true. Deregulation began in earnest in 1984. With restrictions lifted, television programming licenses were easier to obtain. A direct result of deregulation, the Home Shopping Network devoted itself entirely to advertisements of products people could purchase over the telephone. Thus was "interactive television" born, though some might point to a much earlier form of interactive TV: the old *Winkie Dink and You* show. Children put a special screen over the TV set and drew items to help Winky out with his problems—and many without screens got yelled at by irate parents after drawing on the television screen itself.

Technological Advances Developed because of the popularity of graphical user interfaces on the 1984 Macintosh, Microsoft Windows was introduced in 1986. Users began to see applications that could display and control both text and graphics simultaneously: a major component of multimedia.

At the same time, more computer environments and applications offered WYSIWYG (what you see is what you get) displays of multiple typefaces, styles, and sizes. Along with the displays came peripherals that more practically allowed the input and output of graphics as well as text: mice, scanners, and laser printers. These peripherals have made a lasting impact on the computer industry.

The 1980s also saw the introduction of **hyperlinking**—nonlinear navigation through information—and **object orientation,** which makes complicated operations accessible with point-and-click ease. "Once we could easily navigate information and had access to more powerful hardware, we began to want more sophisticated applications that combine analog and digital video, computer graphics, and sound."[58]

The images of interactive games and video also improved; the blinking, indistinguishable blips of yellow or green lights soon became more cartoonlike, with block animation, like Pacman. Eventually, developers achieved full-motion animation, which continues to improve exponentially.

Even just a few years ago, however, multimedia components were expensive and designed individually and so did not always work well together. With these problems, as well as the lack of standards and consistency among hardware products, most software developers just didn't find it worthwhile to create new multimedia products and software.

Then, in the early 1990s, several vendors joined and created the Multimedia PC Marketing Council (MPC),[59] which set the minimum requirements for equipment capable of running a common set of multimedia applications. So, a multimedia standard came about: MPC machines required at least an 8036SX processor, a CD-ROM drive, support for MIDI and waveform audio, and *Microsoft Windows with Multimedia Extensions (Multimedia Windows)*. In the meantime, Apple continued to expand into the area of multimedia. By 1992, "most of the largest players in personal computing and consumer electronics—Apple, IBM, Microsoft, SONY, Tandy, Dell, Sega, Nintendo—began spending large budgets to advertise and market multimedia products and equipment."[60]

The early 1990s also saw the introduction of the first mass-distributed interactive motion pictures. Some of the presentations were inauspicious, to say the least. For instance, in *Mr. Payback* (1994), the audience could choose whether a guy who parked his car in a disabled zone would either get a flat tire or be disabled himself.

Finally, the late 1980s and early 1990s saw more and more consumers using the term *digital*. The **analog system,** which aims at replicating sound or images via transmitted waves, had been around since 1887, when Edison captured and stored sound on tinfoil cylinders. With digital technology, signals or data are represented as a series of on/off impulses, with information being stored in *bits* rather than in a continuous wave. Digital technology has greatly improved sound and image quality. You might think of an analog system as someone tracing an image with a piece of tracing paper—no matter how steady the artist's hand, the replicated image will still not be exact. Now, compare this with, say, a photocopy of the original image. In this case, you would be much less likely to tell the original from the copy.

Multimedia Today

There is no doubt that interactive multimedia is exploding in a way no one could have predicted just a few short years ago. Many corporations and motion picture production companies boast new multimedia divisions. However, some players have already experienced major financial disappointments. For example, Medio, a company that started strong with its JFK Assassination multimedia CD, experienced huge layoffs barely a year later. At this point, Medio faces imminent takeover by Connectsoft or complete dissolution.

With the creation of Dreamquest Interactive, helmed by the likes of Bill Gates and Steven Spielberg, interactive multimedia will no doubt continue to grow. Will the job market, particularly for writers and artists, continue to grow as well? For now, it looks like it will, though jobs are not as plentiful as some originally guessed. Also, jobs for writing multimedia still tend to be free-lance work lasting from three to eight months.

Whether the new multimedia industry will boom or bust in the near future, one thing is certain: As quickly as new multimedia projects and companies are created, the technology supporting multimedia is itself changing—dramatically.

LIFE AFTER TELEVISION

Since the late 1940s, television has aired programs created mainly by an elite for broadcast to the multitudes. With digital technology, the future could hold online, interactive television, making information accessible electronically via computers, cable television, or telephone lines.

In his book *Life After Television*, George Gilder shares his view of the future of interactive technology and the "telecomputer"—"a new system that can transform the possibilities of all human society."[61] He continues,

> Tired of watching TV? With artful programming of telecomputers, you could spend a day interacting on the screen with Henry Kissinger, Kim Bassinger, or Billy Graham. Celebrities could produce and sell their own software or make themselves available for two-way personal video communication. [This has already begun in a sense with a number of current rock stars, communicating with their fans during certain specified times on the Internet—Ed.] You could take a fully interactive course in physics or computer science with the world's most exciting professors, who respond to your questions and let you move at your own learning speed. You could have a fully interactive workday without commuting to the office or run a global corporation without ever getting on a plane.[62]

Thomas Furness takes the idea even further. The founder and director of the Human Interface Technology Laboratory at the University of Washington, he is considered one of the fathers of *virtual reality* (VR), an immersive computer simulation experienced through headgear, goggles, and sensory gloves that allow the user to feel as if he or she is present in another environment. Furness, who began his work in VR creating flight simulators for the U.S. Air Force, feels that the biggest boon for virtual reality will be how readily it fits into the merging of broadband telecommunications, computers, and the telephone, which will become one:

> The interface for humans to that ubiquitous channel is going to be a virtual one. When you put (these different media) together, basically what you get is the "virtu-phone," a telephone that you wear. And basically now in your home, even through coaxial cable, you have the ability to disconnect your head from your body and go places—through what we used to have as television, only television wasn't interactive. Now [this new medium] is going to be completely interactive. You'll go to work with it, you'll play with it, you'll go to school with this new medium [which is] two generations beyond the print medium. We'll be taking ourselves—head and body, because we're going to feel as if we're present—to another place.[63]

One might ask, "With the ability to interact with 500 to 1,000 channels, what happens to shopping malls, not to mention the local video stores?" More and more shopping malls may become entertainment centers. But, what happens to the transportation industry if people no longer have to travel by car, train, or plane to get to work? What happens to downtown urban areas where office buildings might stand empty? And will people want to spend even more time in front of their TV sets than they do now? Corporations are betting millions that the answer is "Yes."

But there are deeper, more disturbing questions to address. What happens to social interaction if people literally never have to leave the house? What happens to reality itself? On the other hand, VR could still move in the direction Furness would like: a place where children can create pastoral worlds while learning about the importance of nature and ecological balance.

It seems as though we're all just beginning to understand the effects television has had on us since the late 1940s; we have little more than an inkling of what effect the new media may have. Will there be a true "democratization" of media, where people can broadcast their own programming from their homes and receive instantaneous reactions? Will McLuhan's "Global Village" come to pass, where students in the United States can communicate online digitally with friends in Germany, China—anywhere in the world? Or will the information highway be owned by corporations who will tout their own philosophies over the Net, creating an electronic elite? The "Global Village" could, in fact, turn out to be more of an electronic megalopolis, overseen by new corporate Big Brothers.

On a more mundane level, 500 to 1,000 channels might well offer us new experiences, opening up new vistas for our children: whole new realms of art, entertainment, documentation, and social interaction. Alternately, all these new channels could also only mean that we can watch *Gilligan's Island* 999 times a day. Certainly, in any case, the digital/media revolution is changing the landscape of our culture. It will certainly affect the way we interact with each other as well as the way we think and perceive ourselves. As Isaac Asimov said, the hope is that "we do not make foolish [or trivial use] of technology. That we use technology wisely."[64]

ENDNOTES

1. Robert Aston and Joyce Schwarz, eds., *Multimedia: Gateway to the Next Millenium* (Cambridge, MA: Academic Press, 1994), 13.
2. Ibid.
3. Michael J. Miller, "Multimedia," *PC* magazine, March 31, 1992, 112.
4. Robert Bell, "Introduction," in *Multimedia Studies Program Catalogue* (San Francisco: San Francisco State University, 1994), 1.
5. Ibid.
6. Erik Holsinger, *How Multimedia Works* (Emeryville, CA: Ziff-Davis Press, 1994), 3.
7. Amy Harmon, "The 10% Solution," *Los Angeles Times,* D1.
8. Natalie Jacobson McCracken, "Is It Still a Book?" *Bostonia* magazine, 1994, 49.
9. Ibid.
10. Ibid., 50.
11. Richard F. Snow, "American Heritage On-Line," *American Heritage* 46, no. 4 (July-August 1995): 7.
12. From Dataquest's online information—webmaster@dataquest.com.

13. Tim Hulley, Media 101 paper, 1994.
14. Ibid.
15. Charles Platt, "Interactive Entertainment: Who Writes It? Who Reads It? Who Needs It?" *Wired,* September 1995, 195.
16. Donald L. Miller, "The White City," *American Heritage,* July–August 1993, 83.
17. Margaret Cheney, *Tesla: Man out of Time* (New York: Dell Publishing, 1981), 70–73.
18. H.G. Wells, *The Time Machine,* in *Three Prophetic Science Fiction Novels of H.G. Wells* (New York: Dover Publications, 1960), 278.
19. Charles Dickens, *The Annotated Christmas Carol* (New York: Clarkson N. Potter, 1976), 93.
20. Terry Ramsaye, "Paul and the Time Machine," in *Focus on the Science Fiction Film,* ed. William Johnson (New Jersey: Prentice-Hall, Inc., 1972), 24.
21. Ibid., 21.
22. John Clute, *Science Fiction: The Illustrated Encyclopedia* (London: Dorling Kindersley, 1965), 46. If you want to explore what might have happened had the technology been available, you might read William Gibson and Bruce Sterling's *The Difference Engine,* a novel about an alternate world in which the industrial and the computer revolution occur at the same time.
23. William B. Meyer, "Life on Mars Is Almost Certain," *American Heritage* 38, no. 4 (February–March 1984): 41–42. Whether this means that like minds think alike or that every genius is a little on the loopy side I'll leave up to the reader.
24. Angelica Shirley Carpenter and Jean Shirley, *L. Frank Baum: Royal Historian of Oz* (Minneapolis: Learner Publications, 1992), 96.
25. Joseph J. Corn and Brian Horrigan, *Yesterday's Tomorrows* (New York: Summit Books, 1984), 24. It is interesting to note that the very predictions Corn and Harrigan (and many of us for that matter) treated cavalierly in their 1984 book have already come to pass, with the age of television now entering a new, interactive phase.
26. Ibid., 25.
27. Frederick Simpich, "Spin Your Globe to Long Island," *National Geographic* 75 (April 1939): 437.
28. Peter Adams, writer-producer, *Art in the Third Reich* (BBC documentary, 1989).
29. Vannevar Bush, "As We May Think," *Life,* September 10, 1945, 121.
30. Ibid., 116.
31. Lynne S. Gross, *Telecommunications: An Introduction to Electronic Media* (Dubuque, IA: Brown, 1991), 96.
32. Ibid.
33. Erik Barnouw, *Tube of Plenty* (Oxford: Oxford University Press, 1990), 300.
34. Carolyn Bennett Patterson and Thomas Nebbia, "Seattle Fair Looks to the 21st Century," *National Geographic* 122 (September 1962): 407.
35. Bruce Wolcott, interview with the author, August, 1995.
36. Jerry Mander, in his book *In the Absence of the Sacred,* noted eloquently that McLuhan was, in effect, saying that the mere existence of new media, of television, "causes society to be organized in new ways. As information is moved through different channels its character and its content change; political relationships, concepts, and styles change as well. Even the human spirit and body change" (p. 40).
37. Stewart Alsop, "Requiem for the Post," *Newsweek,* January 1969. Also in *This Fabulous Century: Volume 7: 1960–1970* (New York: Time-Life, 1970), p. 130.
38. *1965 Official NY World's Fair Guide* (New York: Time Inc., 1965), 90.
39. Kendra Howe, a representative from Watts-Silverstein and Associates, in an interview with the author in February 1995, spoke of how this CD-ROM product profiles a group of statistically average families from countries around the world and shows all aspects of their daily lives. It is basically an educational tool or "browsing product" with its primary target audience being families, especially those with children. In comparing families around the world, the producers of the program thought they would find many differences and were surprised to find, in terms of overall values, many similarities. It is interesting when browsing through the Lifestyles section of the Suitcase Menu to see six different

bathrooms, from one with mink-lined toilets in Kuwait to another in Uganda that is just a hole in the ground.

40. Ibid.
41. Bruce Wolcott, interview with the author, August 1995.
42. Ralph J. Gleason, *The Jefferson Airplane and the San Francisco Sound* (New York: Ballantine Books, 1969), 3.
43. Ibid.
44. Barbara Kantrowitz and Adam Rogers, "The Birth of the Internet," *Newsweek,* August 8, 1994, 56.
45. John Kronenberg, "Push-Button Movies: The Video-Cassette Revolution," *Look,* November 3, 1970, 94.
46. Bruce Wolcott, interview with the author, August 1995.
47. Ibid.
48. Ibid.
49. S. M. Shelton, "Multimedia," *Technical Communications,* Fourth Quarter 1993, 695.
50. Richard A. Lanham, *The Electronic Word* (Chicago: University of Chicago Press, 1993, ix.
51. Platt, "Interactive Entertainment," 146.
52. Ibid.
53. Gross, *Telecommunications,* Plate 8.
54. Michael J. Miller, "Multimedia," *PC* magazine, March 31, 1992, 114.
55. Ibid.
56. Donald A. Norman, lecture delivered at the University of Washington, 1989.
57. Postman, *Amusing Ourselves to Death,* 155.
58. Ibid.
59. Miller, "Multimedia," 117.
60. Randy Haykin, ed., *Multimedia Demystified* (San Francisco: Random House, 1992), 2.
61. George Gilder, *Life After Television: The Coming Transformation of Media and American Life* (New York: Norton, 1992), 40.
62. Ibid.
63. Dr. Thomas Furness, interview with the author, October 1993.
64. Dr. Isaac Asimov, interview with the author, April 1977.

2

The Written Word in the Digital Age

"Perhaps the real question for literary study now is not whether our students will be reading Great Traditional Books or Relevant Modern ones in the future, but whether they will be reading books at all ... Digitized communication is forcing a radical realignment of the alphabetic and graphic components of ordinary textual communication."

— Richard A. Lanham, *The Electronic Word*

"In my case, [using a computer to write] reduces the fear of making marks on a clean piece of paper—electrons are less permanent."

— Neil Gaiman, interview with the author

"Books have had their day."

— Gore Vidal

Whether the written word in the age of interactive media will become anachronistic as Donald Norman, a vice president of Apple, has speculated, remains to be seen.[1] What is unarguable is that the written word is changing, in large part because of the so-called digital revolution occurring in modern media. New Media, or multimedia, is changing the way we interact and communicate, affecting the use of words in everything from advertising to textbooks. As Neil Postman pointedly states, *USA Today* is essentially a newspaper laid out like a television screen.[2] Many new textbooks and magazines share this quality. For example, in the magazine *Wired*, the pages are laid out as if on a computer screen.

A hundred years ago, people wrote clearly and poetically. One only has to watch an episode of Ken Burns' *The Civil War* to see such expertise in common correspondence from the time. Wives and daughters of soldiers in Georgia, infantrymen from Maine, and slaves on the run: These people wrote of their experiences in sweeping, beautiful prose:

> August 30, 1863. Hospital near Gettysburg.
>
> My Dear Father:
>
> It has pleased the God of Battles that I should number among the many wounded of the great and hotly contested battle fought near this place on the first, second, and third of July. But through His infinite kindness and mercy I am once more permitted, after an almost miraculous escape and recovery, to inform you that I have so far recovered that I am able to go about, morning and evening. . .
>
> Your devoted son,
> Albert Batchelor[3]

In those days, people learned to read from the Bible and the works of Shakespeare and Milton. They spoke as they wrote, with phrases that now read and sound odd, anachronistic, and perhaps a little genteel, such as "Are you having me on?" or "Perhaps you should take a lie down."

As the people of the mid-twentieth century would be influenced by the speech patterns they heard in motion pictures, on radio, and on television, so people of the last century were influenced by the written word. I believe the written word can still be powerful and effective and will continue to be so, perhaps for a long time. Not everyone shares Norman's pessimistic speculations concerning the written word. However, as various media directly influenced and changed the written word in the twentieth century, computers, online services, and digital effects will affect the written word of the future.

Multimedia Needs Good Writers

There are, for certain, ways this new technology can help people learn, communicate, and become involved with the world around them. Often, though, these new digital resources remain untapped or are used merely for new forms of entertainment. For instance, movies such as *Jurassic Park* and *Waterworld* take on the attributes of giant amusement park rides. They're great fun while they last, but their impact melts away like cotton candy. Now better than ever with digital technology, special effects have become, in the words of Harlan Ellison, "A tail that has come to wag the dog till it's dizzy as Huckleberry Hound." Ellison goes on to write, "Producers conceive of imaginative fiction as just another shoot-'em up with laser rifles. They have a plethora of hype but a dearth of inventiveness."[4]

Like film, New Media cannot survive on just hype and effects. It needs stories just as much as a book, play, or film does. New Media needs nonlinear perspectives and continual input on given subjects. Most of all, New Media, particularly interactive multimedia, needs *writers*.

As Steven Spielberg rightly noted before filming *Schindler's List*, "It all begins with the word."[5] Saddled with a weak screenplay, a motion picture with the greatest special effects, the most wonderful music, and the most attractive actors will fall flat. Multimedia producers are just beginning to realize the importance of good writing. In recent years, a software manufacturer hired me to write the script for a new CD-ROM program. Like other projects I've worked on, it was based on a successful "linear" or traditionally written series and had an army of talented computer and animation people working on it. The only trouble was, they'd been tooling it for over six months without a script. But then they hired me as a part of a team of writers. Even so, the company found their product greeted with somewhat unenthusiastic reviews and fewer buyers than they had hoped to attract. They'd done it backwards: The script (the "word") should have come first.

Paul Saffo directs the Institute for the Future, a management consulting foundation. According to Saffo, the sort of experience I had with the software company occurs all too often: "Writers are vital to interactive media creation. Publishers understand this, but companies outside publishing often do not. Bad writing and underuse of good writers is a sad norm in companies today."[6] Fortunately, this is changing. As developers learn the medium, they come back to basics, such as the idea that good writing will create good products.

As more and more multimedia producers realize the importance of writers to their products, writers will find themselves in greater demand by this new digital medium. Many of these writers come from film and television, or "linear" entertainment. Others have worked in print-oriented fields, such as technical writing and journalism. In each case, writers often find it hard to begin the task of writing something "nonlinear."

Writing for nonlinear, interactive multimedia is certainly challenging, but it can be as effective, as powerful, and as dramatic as material written for *any* medium. New Media writers can do more than just provide information. The best New Media writers can teach people (as shown by various interactive kiosks), make people laugh (*Leisure Suit Larry*), awe their audience (*Myst*), and have a profound and dramatic emotional effect on the user (*Vietnam*). The writer must engage an audience and make them think and feel. Not an easy job for even the best writers. However, well-written pieces can open up new worlds for an audience and can profoundly affect the way people experience ideas and emotions. With new delivery systems, one could see these programs literally anywhere in the world. Can you imagine the impact this could have on global society? You don't have to look any further than the invention of movable type to see the exponential change a new technological innovation can bring to both a medium and the general population.

Changing the Way People Read and Write

READERS BECOME WRITERS

Printing created new forms of literature and new styles of writing. When manuscripts no longer needed to be handwritten, texts were suddenly available to many more people than before. In the same way, new digital technology has already engendered new art forms, new disciplines of writing, and new ways to use the written word. Jay David Bolter writes, "The shift from print to the computer does not mean the end of literacy. What will be lost is not literacy itself, but the literacy of print, for electronic technology offers us a new kind of book and new ways to write and read."[7]

Richard A. Lanham takes this thought a step further in *The Electronic Word:* "What happens when text moves from page to screen? First, the digital text becomes unfixed and interactive. The reader can change it, become the writer. The center of Western culture since the Renaissance—really since the great Alexandrian editors of Homer—the fixed, authoritative, canonical text, simply explodes into the ether."[8] In other words, the reader—that is, the user—is engaged, becoming as integrally involved in the process as the writer.

WRITING FOR NEW MEDIA

Paul Saffo is optimistic about the writer's role in New Media: "Recent events in the information revolution are great news for writers. The arrival of the Internet as a full-fledged medium—the Web in particular—amounts to nothing less than a full employment act for writers. Meanwhile, optical media are also generating more demand for writers as well, as publishers large and small put out new titles."[9]

Saffo also states that problems inevitably arrive with the introduction of new technologies. "The hitch is that writers will still experience wrenching shifts in work style. Writing in an electronic medium is very different than putting words to paper. And the problem is that most writers—most of us in fact—echo the sentiment behind Mark Twain's observations that 'I am all for progress; it's change I don't like.' *Basically, we are reinventing writing as a medium.* It will be a wonderful, amazing ride for wordsmiths who love change, but stubborn traditionalists will hate it [italics mine]."[10]

Experts Discuss the Digital Word

People fear this reinvention of writing; they feel that digital technology can only hinder the written word. For instance, Stephen L. Talbott writes of "the tyranny of the detached word":

> Even the word-processing capabilities that might favor my more active involvement all too readily serve other ends. For example: the ease and rapidity with which I can cut and paste text enables my hands to keep up more closely with my mind, but also encourages me to reduce my thinking to the relatively mechanical manipulation of words I see in front of me. To edit a text, then, is merely to rearrange symbols ... .
>
> The computer is becoming even more sophisticated in its drive to detach the word from thinking. ... More aggressively, new, experimental software guides our writing by continually offering up words and phrases to extend the last thing we typed. This generosity is made possible by an analysis of our previous patterns of use. ... But the analysis works only on the external form of our words, not their shades of meaning; it trains us in the repetition of familiar forms that do our "thinking" for us. ... Ironically, technology that was supposed to liberate us from the

'tyranny of linear, rationally structured words' in favor of image, intuition, and pattern, is guaranteeing that whatever words remain are as linear and, in a superficial sort of way, as rationally structured as possible. After all, the essence of linearity is not that words should be stuck in a fixed order, but rather that their meanings should be stuck, so that all ordering possibilities are precisely defined and mechanically executable from the start. That is exactly what the programmable and information-processing computer asks of us. We must leave our words alone—sleeping—and may bestow no imaginative kiss upon their inert forms, lest they waken and dance free of the predictable structures in which the machine has snared them.[11]

What do other writers, and those who teach writing, think of the digital word and its effect? Theolene Bakken, a writing instructor at Seattle Central Community College, has seen a somewhat negative impact of digital technology on the linear composition writing of many of her students:

Because revision is such an important part of the writing process model, composition teachers embraced the new technology almost immediately. The thought was that computers would make brainstorming, drafting, revision, and editing easier, and that students would make more deep revisions to content, moving text and trying multiple versions of documents because they would be spared the burden of recopying. However, most beginning writers ignored the flexibility that modern programs allowed. Some were intimidated by the technology, even distracted by it, and the quality of writing suffered because most of their creative energy went into navigating the program or trying to type. Others saw the computer as nothing more than a high quality typewriter and wouldn't use it until the final draft. A more pervasive problem was that students were able to produce finished-looking documents, with crisp typeface and justified margins, without having to think about content; even a rough draft "looks" good when it comes off a laser printer. In other words, students were paying attention merely to surface correctness and not making the kinds of deep revisions so necessary to creating truly effective prose. Ironically, some of the best-looking essays receive the lowest grades because students pay far more attention to fonts and title pages than focus and the development and arrangement of ideas.[12]

Emma Bull, a professional fantasy and science-fiction writer, has also taught writing. To a question that she says is usually phrased "How have digital technologies impacted on the craft of writing?" her usual answer is:

They've produced an unfortunate number of people who use the word "impact"as a verb. Yes, we take the bitter with the sweet; we've got a lot of bad business user jargon on the street that we all should have had the sense to squash before it leaked out of the conference room with the Suits.

But the sweet is very sweet indeed. The human brain created digital technology, and in some measure, was its first model of operation. Now the child is teaching the parent new tricks, new ways of seeing, new solutions to old problems. We had to invent words, pictures, concepts to explain to each other how our new technology works. And once a word exists, it's possible for people to think about the thing it represents and to enlarge on it, make metaphors with it, expand it until both concept and user are big with possibilities. The ideas dreamed up to move packets of information over infinitesimal spaces can change the way we think of people and of ideas themselves. They can apply to the way we organize, communicate, transport ourselves. Asking how digital technology has changed writing is really trying to get at the answer back to front. Digital technology has changed *us,* the writers and the audience, our lives, our values, our very thought processes. Writing—both how we do it and what we say with it—changes with us naturally.[13]

Susan Palwick, an award-winning author of fiction and poetry and an instructor at Yale, has her own thoughts about the craft of writing and new technology.

When trying to teach literature and writing, prose-based skills, to a video-based generation, you begin to encounter problems. Digital technology doesn't make people better or worse writers, it just makes them better or worse writers differently. People don't proofread, and because they don't have to retype it encourages them to focus on local problems, so if you've asked them to change a paragraph and incorporate it into rest of story, they will only revise paragraph and leave rest of text as is. A lot of people say because of screen size you can't see whole document at once, which makes it harder to think of it as a whole—writing becomes localized—good to get students to do line by line writing but it is hard to get them to look at larger picture. Some of this is also because we've moved out of the print culture—a technological change from print culture—students get info from tv—we don't read like they do. Someone writing passionless prose might be more adept at passionate video with computer technology. This isn't necessarily good or bad—it just is.[14]

The writer and instructor William Shetterly, author of the books *Elsewhere* and *Never Never* and the comic series *Captain Confederacy,* has the following to say about the impact of new technology on writing:

I'm sure scribes who wrote on clay tablets then baked them were very suspicious of the work of writers who used that new-fangled parchment, which let writers compose too quickly and easily for true depth of thought.

A great many things have changed since the invention of the word processor. If students' writing has become bland, it is probably a mistake to blame the word processor. Tools have some effect on an artist's work, but tools are only tools. Someone who loved technology as much as Leonardo Da Vinci would be doing digital art today. ... Would that reduce the quality of his work?

It is conceivable that many people have not learned how to use the new tools well. The word processor is a wonderful device for revision, but our education system often doesn't stress revision in the creative process. It's possible that some students are revising too much, and more are revising too little—but that's been true since people began to paint on cave walls.[15]

Emma Bull concurs:

I'm sure there were literary pundits who declared in 1873 that the typewriter would be the death of decent prose style. Why are we so determined to confuse the tool with its user? If you find that you like to write with a word processor, if you find that it's easier and more fun for you, then use it. If you find it intimidating, or if part of your pleasure in writing comes from feeling the pen move across the paper, then don't use it.

The editor who bought my first short story told me in the acceptance letter that she'd edited the story a little for length, because 'it's so easy to overwrite when you're using a word processor.' No, it's easy to over-write when you're new to your craft and haven't yet learned that the one right word is better than six not-quite words. Instead of blaming my tools, she would have done me more good to have sent me the marked-up manuscript, so I could see where I'd gone off the rails.[16]

COMPUTERS AND ART

Terri Windling has won five World Fantasy Awards for such works as *The Armless Maiden and Other Tales for Childhood's Survivors, The Wood Wife,* and *The Green Children.* Her art has been exhibited in the Boston Museum of Fine Arts and in galleries across the United States and the United Kingdom. Windling did not begin using a computer for anything, let alone her work, until 1990, by which time virtually everyone she worked with in the publishing industry had been using computers for a while. "[They] considered me deucedly peculiar for not [using a computer] myself," she says. "The reason for my delay was simple fear of technology."[17]

Windling inherited an old Apple computer from colleagues. It sat on her desk gathering dust for two years.

> I became a born-again computer convert when I discovered laptops. In 1990, I left a rather stationary life in Boston for a vagabond life—splitting my time between a winter house in Arizona, a summer cottage in England, and travels to other places in between. A laptop was the perfect way to carry my writing/editorial office with me wherever I went. ... [I] joined an international online service so that I could communicate with my New York publishing office (and various writers whose work I edit) no matter where I was during any given month.[18]

In spite of her initial reluctance, Windling believes digital technology will create new forms in fiction as well as other arts:

> [It will create] new ways of disseminating fiction, bypassing altogether the large corporate-run media empires that dominate the publishing world today. ... I find this exciting even though my own heart is firmly given to traditional, old-fashioned books. And despite these digital innovations, I believe there will always be an audience for traditional books—for the book as a tactile object will continue to hold a romantic appeal for many readers. ... It seems to me to be no accident that the Book Arts movement (creating fine limited editions and single-edition works) is growing in popularity at the same time that computer technology begins to create new ways to tell stories without the use of printers' ink and binders' glue.[19]

Some have remarked that Windling's art, specifically her collages, looks to some extent like the menu screens for multimedia programs (see Figure 2-1).

> My collages are tactile objects, created by hand and not by mouse; they use pages of text from old books (damaged ones, I hasten to add—I don't set about damaging old books myself!) juxtaposed with painted imagery, natural objects, and the anonymous "women's work" of sewing, lace making, and embroidery. ... This said, however, one could also explore, in a similar visual, nonlinear way, the evolution of stories from the printed page to the digital screen. Thomas Canty, a contemporary artist whose work I admire a great deal, does this in his illustrations and designs, which

FIGURE 2-1 | *Dust jacket collage for* The Armless Maiden. *By permission of Terri Windling.*

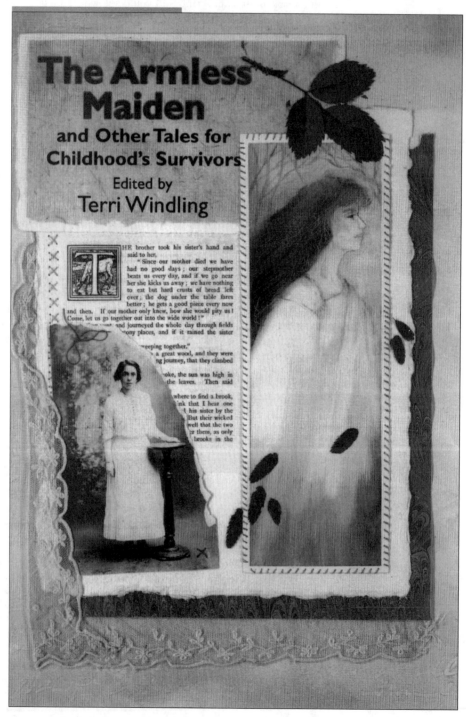

make deft use of computer technology while incorporating icons from the Arts-and-Crafts and Golden Age illustration movements at the turn of the last century. My own work is often in a kind of dialog with Tom's—so a good case could be made that there is more of a digital influence on my collages than I am conscious of as a result.[20]

Delia Sherman, the author of *Through a Brazen Mirror,* the award-winning *The Porcelain Dove,* and numerous fantasy and science-fiction short stories, recently taught first-year composition and "Fantasy as Literature" at Boston University. Now she has "given up the bright lights of Academia to become a contributing editor at TOR Books." Sherman feels that software must travel far before becoming sophisticated enough to help writers:

> It would be nice if [developers] could invent a program that genuinely helps someone avoid common grammatical errors like comma splices and dangling modifiers, but until computers can become case-sensitive, I live in fear of grammatical parallels to spelling bloopers. A friend of mine, a lady and a fine writer and crafter of plots, swears that she can only figure out what happens next with the help of her handy-dandy plotting program. The fact that she wrote the program probably helps keep things from getting too mechanical.[21]

THE BASICS OF WRITING

So, what kind of impact will digital technology have on the basics of writing: story, character, theme? Will writers simply press a key for "Hemingway Style?" Or could the technology lead to an ever greater change in the use of the written word?

Some speculate that once multimedia and digital technology become as much a part of people's lives as the telephone, the written word could become unnecessary. Frank Catalano, the principal of Catalano Consulting, comments on digital media trends in the weekly "ByteMe" column for Seattle's *Eastsideweek* and PC World On-line. He also spent fourteen years as a broadcast news reporter and anchor, and his fiction, essays, and columns have appeared in *Omni, Analog,* and the *Seattle Times.* When asked if he thought the written word would become unnecessary, Catalano replied,

> Hmmm. I guess that means oral storytelling died completely when Gutenberg came along. Tell that to radio. Or novels went away when film came along. I think Random House would be interested in that.
>
> Every [medium] has its own place in terms of convenience, type of story it tells best, cost of delivery, and market. Interactive multimedia might force other types of writing (or media) to become more focused on what they do well, but it won't supplant them, even in the next fifty to one hundred years. That will be more an issue of economics (rising paper costs, for example) rather than the new technologies. And storytelling goes back thousands of years and shows no signs of going away. It's a basic human need, as much as food, shelter, and companionship.[22]

Others feel digitization can open up the arts to more people, in the same way the printing press allowed many more people to read books than ever before.

In writing about someone accessing *Paradise Lost* from a CD-ROM, Richard Lanham asks, "Wouldn't you begin to play games with it? A weapon in your hands after 2,500 years of pompous pedantry about the Great Books, and you not to use it? Hey, man, how about some music with this stuff? Let's voice the rascal and see what happens. Add some graphics and graffiti! Print it out in San Francisco [typeface] for Lucifer, and Gothic for God. Electronic media will change past literary texts as well as future ones. The electronic word, for both literature and literary history, works both ways."[23]

Nonlinear Storytelling

Obviously, the effect of technology on the way people write and read will be enormous. This could mean the creation of new definitions for *story* and *script* and *screenplay*, because one of the basics in these media is that *all* stories must have a beginning, a middle, and an end. Of course, anyone can read them in any order; think of the last time you took up a murder mystery and had to read the last page first.

Alternatively, adults may simply be learning from children: Listen to any third-grader tell or write a story and you will see the true meaning of *nonlinear:* "Well, we went to the house and we hid from the wolf and, oh wait! I forgot! We also met a snake on the way ... " The story is great if you happen to be another third-grader (or the parent of the child telling the story), but most of us still find such nonlinear storytelling pretty confusing. Still, instead of using the child's "Wait, I forgot" motif, what if one uses "Here's even more information, if you'd like it" or "You can move to another part of the story if you want to find out about the snake we met on the way."

GRAPHIC NOVELS (COMIC BOOKS)

There are some who feel that nonlinear writing for a mass medium began with comic books, now often referred to as *graphic novels.* As in today's CD-ROMs, comics have always had less room for dialog and description than movies, books, and radio. In comics, the writer and artist can condense and reorder time and space. Of course, comics aren't really interactive. Even so, Douglas Rushkoff argues well that Frank Miller's Batman series, *The Dark Knight Returns,* was not only nonlinear but, on a certain level, interactive as well. Rushkoff writes, "The iterative quality of the media within the comic book story creates a particularly cyberian,* 'looking glass,' milieu that has caught on with other comic book writers as a free-for-all visual sampling of diary entries, computer printouts, television reports, advertisements, narratives, and other characters as well as regular dialog and narration."[24] Rushkoff goes on to state that comics have always been an ideal form of visual collage:

---

* As in cyberspace—the digitally created "space" or shared virtual environment found on the Net.

Miller initiates a reexploration of the nonlinear and sampling potential of the comic book medium, pairing facing pages that at first glance seem unrelated but actually comment on each other deeply. A large, full-page abstract drawing of Batman may be juxtaposed with small cells of action scenes, television analysis, random comments, song lyrics, or newsprint. ... *The eye wanders in any direction it chooses.* ... The comic book reader relaxes only when he is able to accept the chaotic, nonlinear quality of Miller's text and enjoy it for the ride [italics mine].[25]

Interestingly, another major talent in the art of the graphic novel disagrees. Neil Gaiman won the World Fantasy Award in 1991 for best short story—an issue of his Sandman comic series.[26] His other works include *Black Orchid, The Books of Magic,* and *Good Omens* (coauthored with Terry Pratchett). When I asked him about the idea of comics being nonlinear, he said, "That's not nonlinear. Or, if it is, then *all* books are nonlinear. Most comics, most prose, most words, you start at the beginning and go on to the end. A dictionary is less linear than a graphic novel."[27]

However, if Gaiman's work isn't actually nonlinear, some of his newer material certainly seems inspired by multimedia. His most recent graphic novel, *Mr. Punch,* presents a disquieting story about childhood, brutality, and puppets. The artist Dave McKean uses many fonts to make Neil's text a graphic element among photographs, drawings, and models. Many of the panels look like a menu screen for a richly textured, particularly artistic dramatic multimedia presentation. Though this work isn't strictly multimedia, those who hope to write multimedia should nonetheless steep themselves in Gaiman's graphic novels and comics, as well as other comics, to begin to see the variety and richness of visual language.

IS NONLINEAR STORYTELLING NEW?

Will Shetterly echoes Gaiman's opinion about interactivity, though he takes it a step further:

All writing could be seen as non-linear. We, the reader/observers, receive information from the artist and put the pieces together in our minds. It's true that comics allow the reader to choose the order in which information within a panel is received. Do you read the words first, or look at the art, or scan one, study the other, then study the first again? But readers of fiction also have different ways of receiving information; some read every word, some scan; some scan a work once, then re-read it again more slowly. Either all art is "non-linear," or none is.[28]

On the other hand, Emma Bull states,

Multimedia is a whole new storytelling form. It looks as if it's only fusing a handful of others—print, cinema, still photography and illustration, music, speech—but those elements in combination reach our minds in a way that any one element in isolation won't. Not that multimedia is automatically better than its parent forms; it's just different, as movies with sound are different from silents. Because it's different, people who want to create multimedia need to embrace that difference if multimedia is going to be everything it can be. Multimedia creators have to avoid doing things that could be done as well or better in print, in film, in comic books. Remember that multimedia offers a unique chance for creator and audience to collaborate, to decide together how the work occurs in time, and even how it occurs, period.

Not that all the bugs are out of the form yet. Steve Hannaford, in *Adobe* magazine [September–October 1995], points out that we haven't got a dependable way for would-be buyers to "leaf through" a CD-ROM, as they would a paperback they were thinking about buying. Publishers can offer samples of multimedia projects at Web sites, but that only covers the equivalent of the home shopping channels. We need an easy way to browse the multimedia at the local computer store.[29]

Despite the current problems in multimedia, Richard Lanham sees digital technology soon providing completely new ways to communicate.

First, the essay will no longer be the basic unit of writing instruction. ... Second, we can back off a turn or two on the thumbscrew of spelling instruction, spelling checkers being what they are. ... Third, the nature of punctuation will change. ... I am thinking of the use on electronic bulletin boards of "emoticons," certain letters and symbols employed as tonal colorizers to indicate the spirit in which to read. ... Fourth, writing will be taught as a three-dimensional, not a two-dimensional art. Hypertext does this in one way; computer animation in another. ... Given the current state of digital animation programs, I think we'll come pretty soon to three-dimensional modeling of basic argumentative patterns. And we will add the dimension of color. ... And with better compression techniques and gigantic memory storage, we can add sound to our reading as well. Word, image, and sound will be inextricably mixed in a dynamic and continually shifting mixture.[30]

Lanham's description provides a solid definition not only of multimedia, but also of how one can use multimedia to communicate more creatively and efficiently. Lanham also states how multimedia will change the very nature of "writing"—how the symbols we use, the letters themselves, will be replaced.

"We will always have different levels of symbols that we use to communicate," Thomas Furness told me.

The emphasis on symbols, however, can change. We're much more visually oriented today. We're wanting compressed information: bytes, both sound and visual. Don Norman, to some extent, may be correct: There will be less and less emphasis on reading the classics, which is a shame. But New Media does not have to replace old media. After all, new technology doesn't necessarily replace old technology. We still have travel even though we have telephones. Radio was not dead after television came on the scene. In fact, in some ways, it's more alive than ever. Also, movies did not die with television. What could happen with a new medium added is a changing emphasis somewhat in the written word. This could dilute attention to reading, but there will be a rediscovery of reading. We'll cycle.

In the meantime, there will be another kind of reading. We're beginning to see this in fact on the Internet. An *imbedded narrative*—using spatial organization of information. In other words, the information you're organizing is narrative, but instead of just text, it will also be visual—a picture, like a cartoon. You look to a particular location to select a visual link to hypertext—you search out the text pieces. This is a new hybrid link of using written textual material along with three-dimensional visual worlds. But I do believe we won't end up replacing the written word; we'll end up changing it only to come back to it once again. The written word will, for a time, be deemphasized. But there will be a reemphasis.[31]

Paul Saffo concurs:

> The written word will continue to evolve, of course. It has been evolving at an accelerated rate ever since the invention of movable type. Annoying neologisms* will become artful fixtures in our language. We will love some and hate others—for example, I detest the use of "impact" as a verb [see Emma Bull's thoughts on this earlier in the chapter]. "Affect" strikes me as far more euphonious, and accurate besides. Give me thirty years and I'll get used to it.
>
> Technology has always had a profound effect on writing sensibilities. Hemingway developed his style because of years of filing reports via telegraph and having to put lots of information and visual imagery in a medium that cost his employers on a per-letter basis. TV affected reader sensibilities and writing styles. Now New Media will do the same. But the level of surprise this time may be greater than we imagined: What does writing look like in a medium where words and images can all be animated? We already talk of nonlinear writing, but I think that term is incomplete: Writing is not so much nonlinear as it is becoming weblike. And of course this will affect the trajectory of cultural trends just like every earlier medium has. Where exactly it ends up though is hard to guess at, though it is clear that words will play a key role in a strange new world of cyber-communities—rich social environments where people interact with people in information-rich contexts.[32]

Will Shetterly feels that art evolves whether the technology does or not. "Multimedia fiction may go the way of the silent movie, but if it does, the great creations will be remembered as fondly as the great creations of Keaton and Chaplin."[33] According to Shetterly, verbal linear construction will never entirely disappear. He also doesn't think that entirely free-form fictional environments, where the user can choose any result, are ultimately viable. "The point of art is to experience the artist's vision, and an artist's vision must have a moral coherence. Could you decide halfway through MacBeth that it should become a slapstick comedy and still have a satisfying experience? Artists can create multitrack fiction that would allow some degree of selectivity, but each track, to be interesting, would have to tell us more about life than which character succeeds and which fails."[34]

Multimedia and the User

The writers play as important a role in New Media as technicians and software. Just as critical to New Media is the user or audience. Writers will have to change their mode of operation to take such users into account: What information must the writer provide for the user and what will the user do with it? The writer of New Media has to make the audience think and feel not just by reading but also by doing; the "digital writers" must provide the user with the tools necessary for true interaction. Most important, the digital writer has

---

* *Neologisms* are new words. For example: Milton needed a word for his principal city in Hell. He combined the word *pantheon*, a temple dedicated to all gods, and *demon*, creating the word *pandemonium*, or place of all demons. Today it means a wild and unrestrained uproar or tumultuous assembly. One modern neologistic phrase is *channel surfing*.

to understand that once the user begins to interact with what is presented, the experience then becomes the user's, not the writer's. In essence, the writer must involve and engage the user actively by providing both hidden and visible resources. At present, some of these tools remain limited, particularly those involving CD-ROM technology, which has been available for the past eight or so years.

"CD-ROMs are a medium in search of content,"[35] says Neil Gaiman. But multimedia is still very young, and CD-ROMs are only one particular (and limited) storage medium. Motion pictures are only a little over a hundred years old, television perhaps fifty. It took the cinema over fifteen years to produce a D. W. Griffith. It took another twenty-five years for the young Orson Welles to produce *Citizen Kane*. In the world of interactive multimedia, one has yet to see the equivalent of an H .G. Wells, let alone an Orson Welles. There can be no doubt though that when a history of multimedia productions is written some time in the early twenty-first century, some of the people now reading this text will be considered the first great talents of an entirely new and wondrous art form.

E N D N O T E S

1. Donald Norman, "In the Future of Interactive Multi-Media, Who Needs Reading and Writing?" Talk given at the University of Washington, February 1989.
2. Neil Postman, *Amusing Ourselves to Death: Public Discourse in the Age of Show Business* (New York: Penguin Books, 1985), 111.
3. Geoffrey C. Ward (with Ric Burns and Ken Burns), *The Civil War: An Illustrated History* (New York: Alfred Knopf, 1990), 234.
4. Harlan Ellison, "An Overview of the Science Fiction Cinema," in *Omni's Screen Flights/Screen* Fantasies, ed. Danny Perry (New York: Doubleday, 1984), 3, 11.
5. Quoted from the Academy Awards ceremony, 1991.
6. Paul Saffo, interview with the author, October 24, 1995.
7. Jay David Boulter, *Writing Space: The Computer, Hypertext, and the History of Writing* (Hillsdale, New Jersey: Erlbaum, 1991), 2.
8. Richard A. Lanham, *The Electronic Word* (Chicago: University of Chicago Press, 1993), 31.
9. Saffo, interview with the author.
10. Ibid.
11. Stephen L. Talbott, *The Future Does Not Compute: Transcending the Machines in Our Midst* (California: O'Reilly & Associates, 1995), 191–192.
12. T. O. Bakken, interview with the author, September 1, 1995.
13. Emma Bull, interview with the author, September 26, 1995. She also told me, "Remember, wearing a tie reduces the flow of blood to the brain."
14. Susan Palwick, interview with the author, September 10, 1995.
15. Will Shetterly, interview with the author, September 13, 1995.
16. Bull, interview with the author.
17. Terri Windling, interview with the author, October 5, 1995.
18. Ibid.
19. Ibid.
20. Ibid.
21. Delia Sherman, interview with the author, September 10, 1995.
22. Frank Catalano, interview with the author, September 2, 1995.
23. Lanham, *The Electronic Word*, 7.

24. Douglas Rushkoff, *Cyberia: Life in the Trenches of Cyberspace* (San Francisco: Harper Collins, 1994), 183.
25. Ibid.
26. Since then, those who run the FantasyCon have rewritten the rules so that no "comic book" can ever again be nominated. See Harlan Ellison's introduction to the Sandman collection *Season of Mists,* DC Comics, New York, 1992.
27. Neil Gaiman, interview with the author, September 11, 1995.
28. Shetterly, interview with the author.
29. Bull, interview with the author. Regarding browsing, when I was exchanging a faulty CD at the local Egghead store, the salesperson wouldn't even let me check the new copy I had to see if the problem was in the CD or my machine.
30. Lanham, *The Electronic Word,* 127–128.
31. Thomas Furness, interview with the author, September 22, 1995.
32. Saffo, interview with the author.
33. Shetterly, interview with the author.
34. Ibid.
35. Gaiman, interview with the author.

3

The Interactive Piece

"Multimedia electronic documents can be enormously useful adjuncts to the existing teaching, research, and learning tools of scholars, but to do this they must provide facilities that are different and more powerful than those of paper books. These facilities ... include tools to promote connectivity, enhance audiovisualization, aid in the creation and revision of information, facilitate the search for and retrieval of data, and maintain historical integrity of materials."

— Nicole Yankelovich, Norman Meyrowitz, and Andries van Dam,
Reading and Writing the Electronic Book

The Case for an Interactive Piece

The first thing writers of multimedia should ask themselves is why exactly does the piece being written need to be interactive? Does the project lend itself to multimedia and interactivity? Will multimedia truly enhance it? If so, what kind of interactivity would be best?

These days, it seems that every other book and every motion picture ties in to a multimedia product. In many cases, producers take linear products and fit them uncomfortably into an interactive multimedia format.

One thing multimedia provides is the capacity for in-depth research of a subject—*if* the material is in text form. The number of images and sound stored on one CD-ROM is still limited. Even so, multimedia today offers a powerful and artistic venue.

THE LANGUAGE OF MULTIMEDIA

Before I go any further, I must discuss the "language" of multimedia, or how one communicates ideas, both visually and verbally, within a multimedia program. For instance, because multimedia allows less time to say something than linear forms of writing do, writers must use a sort of sound bite or "quicktalk," which I'll explain in greater detail later on. However, it is the look and "feel" of the program that create the true language of multimedia, described by the following terms: *menus, metaphors, symbols,* and *icons.*

A multimedia **menu** allows users to select, through either pictures or words, where they want to move through the program.

A **metaphor** is a figure of speech in which a word or phrase that denotes one thing is used in place of another word or phrase to suggest a comparison, as in "A mighty fortress is our God." In multimedia, the metaphor becomes the scenario that depicts the theme or setting in which the particular module is taking place. An example of a multimedia metaphor is the mandala in the *Rebirth* project (see Chapter 5). The general shape of the mandala makes it an effective menu icon while reflecting the Tibetan religion.

A **symbol** is an object that stands for something else but doesn't necessarily resemble what it represents. For example, the eagle symbolizes the United States. An **icon,** on the other hand, is a sign or representation that stands for something by virtue of a resemblance or analogy to it.

The first questions writers must ask about the language of their program are "How is the menu to be set up?" and "What kinds of metaphors, symbols or icons will be utilized and how will they be placed on the screen?" With answers to these questions, writers can enrich and improve the language of a multimedia project. Without them, writers have no way to fit what they have into a multimedia environment.

INTERACTIVE WHALING: A PROPOSED ADAPTATION OF MOBY-DICK

Media analysts continually focus on the plummeting attention span of children. From Neil Postman to Bill Moyers, theorists and commentators point to how visual our society has become, and how people read much less. Several people I have interviewed believe that with the coming of multimedia and a completely visual society, classic literature may be read only rarely, if at all, for some time to come. However, this same technology may encourage students to both read and recognize great writing.

For example, imagine that a company has decided to take *Moby-Dick* and make it into a multimedia program. *Moby-Dick* is a classic—an amazing novel about humanity versus nature, the rage of obsession, and the whaling industry. At first glance, one would assume that no one could ever improve on Melville's masterpiece, particularly with the bells and whistles of new technology! It has been said that the most convenient piece of interactive entertainment is a book. If you wonder what this means, just think about the experience of reading. At first, you're just seeing and comprehending words. Then, slowly, as you read, you begin to hear the voice of the author or narrator, then the voice of each character. You also begin to visualize the setting and the look of each character. Before you know it, you can hear the sound of waves crashing, men shouting, and wood breaking as the great whale destroys the *Pequod.*

Enhancing the Novel Adapting Melville's epic for multimedia does not mean allowing the user to choose alternate endings, which might strike people as unethical. If a company, most likely involved in education and training, were contracted to put *Moby-Dick* on a CD-ROM or laser disc, they would strive to clarify and heighten the reading experience. For instance, an actor might present the opening lines in the author's "voice" accompanied by the words on screen, immediately pulling the user into the virtual world of Moby-Dick.

Along with instantly grabbing the user's attention, the writer would want to make *Moby-Dick* accessible, going beyond the traditional annotations and indexes. To this end, he or she might include a glossary, so when readers come upon an unfamiliar word or phrase, they could click directly on it and have the meaning revealed. The developer might also include a way for users to move around in the text easily. On the top of the screen a line would appear with page or chapter numbers on it. The user could select a specific chapter or page to bring it onto the screen along with helpful information.

Because the novel has 135 chapters, developers might divide the multimedia program into four main segments: Ishmael's quest for a ship, the introduction to the *Pequod* and Captain Ahab, life aboard the *Pequod,* and the confrontation and chase for Moby-Dick. Each segment would have its own main screen or menu. Let's assume the producers can put the entire text on a few discs. Along with the glossary, developers might include annotations and a written or spoken commentary. To this end, the multimedia producers might choose to secure the multimedia rights to the most complete annotated edition of the text[1] as well as the rights for John Huston's classic film based on the novel.

Through multimedia, developers could enrich *Moby-Dick* as literature by providing in-depth commentary on the characters, showing how Melville develops them and how they fit into the plot. This would actually help teach users how to write as well as gain a greater appreciation of the literature.

The writers and designers might then decide where they want to provide graphics along with the text. Short clips from Huston's film might work, though they would use a lot of memory. For example, one scene involves the Whaleman's Chapel, where Orson Welles gives a sermon that comes directly from Melville's text. Users might also have the option of taking a "tour" of the chapel at the point in the novel when Ishmael stops there before setting sail.

Bernard Herrmann's *Moby Dick Symphony* might be used as the soundtrack to part of the text. One might also hear a sea chantey or two.

Other possible pathways might allow users to read a short history of New Bedford, see some examples of scrimshaw of the period, view a short documentary on how the old whaling vessels were built, or read a biography of Melville. They could also read about whales, endangered and not, or see how whaling today differs from whaling 150 years ago. Users could even plot the voyage of the *Pequod* on an interactive map.

Thus, the entire program would not replace the reading experience, but greatly enhance it. The student could also extend his or her vocabulary and learn about history, folklore, art, and music. Of course, the writer must always be aware of the available technology and the overall budget of a project. However, even the most basic programs can provide a great deal of information, enhancing and facilitating a user's appreciation of a given work.

A Sample Page   As an example, let's look at how a writer might design a page from the novel (this type of structure will be explored in greater detail later in the text). First, the user has the opportunity to lay anchor at the written text of Chapter 6 by clicking on the icon shown at the left.

Chapter 6

THE STREET

If I had been astonished at first catching a glimpse of so outlandish an individual as Queequeg circulating among the polite society of a civilized town, that astonishment soon departed upon taking my first daylight stroll through the streets of New Bedford.

At this point, the user can click on the icon shown at the left to view a short video of historic New Bedford, accompanied by audio narration from the book: "In thoroughfares nigh the docks, any considerable seaport will frequently offer to view the queerest looking nondescripts from foreign parts. Even in *Broadway* and *Chestnut* streets, Mediterranean mariners will sometimes jostle the affrighted ladies. Regent street is not unknown to Lascars and Malays; and at Bombay, in the Apollo Green, live Yankees have often scared the natives. But New Bedford beats all *Water street and Wapping*."

The opportunity arises here for the user to click on to *Broadway, Chestnut,* and/or *Water street and Wapping* to provide the following information: "Melville is referring to New York's Broadway, Philadelphia's Chestnut Street, and England's Wapping and Water streets—Wapping being in London, Water in Liverpool." The user can then click back to the Chapter 6 audio narration: " ... In these last-mentioned haunts you see only sailors; but in *New Bedford* actual cannibals stand chatting at street corners ... "

The user can click on *New Bedford* to see photos of New Bedford and sailors from the nineteenth-century places. With another click, the narration continues: "... savages outright; many of whom yet carry on their bones unholy flesh. It makes a stranger stare."[2]

The book symbol shown at the left appears, alerting the user to click on the icon to return to the text.

BEETHOVEN ON CD-ROM

A good example of this kind of enhancement is Microsoft's *Multimedia Beethoven: The Ninth Symphony.* Here music is enhanced by multimedia. This Microsoft CD-ROM, produced by the Voyager Company, has been around since 1991! In fact, many consider this program to be the first consumer CD-ROM product.[3] Though I provide here a description of the program, I strongly urge you to experience it for yourself. This brings up an important rule that will be mentioned many times in this text: If you haven't seen any multimedia products, then you have no business trying to create one. The same goes for any form of visual art. How could you expect to be a great painter if you've never visited an art gallery? How could you expect to write a great screenplay if you've never seen a movie? So, before going any further, start using some of the CD-ROM products firsthand.

Getting back to *Multimedia Beethoven*: The program is divided into five segments. The Pocket Guide lists the major sections in each of the four movements of the symphony. When you click a section's name, you'll hear its music. Beethoven's World is a historical introduction to the time and place Beethoven lived, detailing the influences that shaped his music. The Art of Listening explains basic musical concepts by focusing on sections of the Ninth Symphony. A Close Reading plays the symphony in its entirety, but allows the user to stop and start the music at any desired point. Text on the screen describes the section the user is listening to. Finally there's The Ninth Game, a question-and-answer game about Beethoven's life and the music in the Ninth Symphony. Whenever the user answers a question correctly, Ludwig smiles and tells the user he or she has done well (in German, of course). The Ninth Game is based on *stealth learning*, which I shall discuss in detail later.

Of course, there's also a Help menu that allows the user to display information for any segment of the program while displaying miniature sample pages.

Multimedia Beethoven is as fresh today as the day it first appeared on the shelves. It is fun and educational with interesting but easily understood graphics. In short, it is the perfect interactive multimedia product.

Voyager has also created Expanded Books, or books published on floppy discs. They contain the complete text of hardcover editions, can be loaded on the hard drive of a laptop and be read anywhere, and can be navigated easily. The user can underline passages, write and save margin notes, copy passages into a notebook and print or export them to another document, dog-ear or paper clip pages, enlarge or change the typeface, and search for specific words and phrases. Recently, the Expanded Books have been given added capabilities that allow the user to call up pictures, sounds, author's annotations, and endnotes.

Like Expanded Books and *Multimedia Beethoven,* future multimedia products will have to take advantage of the available technology and allow the artists involved to create new visions and open up new vistas. In this way, new products can be both marketable and imaginative.

Multimedia Formats, Design, and Genres

CHOOSING A FORMAT

After the first step of deciding if your project lends itself to this new digital entertainment, you will have to consider and decide what kind of interactive multimedia presentation you are going to create and exactly who your audience (or market) will be; that is, a *needs analysis* will have to be done. Will your piece be a documentary, a game, a theatrical release, or an informational kiosk? *Moby-Dick* would, most likely, be considered a CD-ROM edutainment product.

Again, developers must know and understand the available technology. For instance, CD-ROM technology is limited and, as noted, may become obsolete once the **information superhighway** arrives. In the meantime, developers will have to know how much information they can put on a CD-ROM, and if their product will have more than one CD per package. They will also need to know how to keep the user engaged, making the piece simple enough not to frustrate, but interesting enough to make the user want to continue.

Initially, the writer will have to ask some pointed questions, such as

1. What is the problem to be solved?
2. What idea am I trying to get across in the multimedia piece?
3. Exactly what am I using the interactive multimedia technology for?

The problem solved, the idea put forward, and the use of the technology will help one determine exactly what format to use. (Multimedia platforms and formats are discussed in detail in Chapter 4.)

Within the multimedia program, developers also link a variety of sensory modes. For example, they must decide what role audio will play in a program. They don't merely decide whether or not to use audio, but exactly how the audio component will stimulate the user and tie into the other modes such as graphics and text. In short, they ask themselves why the audio is needed. By answering, they make the decision.

One benefit of multimedia is that, like a book, a multimedia program is an intimate experience. You might not think to use the word *intimate* with *multimedia,* but by nature, multimedia is intimate. The best multimedia programs take you to other worlds, other landscapes. You and only you explore these new worlds and new possibilities with a CD-ROM system. Even online programs that make use of both the Internet and CD-ROM technology, like the Worlds Incorporated chat rooms and their future World's Fair, still create intimate environments where you can choose to "talk" with as many people, or with as few people, as you'd like. The best multimedia worlds, even without the benefit of virtual reality gear, can engage you to the point that you actually "feel" like you're in a different environment. It will be up to the writers to lay the foundations for these new worlds, to make them come alive in the minds of the users.

DESIGNING A MULTIMEDIA PRESENTATION

Trip Hawkins, the president of SMSG, Inc., and chairman of Electronic Arts, has discussed a number of important multimedia design goals. Hawkins points specifically to using multimedia for education: "The United States has the world's worst education system. It's expensive and it takes the longest to complete. ... The solution is interactive multimedia. In the sense that audio is the medium of hearing and video is the medium of viewing, multimedia is the medium of "doing." ... The fact that we learn by playing is a concept that is fundamental to all mammals."[4]

He then gives a list of seven multimedia design goals. They are (1) make the project innovative, (2) make it simple, (3) make it hot, (4) make it cool, (5) make it deep, (6) make it fun, and (7) make it cheap.

Make It Innovative Hawkins' first design goal is echoed by many heavy hitters in the multimedia landscape. One problem for writers and designers of interactive multimedia is to make whatever they're doing original and not just a retread of linear material. They should present a new experience, just as exciting as reading a book or watching a film, but in a unique way.[5]

Al Lowe of Sierra On-Line speaks of two problems in this regard. First, many multimedia producers today are so swept up by the technology that they pay scant attention to things such as plot, story, and character. Second, many multimedia personnel still retain a completely linear point of view. "I have a term for Hollywood taking a movie and attempting to repackage it as multimedia—**"sprocketware"**—you just shovel all that film onto a CD—you just shovel that footage onto there."[6]

To put it another way, "Don't Repackage—Redefine!" as Barry Miller writes.

> Taking a movie like *Jurassic Park* and turning it into a videogame— that's repackaging. Taking a bestseller and putting it on tape—that's repackaging. ... We will fall short if we impose our own familiar business models on the coming convergence. Telephones were not just telegraphs with voice. Computers weren't just calculators with keyboards. ... We have to resist media imperialism—the tendency to colonize, to define new technologies in terms of the old. ... To define television as radio with pictures may have been accurate, but it missed the point entirely. ... It took someone like Ed Murrow to shift the paradigm, to use the television as an eye, to take you, the viewer, into other people's homes. It was the first use of the technology of television fused to imagination: TV as a medium to create intimacy.[7]

In the same way, multimedia must redefine itself as an entirely new medium, one that can merge learning with enjoyment, absorption of facts with interactivity, and interest with excitement.

Make It Simple Hawkins next makes the point that, while most people know how to use the telephone, a lot of people still don't know how to program their VCR. He then lists a number of ways to keep a user engaged while making the product simple enough for interactivity:

1. Present the user with one way of doing things—in other words, there should be only one way the user can accomplish a given task. But be careful: Within an educational program you want to do many things with the learner—teach inquiry, decision making, problem solving, etc.[8]
2. Eliminate clutter on the screen. This includes making all icons clearly readable and not having too much art work on each individual screen.
3. Give the user both audio and visual feedback while he or she is working with the program, and let the user know just what he or she has done correctly or incorrectly.

Make It Hot and Cool   Hawkins goes on to write that a multimedia product must be both "hot" and "cool." To make a program hot, Hawkins means that the piece should use both high resolution and brilliant color. Making a program "cool" means that people must participate to get full value from the program. In other words, they must be engaged enough by a product to want to *use* it.

Make It Deep, Fun, Cheap   Hawkins ends his list of guidelines by writing that multimedia should be "deep," or involving. He stipulates that the user should make the decision how deep into the program he or she wants to get. Of course, it must also be fun. Tim Rohrer, a philosophy instructor at the University of Oregon, writes, "The payoff of fun [in multimedia] is productivity."[9] In other words, the more engaging the user finds a program, the better and more intensely the user will work. And, of course, the product must be inexpensive enough for the user to buy in the first place.

Tony Bove, one of the creators of the CD-ROM *Haight-Ashbury in the Sixties,* says that the design for that particular CD-ROM title was a collaborative process: "[The design was by] artist Jim Collins with input from [Tony Bove], David Biedny, and Mark O'Hara, with an eye toward the original design of the *San Francisco Oracle* [a sixties underground newspaper] with its many mandalas—many of the menu screens are mandalas. We used Timothy Leary's 'Turn on, Tune in, and Drop out' slogan as the organizing metaphor for the different sections."[10]

Of course, multimedia design is to some extent affected by the type of program being created. In other words, the program's design depends in part on the program's genre.

GENRES

The multimedia writer must know exactly what type of presentation he or she is writing for. As mentioned, to figure this out, one must define the goal of the program and discern the inherent problems in presenting the program and having the user reach the goal. In fact, the problems the writer is trying to solve will determine not only the format, but also the exact type of multimedia presentation to be used.

Let's again use *Multimedia Beethoven* as an example. The basic problem the multimedia writer and producer face is how to help the user understand not only Beethoven and his music, but also Beethoven's era and how it might have affected his compositions. One good way to do this is through a CD-ROM disc for a home CD-ROM unit that individuals can use. However, a presentation to a larger, more general audience at a kiosk or pavilion would probably allow one to share more information, but in a more extensive and expensive format.

Writers also need to understand how the various modes of multimedia will work within their piece, such as which sounds or music to use with which images. Alex Shapiro, a content editor in the games division of Microsoft,

discusses the role of the writer in multimedia and the different kinds of multimedia presentations one can use.

> Interactive pieces depend on what the purpose and who the audience is. Is it to
> entertain? [Then] what is the genre? Is it a game, an educational product, a refer-
> ence title?
>
> So, number one—*know your audience*—number two—*know your purpose*—and
> number three—*know the media at hand.*
>
> After a writer knows both the audience and purpose, he should look at every sin-
> gle thing that is in the particular genre he's interested in or writing for so that he
> can understand it thoroughly. You can't write a screenplay if you haven't seen a
> movie, you can't write a good book unless you read. It's amazing how many people
> apply for positions who have never even looked at a CD-ROM, and that amazes me.
>
> As a writer, you also need to know exactly what kind of writing you do best: based
> on your background, based on your experience, based on your interest. Narrow
> it down before you begin looking for work. Writers need to understand that there
> are many different genres within the field of CD-ROMs: You've got games, you've
> got instructional material, you've got reference titles, you've got edutainment,
> you've got interactive fiction, you've got adventure games, you've got role-playing
> games. ...Even within children's titles, you have a number of subgenres, like edu-
> tainment, entertainment (which I define as a straight game where the player isn't
> learning anything), role-playing games, and arcade games. Even children's titles that
> are leaning towards edutainment are becoming games because in order to educate
> through interactivity, you have to more or less make the product like a strategic
> game or a role-playing game.
>
> Now, there are other types of multimedia programs as well. There are reference
> titles like *Encarta. Encarta* is hyperfiction but it's not necessarily interactive. You
> could almost draw a graph designating the ratio of interactivity of multimedia titles,
> beginning with titles that are the least interactive and going to the titles that are
> the most interactive. And something like *Encarta* or Microsoft's *Cinemania* are on the
> low end of interactivity graph while *Doom* is on the high end of the interactivity
> graph. In any case, that's one way of looking at what's interactive and what isn't.
> Within that graph, you could then pinpoint what you'd be best at writing [italics
> mine].[11]

Shapiro also uses *Moby-Dick* as an example:

> So, let's say you're more interested in looking at *Moby-Dick* as an interactive
> title. [If you decided to make it primarily text based], perhaps with some shots from
> the John Huston film included ... there might be a hypertext leap into cultural
> history about New Bedford. But this would still be considered low end on the inter-
> active scale or graph.
>
> In the middle of the graph you'd find an adventure game like *Under the Killing
> Moon.* This is a detective story primarily where you're encountering different
> options, different places to go. Basically there are probably branching story lines that
> take you to different modules within the main story line. There are definitely differ-
> ent ways to graph adventure games—what you might call interactive fiction. You
> might, for example, do a web structure or an intelligent agent structure.[12]

Such structures use **pathways,** or the various routes a user can use to get
from one point in a program to another. Pathways will be covered in detail in

the chapter describing multimedia navigation, which also includes access and manipulation.

Categories of CD-ROMS Shapiro has divided CD-ROMs into categories. Each of the categories branches out into a series of genres or subgenres. For example, a computer-based training program on fixing a light socket could easily fit within the second category, Sports/Simulation. Each multimedia program or show utilizes a certain story structure. Even within television writing, there's a tremendous scope—sitcom writers, movie-of-the-week writers, commercial writers, documentary writers. The same thing is now true in CD-ROM writing. Here are the main categories of CD-ROMs:

1. Adventure: Includes working-through or more linear adventure games; involves pointing and clicking, finding lost objects
2. Sports/Simulation: Such as football or a purely simulated situation (being a doctor) or environment (*SimCity*)
3. Arcade: Like the adventure category, but more immediate, more like the game *Doom*
4. Children's educational, edutainment: Includes comprehensive learning programs, where teachers write the curriculum, and edutainment

Each of the categories mentioned has different elements of interactivity. Something like Sierra's *Pinball* game is the most *real-time* interactive piece. With real time, the computer can keep up almost instantaneously with the user. So, in *Pinball,* you actually get your body motions going; you're moving as if you *are* playing pinball. On the other hand, in most adventure games, real time is not necessarily of the essence. The objects a user may be looking for will always be there; it doesn't matter if you find it immediately and click on it or not.

For example, in Sierra On-Line's *Shivers,* users find themselves in an eerie museum that's been closed for years. As they maneuver through musty halls, they must find mysterious artifacts from all over the world that now contain the essence of Professor Windlenot. Once the artifacts are collected, the Professor will live again. Unfortunately, the evil spirits that originally stole the Professor's life essence are still lurking in the museum. The program certainly sounds interesting enough as is, but while exploring the museum and fighting evil spirits, the users have their reasoning and problem-solving skills challenged. On top of that, users learn about history and geography. They have to in order to play the game! This is what Alex Shapiro aptly refers to as **stealth education.**

Storytelling Modes Along with the four main categories of multimedia, there are also different storytelling modes within each multimedia classification. Charles Platt has divided interactive multimedia into three specific ways of telling a story and stated the degree of interactivity in each:

1. The user as observer: "The user doesn't control characters but may select one plot path or another at preset story branches. As in *Where in*

the World Is Carmen Sandiego?, the user can sample different viewpoints in a single story thread."

2. The user as director: "The user controls the decisions, speech, or behavior of one of more characters. This is the style of *King's Quest.*"

3. The user as actor: "The user becomes a character (usually the central character). *Myst* functions this way."[13]

There are also different kinds of story structures within multimedia writing:

1. Linear: Like any movie, play, or book, with a beginning, a middle, and an end. In such a structure there is rarely "audience participation."

2. Linear/Interactive: Though you can go on some different pathways, you always follow the same general story line and always arrive at the same ending.

3. Linear/Interactive/with Multiple Pathways: Though you start at the beginning, the ending can change according to the pathways you chose.

4. Nonlinear/Interactive/with Multiple Pathways: You go at your own speed and create your own situations. Utilized often in **edutainment** and instructional multimedia.[14]

Conclusion

In summary, when you wonder if you want to create an interactive product, you can consider design, format, and genre, as well as the question, "Could I do it without interactivity?" If the answer is "No," you're on your way. In the next chapter you'll see the types of multimedia products presented in detail, learning about how people came to choose careers in multimedia writing, as well as what each genre involves.

ENDNOTES

1. See Herman Melville, *Moby-Dick or, The Whale,* eds. Harrison Hayford and Hershel Parker (New York: Norton, 1976).
2. All material from H. Melville, *Moby-Dick or, The Whale.*
3. From Voyager's online information—"Where Minds Meet."
4. Trip Hawkins, "State of the Media," in *Cyberarts: Exploring Art and Technology,* ed. Linda Jackson (San Francisco: Miller Freeman, 1992), 12–13.
5. Ibid.
6. Al Lowe, interview with the author, August 1995.
7. Barry Diller, "Don't Repackage—Redefine!" *Wired,* February 1995, 83.
8. Hawkins is writing of multimedia as more of a presentation than a self-study medium. In computer-based education programs, the writer and designer can provide tools. That is, each screen can present a scenario that requires the learner to use tools to enhance what is being shown and to provide the depth required for serious study, including reference notes, glossaries, measurement instruments, and data-collection facilities. All these tools enable the student to interpret and interact with the content.

9. Tim Rohrer, "A Brief Paper on Metaphor Generation," Internet, April 1995 (by permission of the author).

10. Tony Bove, interview with the author, October 3, 1995.

11. Alex Shapiro, interview with the author, June 29, 1995.

12. Ibid.

13. Charles Platt, "Interactive Entertainment," *Wired*, September 1995, 148.

14. Ibid. (Though most of this comes from Platt's article, I've also incorporated some of Alex Shapiro's and Sierra On-Line's categorization of interactivity. Ed.)

4

Case Studies

"An interactive movie is not a movie. A movie acts on you, you do not interact with it."
— Roger Ebert, from his television review of
the interactive film *Mr. Payback*

"From Disney's point of view, we still think content, content, content! And so, the story, the characters, the world (the user) gets to move around in, those are always the things that drive the properties no matter where the technology goes."
— Kendal Lockhart of Disney during
a CNN interview

In this chapter, I'll present a more in-depth look at the specific multimedia genres and subgenres by discussing each. This section will also introduce the reader to some of the many people producing and writing in these genres, to show you how diverse their backgrounds are.

Interactive Books and Enhanced CDs

HYPERTEXT AND HYPERFICTION

First of all, I need to distinguish the difference between interactive books and hyperfiction or hypertext. **Hyperfiction** is text that is online and that any number of different people can become involved with, either as participants, readers, or writers.

Hypertext is sometimes described as nonsequential writing.[1] The term *hypertext* was first used by Theodor H. Nelson during the 1960s. He and Douglas Engelbart were among the first to theorize that electronic documentation could revolutionize "the word" through interconnectivity: the creation of webs of interrelated information. As George P. Landow and Paul Delany state, "So long as the text was married to the physical media, readers and writers took for granted three crucial attributes: that text was *linear, bounded,* and *fixed.* Generations of scholars and authors internalized these qualities as rules of thought, and they had pervasive social consequences. We can define *Hypertext* as the use of the computer to transcend the linear, bounded, and fixed qualities of the traditional written text."[2]

Like **hypermedia,** hypertext has a number of different links and pathways or webs of information the user can follow in any number of directions. As the delivery systems for online services increase in terms of speed and the amount of information that one can access, hypertext will truly come into its own.

THE ENHANCED CD

Another type of interactive book is the *Enhanced CD,* a marriage of music with multimedia. This was being done on such CDs as *Multimedia Beethoven* in 1991 (ancient history for multimedia). However, enhanced CDs bring "hi-fi audio to low-fi CD-ROMs. And the difference between CD-ROM audio and CD audio is as dramatic as the difference between listening to an old 78 on an aging Victrola and attending a live concert."[3]

The material incorporated into most of the enhanced CDs includes what would ordinarily be album liner notes—photographs, biographies of the musicians, lyrics, and painted or drawn images. Some also include digital music videos, and many now include the sheet music for the songs on the discs.

According to Daniel Tynan, "In an ideal world, the enhanced CD will provide musicians with a new means of artistic expression, a new way for them to reach out to their audience. Imagine what music videos could be like if their style and content wasn't dictated by MTV. On the other hand, if the enhanced CD becomes just another tool in the hands of visionless marketing execs, it could go the way of the linear-tracking turntable or the 8-track tape player—yet another technology that seemed like a good idea at the time."[4]

The way to use enhanced CDs to their fullest potential would be, first of all, to make the authoring tools available to the artists and musicians. The next step would be to give those same artists and musicians free reign to create their own programs.

A Recent Example   *Songs from "The Gypsy"* is a new variant on the enhanced CD. The story of how this CD came about serves as an excellent example of how creativity works among various media: literature inspires music which in turn engenders a novel that leads directly to an enhanced CD.

In 1986, the adult fantasy writer Steven Brust published his novel *The Sun, the Moon, and the Stars,* a new take on a Hungarian folktale. In this story, a kingdom lay in darkness because the sun, moon, and stars were hidden in a box in the belly of a sow somewhere at the end of the world. With Brust, Adam Stemple, the lead singer and guitarist of the Celtic rock band Boiled in Lead, wrote a series of songs based on characters created for Brust's novel. In 1992, TOR books published the novel *The Gypsy,* which Brust and the science-fiction/fantasy author Megan Lindholm based on the music Brust and Stemple had written. Boiled in Lead recorded the songs. Then, spurred on by their bass guitarist, Drew Miller, they packaged them on a CD-ROM.

What emerged was a disc, *Songs from "The Gypsy,"* containing the entire novel along with over eighty sound bites that the user can access from the text. Also included are album notes, graphics, and artwork. Plans had originally included video on what has been called an "elegantly designed" disc.[5] "Originally I just wanted to stick a text file and a couple of pictures on there, using the extra space in the hope that someone would be able to read them someday. The project grew from there," states Drew Miller.[6]

The CD-ROM does indeed enhance the novel. Miller explains, "The book quotes from the songs, so making the songs available while reading the book was a natural feature to have. The centerpiece of the data is the text. If we had designed it as a CD-ROM from the ground up, we might have done more, but it happened very quickly, with us adding features as we went and trying to figure out what would work."

At least for now, Miller doesn't see the cost of adding video justified. "I suppose once I get my hands on some multimedia authoring tools, though, I could create some content for a disc myself … if there were dollars and enough time."

Thoughts on the Future   As for the near future of interactive multimedia, Miller sees "getting the bugs out" to be the most important part of the agenda. "The hardware is only now beginning to catch up with the demands programmers and designers are putting on it. It's frustrating to run [a program] if it's slow. There are compatibility issues too; some CD-ROM drives, for example, have firmware that make them so they can't read *Gypsy* and other mixed-mode CD-ROMs [in other words, CD-ROMs that are supposed to be readable by both Macs and IBM-compatible PCs]."

Like many others, Miller feels that advancing technology—the use of the World Wide Web, cable modems (using cable TV to provide fast Internet access), multimedia database applications, and Internet database publishing with "smart links" to make information in a database available through the Web—will all enhance interactive multimedia technology. "CD-ROMs will eventually be replaced by 'on-demand' services, once enough people get wired with sufficient bandwidth. Five-gigabit movie CDs will also make more and flashier content possible [as long as the hardware can keep up]," Miller claims.

For now, however, *Songs from "The Gypsy"* has some wonderful music played by one of the most interesting and energizing groups around along with a suspenseful and well-written novel by two of the premier authors of modern fantasy fiction. The CD is well-worth having as part of your collection if you're looking to have your written text enhanced by other media.

Though *Songs from "The Gypsy"* is well designed, it is still mainly text-based. However, most multimedia is becoming less and less so. True, the first computer games were entirely text-based, with worlds created, as it were, in the user's head. As software became more sophisticated, graphics, animation, and video soon accompanied the text.

Games

One major player in the field of interactive entertainment and educational software is Sierra On-Line. Founded in 1979 as On-line Systems, the company's first product was *Mystery House* for the Apple, written by Roberta Williams and programmed by her husband, Ken Williams. The first computer game to combine graphics with text, *Mystery House* sold thousands of copies within months of its release.

In 1982, Sierra On-Line collaborated with Jim Henson to design a computer game based on Henson's feature fantasy *The Dark Crystal.* Two years later, the company released *King's Quest I: Quest for the Crown,* the first 3D animated adventure game. To date, the series has sold over three million copies. *King's Quest IV,* which garnered the Software Publishers Association Award in 1989, was the first game to contain **VGA** graphics* and to take full advantage of the new music card technology with a fully orchestrated stereo soundtrack. The game was also significant in that, unlike most games then, it featured a female protagonist.

In 1990, Sierra combined text, graphics, sound, voice, and animation on a single compact disc for *Mixed-Up Mother Goose.* In 1995, Sierra released *Phantasmagoria,* an adult interactive horror program combining live actors with realistic backgrounds. (See Figure 4-1.)

THE CREATIVE PROCESS

Al Lowe has a master's degree in music education and was a high-school band director and orchestra teacher for years. Lowe's official biography from Sierra On-Line states that he is "widely acclaimed for single-handedly corrupting the computer game industry." He created what is arguably the first "adults only" computer game. In *Leisure Suit Larry,* the main character attempts to get various damsels into his bed. Larry was so "successful" that the State of California actually introduced a bill that would have prohibited adult themes in any computer game. The legislation died in committee, though, and in 1987, *Leisure Suit Larry in the Land of the Lounge Lizards* won the Software Publishers Award for the best adventure game. Since then, there have been five more Larry adventures, and the Larry series is still a best-seller.

In 1992, Lowe created another game, *Freddy Pharkas, Frontier Pharmacist.* Set in California after the Gold Rush, the players find themselves in the shoes of Freddy, a beloved but meek pharmacist who must once again become a gunslinger in order to save his town.

When I spoke with Lowe, he was busy working on a new and very different project, *Torin's Passage: The Sky Above, the Sky Below.* In this fantasy game the young Torin must rescue his parents from an evil sorceress's magic spell. For *Torin's Passage,* Lowe has created a series of Escher-like worlds within worlds

---

* Video graphics adapter, the standard for display.

FIGURE 4-1 *Pushing the envelope of interactivity*—Phantasmagoria.

within worlds, making use of interactive multimedia's best aspects. Here, Lowe shares the process of creating a multimedia program:

> Well, in anything that's creative, there's no one way to do something. People have ways that work and people have different ways based upon differing requirements. I've done a lot of products over the last thirteen years; and out of twenty products, no two of them are done the same way. Part of it depends on what pushes the product and what pushes the story. Sometimes it's the subject matter, sometimes it's a plot, sometimes it's a character. This was true in *Leisure Suit Larry,* where I had a character who'd get into numerous situations and then I'd write up his reactions to the situations.[7]

Torin's Passage is interesting because Lowe wanted to have plot development but give some control of the plot to the user. That is, he wanted users to see their progress toward a final goal but still have several ways to reach that goal. To do this, Lowe literally split the game into five distinct "worlds."

> Of course, I [look] to build a game that could be sequelized, because (I don't know how other publishers work but I suspect it's the same) our sequels always sell better than our originals. You pick up a few people with the first one and you pick up a few people with the second one, but on the second one you also pick up all the

people who played the first one. And so, the only thing I can figure is that you attract some people each time because of the story or package. But then, if they like the first one and then if they come back for the second one, you've got to make them like the second one too; of course, you're only as good as your previous product. If the third in a series is a loser, it'll sell, because the second one was good. But the fourth one, even though it might be a great game, won't sell, because the third one was a loser. So, you have to maintain your consistency.[8]

Lorelei Shannon, also at Sierra, relates her view of writing an interactive multimedia piece:

Well, it seems to me that every designer I ever met [formats their writing] a little differently—we all have our own way of doing it. Most of us at this point are using the **screenplay format** with different ways of indicating the interactive branches. The main thing is [these branches] have to be clearly marked. With as many people involved on a project as there are, boy, there's no room for confusion.

On *King's Quest VII*, as far as plot and story goes, Roberta and I designed that together, we're pretty much coconspirators on that one. I wrote all the text and dialog, everything you hear in the game.

These are generally "entertainment products." I come from a fiction-writing background. Frequently, what will come to me first are one or two basic concepts. For example, I'll get an idea for a really neat character and a really strange situation and build from that and the things I design are quite story oriented. They're not like *Doom* where you're going and just shooting things and having a good time. Now, with the projects I work on, you're having a good time too; you're also unfolding a story and making it change and react to you. It's very difficult, very challenging, but it's a lot of fun.[9]

Interactive Movies

According to Roberta Williams, the cofounder of Sierra On-Line and creator of *Phantasmagoria,* the actual writing time for the script for *Phantasmagoria* took about three months. However, it took about a year to go from conception to the final multimedia product.

Echoing Roger Ebert's opinion, Williams is not a fan of the phrase *interactive movie.* "There is no such thing as an interactive movie that is compelling, or fun, in any way," she says. "An interactive movie implies sitting in a theater watching a movie that is supposed to be interactive and then pressing a button whenever there's a decision to make. You and all the people in the audience will make your choices, and then some computer will tally them up and make the appropriate move … . That ruins the movie experience."[10]

Even so, Williams did want to push the envelope with *Phantasmagoria,* (see Figure 4-1), creating a new type of interactive multimedia experience for the home user. The thriller unfolds in chapters. Players assume the role of Adrienne, a young woman who must unravel the mystery surrounding an island mansion she and her husband have purchased. According to Sierra's promotional material, "The cinematic design approach coupled with Williams's … storytelling will combine to give consumers the opportunity to not only witness the nightmare but become part of it." As Williams puts it, "I wanted to make the story more compelling, the characters more real, the interface more intuitive, and the game less frustrating. In thinking more about the mass market, I wrote the game in shorter 'chapters'—which breaks the game into smaller, easier to play sections. Each chapter is relatively complete in and of itself, and the player can check to see how far they are into each chapter through an easy-to-use chapter gauge."[11] (See Figures 4-2 and 4-3.)

Phantasmagoria lives up to Williams's hopes for the game. Users can, for example, save the choices they've made in the game and then view them all as a short movie. All in all, *Phantasmagoria* is probably the most compelling

FIGURE 4-2 ▌ *Live actors combined with computer-generated imagery in* Phantasmagoria.

FIGURE 4-3 ▌ *The computer-generated kitchen in the haunted mansion of* Phantasmagoria.

CD-ROM program out as of this writing and may redefine the genre. Ironically, and whether Williams likes the term or not, *Phantasmagoria* is, in fact, an interactive movie, with characters people care about, an intriguing and continually interesting plot, suspense, excitement, and some powerful adult horror—all in all, a good barometer for where multimedia "gaming" is heading. In fact, there have been recent attempts to censor *Phantasmagoria* because of the nature of its intense and personalized horror. Critics contend that it's one thing to view a horror movie, another to make choices that can lead a character to be raped or killed. People who have never played a CD-ROM game are reading and hearing about *Phantasmagoria*. The days of green flashing blobs representing fighter planes on a gridlike screen are long gone. (See Figures 4-4 through 4-6.)

FIGURE 4-4 | *Computer-generated exterior and live actor.*

FIGURE 4-5 | *An animated character tells your fortune.*

FIGURE 4-6 | *The strange and grim architecture adds to the mood of* Phantasmagoria.

Children's Interactive Multimedia

INTRODUCTION

Hoping to teach children or perhaps do some writing, Robin Worley ended up doing both, at first in a traditional classroom environment. Then, she went on to Splash Studios, a company specializing in interactive multimedia for children. As she puts it,

> I didn't have a real firm idea of what exactly I wanted to do as a career—this area [multimedia] was not even in my thoughts. ... I taught in some private schools and ... got my master's degree in psychology with a specialization in child development. So I've always been working with kids and I have always loved writing. ... Then, I started to get interested in computers. ... I began to do a little desktop publishing on my own, and I was getting a little business that way while I was going to school. I upgraded my computer, and then I got a multimedia computer a couple of years ago when they were first coming out. But, again, that was not the area I was thinking about as far as a career goes.
>
> When I heard about this job [at Splash] I was actually running a social service children's program and also working at Snohomish county doing a developmental screening program for children. ... About that time, my sister, who was working for Microsoft, heard about this job. Splash was looking for somebody who had a background in writing as well as in child development who could write the educational challenges that would fit in the CD-ROM titles. So that's how I came to work here. In a way, it was a fluke that I even heard about this position and it just fit with my background in education and work experiences. So, I really got here in kind of a roundabout way; it was not something I had been consciously preparing for. ...
>
> Of course, people are now being trained for [multimedia], but prior to a couple of years ago, nobody knew the area of "interactive multimedia" even existed. The classes weren't available. In a way, it's all still being invented now.[12]

Videoactive Games Splash Studios began by creating children's CD-ROM titles, and that has continued to be their primary focus. Along with new online services, the studios have now set their sights on interactive television and what they refer to as **videoactive** entertainment. In these video-taped programs, live actors move about in realistically rendered environments that look three-dimensional on a screen. Interactive television will allow users to search for, discover, and click on things within this rendered world, which presents a variety of audio and video **pop-ups**: goals, clues, and lessons that appear with each new discovery.

These videoactive games include educational challenges in which the users have to actually solve problems of some sort, as they do in certain computer-based educational programs. During these challenges, live actors won't be seen, but the user will still interact within that rendered environment. The people at Splash hope to have these programs on interactive television as soon as that format is available for consumer use.

Elements of a Good Story Here, Worley comments on the differences between writing a linear script and one geared for interactive multimedia:

> Of course, [writing for interactive multimedia] is very different from writing a linear piece. For example, when I was creating the challenges for the CD-ROM titles, I had to keep my mind on all the possible things that the children, the users, might do. Where they might click, what will then happen—so I couldn't go along in my mind on one linear path—I had to go on what seemed like a hundred paths—and try to plan for what they might do. Then we had to have a response for the choices made by the users designed into the product. For example, say you're in an environment and the challenge is to get across a ravine. ... The children, the users would have five things there that they would need to have in their possession in order to somehow get across the ravine. So, not only would I have to have responses for anything that the user clicked on as far as items they need to help them get across, I would also have to decide how those items would then be combined and what they would do. I also had to plan for other possibilities as well. Such as, what if the user was clicking on the walls or on the ceiling or on the top of the screen where the ceiling wasn't even seen. Basically, I'd have to write for everything that the user might do and have a response planned for that action. And so, I would come up with these huge documents. Now, for our first CD-ROM title, we ended up with eight interactive educational challenges, which ended up with a general time period of two hours for the user to do all the challenges. In this case, there were only eight challenges and I still ended up with a document, my first document, of nearly 200 pages [vs. screenplays, which average 120 pages]. Just writing out every single thing that would happen took up much of the material in the scripts. And I'd have to keep asking myself, when a user clicks on this, what is the response, then where does it go to and what loops might it make. Also, I'd continually be making sure that the writers weren't leaving the user hanging somewhere in limbo from which they couldn't escape. The entire project was just incredibly detail oriented. Writing nonlinearly is just really different—it's more taxing for sure; trying to think of every possibility that other people might have in their heads of what they want to do with the information and trying to write for that is a bigger job, it requires more work and a different kind of creativity. With linear writing, creativity is the writer's own

personal creativity. In nonlinear writing you need to be creative in a different way. You need to be able to get into the minds of other people and try to think of what they may be thinking of while involved in a particular program.

One also needs to set boundaries and parameters, retaining control over the random action of the user.

Regarding the process involved for writing these interactive pieces, Worley says, "First, we have story writers who write the story in linear script format so that the characters are developed and the entire script is basically done and can then be shot as a video or as a movie." In linear story telling, strong characters help create compelling stories. At Splash, the producers want their stories to be just as compelling as those of children's favorite videos, watched over and over. Straight interactivity alone will not be enough to engage the users. Children love interactivity and find it a lot of fun, but to get them really tied in, they have to also care about the characters.

Interestingly enough, Splash's first CD-ROM, *Piper* (1995), has spawned a video that uses a linear version of the story. That would not work with characters too weak to carry the story. (See Figures 4-7 through 4-12.)

Once the writers develop the basic story and characters, Worley, now a manager, looks over the material and decides on places that offer a natural opportunity for a "challenge." "If I was looking at a dramatic story line, the challenge would come at a climactic point in the script where the user would naturally

FIGURE 4-7 | *Live actors shot against a blue screen for Splash's production of* Piper. *Computer-generated streets and houses will be added in post-production.*

FIGURE 4-8 | *Real actors, a real door, and a blue screen.*

want to be involved and want to help have an impact on the outcome. So that's where I develop the interactive challenges and also have educational content come in at that point too."

FIGURE 4-9 | *Live-action director confers with the piper and a rat.*

FIGURE 4-10   *Computer-generated background with live actors in* Piper.

FIGURE 4-11   *A costumed rat in a computer-generated Hamlin Town.*

FIGURE 4-12 ▌ *Cool picture from* Piper.

THE THEORY OF MULTIPLE INTELLIGENCES

For the educational content, Worley follows a theory of *multiple intelligences,* designed by Howard Gardner, a professor at Harvard. According to this theory, education has always focused on the basic learning tools of reading, writing, and mathematics and has always tested students on their knowledge in these areas.

As Gardner states, "These skills in turn play a central role in school success. In this view, 'intelligence' is a singular faculty that is brought to bear in any problem-solving situation. Since schooling deals largely with solving problems of various sorts, predicting this capacity in young children predicts their future success in school."[13]

Gardner points out that this view of intelligence does not help predict success after schooling. He uses the example of two eleven-year-olds: One tested well, the other scored as average. However, once the two were adults, the so-called average student was a great success as a mechanical engineer while the "superior" student ended up working in middle management in a bank.[14]

Gardner goes on to outline seven intelligences that all people possess in different degrees:

1. *Linguistic intelligence* is the ability to use language well.
2. *Logical-mathematical intelligence* includes scientific ability and the ability to logically determine answers.

3. *Spatial intelligence* is the ability to form a mental model of a spatial world and to apply that model to the physical world. Sailors, sculptors, engineers, and surgeons all have highly developed spatial intelligence. Children who learn well by seeing pictures of objects also have good spatial intelligence.

4. *Musical intelligence* is exemplified by people like Mozart and John Lennon. Those who learn best by singing, by having a beat associated with some information, show musical intelligence. Interestingly, this intelligence appears dramatically when an autistic person performs music perfectly, though he can neither speak nor participate in the world around him.

5. *Bodily kinesthetic intelligence* is the ability to learn by moving one's body or somehow doing something physical with information received.

6. *Interpersonal intelligence* is the ability to understand other people and what motivates them and how to work cooperatively with them. Individuals really good at dealing with other people have a high degree of such intelligence.

7. *Intrapersonal intelligence* is the ability to form an accurate, undistorted model of oneself and to be able to use that model to operate successfully in life. People who are very insightful of themselves, of their spiritual self, and of their place in the cosmos show a lot of intrapersonal intelligence.

In Gardner's view, "The purpose of school would be to develop intelligences and to help people reach vocational and avocational goals that are appropriate to their particular spectrum of intelligences. People who are helped to do so ... feel more engaged and competent, and therefore more inclined to serve the society in a constructive way."[15]

By following the multiple intelligences (MI) theory along with new interactive technology, Splash hopes to augment the education process while making it more fun for students. Indeed, the use of digital technology for educational purposes cannot help but promote MI or similar theories. In *The Electronic Word,* Richard A. Lanham writes,

> If we remember how much our education system depends on grades—"grades" both as merit badges and as age and ability groups—and how much grades depend on verbal testing and verbal cleverness (as vocal but not always verbal minorities remind us), we can glimpse the attitudinal and administrative readjustments that will be required. If a "musical" child can be musical without the long and expensive muscular training required, who knows what "verbal" talents may emerge, or what verbal training may be required, when words and images and sounds, when pixeled* print and digital voice, mix in such profoundly metamorphic new ways. Perhaps we will learn the lesson Ovid's metamorphoses sought to teach, see how the literary imagination actually works. One thing is certain: the arts and letters will be one activity as never before.[16]

---

* Pixels are picture elements, tiny dots that electronically make the letters and other images you see on a computer or television screen.

Lanham goes on to show how interactive digital technology could offer extraordinary methods of teaching, from kindergarten to graduate school, radically changing traditional methods.

> A profound revolution in educational techniques is occurring as well. If we truly want to prepare our students for it, though, I don't think we should send them to our local ed school for two years' worth of pedagogical methods. It would make more sense to send them to the firms that are creating the new multimedia programs, firms like the Voyager Company or Lucasfilm. That's where the real revolution in educational technology is taking place, the revolution we would attend to if we wanted to prepare our students for their world rather than ours.[17]

Along with the Voyager Company and Lucasfilm, Splash is considered one of the companies at the forefront of this new revolution in education.

Splash Studios will be using formal focus groups to find out how well both the educational material and the interactivity in their multimedia products work. When Splash's programs do become videoactive for interactive TV, each "episode" will last less than half an hour and each challenge about three minutes. Alternatively, other products are open-ended—one can play them for hours upon hours. Because of both their audience (children) and their future venue (interactive TV), Splash did not choose open-ended formats. In their products, if one doesn't complete the challenge in the allotted time, then a character will step in and take one back into the story line. Viewers can always try the challenge again the next time they play.

Most of the products currently in development at Splash Studios are adapted from children's classics. For example, *Piper* is adapted from the story of the Pied Piper of Hamlin. *Bad Nicky* reflects an updated version of the myth of Icarus. There is also an original Christmas story being produced, but most of the stories worked on are the "tried and true" tales for children.

EDUTAINMENT: INTERACTIVE GAMES THAT TEACH

> "In ten years textbooks as the principal method of teaching will be as obsolete as the horse and carriage. ... Books are clumsy methods of instruction at best, and even the words of explanation in them have to be explained."
>
> —Thomas Edison, 1921—predicting that by the 1930s, most instruction would occur through motion pictures.[18]

The term *edutainment* doesn't bother Alex Shapiro of the Games Division at Microsoft. She explains,

> I wanted to [do something] with both my educational experience and my writing experience, which I was really more interested in. There was an ad in the *New York Times* for someone who had experience in writing and developing educational programs to apply to Macmillan/McGraw-Hill, for interactive educational products, an interactive textbook series, which was still in the experimental phase. This was in 1990, when multimedia was just getting big. This was also right after *Carmen Sandiego* came out, so people were very hot on teaching through interactive games, as was I. So I applied and I must say my cover letter had a lot of good ideas as to how

to put Hamlet into a good interactive program and make it into a game. I got the position and worked there for a year, and that's where I got my multimedia background. I already had a pretty strong background in writing [Shapiro won two fiction awards as well as scholarships at Columbia University. Ed.]. So I did have the necessary background in education, publishing, and teaching. Now, Macmillan is primarily a publishing firm, and the people who were running the technology department were primarily educators, with experience in teaching high school and experience in developing imaginative curriculum guides. So we were all new to multimedia. We did an interactive multimedia title for children called *Sounds of Poetry.* A project I also worked on was showing San Francisco through time—showing the transformation of a city and a culture through time which we could do through photographs and through descriptive narrative. That was really fun; that was my pet project and I loved it.[19]

When Macmillan began to downsize, Shapiro applied for other jobs and made the contacts that would lead her to Microsoft and gaming. "I like the term *edutainment,* because that's what we did at Macmillan/McGraw-Hill. We talked of [edutainment] in terms of 'stealth education'—where the children might not necessarily realize you're teaching them something."

The basic educational environment—i.e., the classroom—is structured for teaching many students at once and helping the greatest number of them learn and remember. However, a CD-ROM product is usually considered extracurricular. In other words, students will be using the CD-ROM product *in addition to* the normal curriculum and classes. Thus, it must be fun as well as educational; otherwise, the students won't bother with it.

The first project Shapiro worked on at Microsoft was *How the Leopard Got Its Spots.* With that program, the writers were essentially transforming the Kipling story into an interactive piece. After that project, Shapiro became involved with editing original material provided for the *Magic School Bus,* based on a popular Scholastic series. (See Table 4-1).

Shapiro stresses that without her background in education, she would never have been hired at McGraw-Hill in the first place. "Microsoft and Macmillan were looking at degrees, but I don't think that's true at other places—that was my route. I think Hyperbole, I think Sierra On-Line will be looking more at the type of work you have produced."

Essentially, writers need certain credentials for a multimedia production company to hire them, such as a degree in education or a relevant portfolio. Shapiro suggests that those who hope to find work in the multimedia industry should get involved in a course or program and, if possible, produce a **prototype** that can then be shown to various multimedia companies and producers (prototypes will be covered in detail in Chapter 9).

Shapiro feels she came into the industry at a good time:

I was really interested in what happens to the story element when you make it interactive and also in how kids learn the best, because I was very interested in finding imaginative and fun ways to teach. So my primary purpose was how can we teach kids in the most fun manner so that the program will be a real exploration and a real learning environment where they feel like they have control and where they remember things because it's a game as opposed to just being pedantic rote memorization. That was my primary concern, and I was coming into it from that angle.

TABLE 4-1 | *Microsoft® Home's*
SCHOLASTIC'S The Magic School Bus™ Explores the Solar Sytem

	Fact Sheet
What/who	Microsoft Home's new *Scholastic's The Magic School Bus Explores the Solar System* is a fully animated, interactive multimedia science adventure for kids ages 6–10. Inspired by the award-winning book series by Scholastic Inc., the product features the irrepressible science teacher, Ms. Frizzle, and her inquisitive class in an out-of-this world exploration of the solar system. The CD-ROM software is designed to entertain and encourage a sense of adventure and exploration. Kids can drive the Magic School Bus to any planet, land and explore the surface.
Product description	This time, Ms. Frizzle's *really* out there—in outer space that is! She's lost (or is she hiding?) and the kids in the class must find her. Together, the Friz, Arnold and his classmates and users explore outer space and learn about the planets and solar system. Along the way kids gather information from science experiments and reports to identify the Friz's whereabouts. To find the Friz, kids play games to win tokens that they use in the special Friz finder to guess the Friz's location. Of course, there are many unpredictable and fun surprises along the way.
Product goal	To make science fun for kids through a multimedia adventure with learning opportunities built into entertaining activities.
Features	• INTERACTIVITY: Kids can control their adventure. Kids drive the bus, allowing them to explore areas of interest at their own pace. Kids also control how they learn. Multimedia reports are presented in several ways to meet different types of learning styles. • SCIENCE CONCEPTS: Teaches kids about science concepts, such as gravity, in ways they can understand. Kids also learn "planetary" information such as the composition of each of the planets and the distance from the Earth and sun to the planets. • AUTHENTIC NASA VIDEOS: Videos of actual planet surfaces from NASA and the U.S. Jet Propulsion Laboratory. Features videos of astronauts on the moon as well as video fly-bys of Jupiter and other planets. • EXPERIMENTS: Interactive science experiments, that can't be done in the classroom, at each of the nine planets. For example, on Neptune kids can cut the planet in half to learn what's inside, or can fill up Jupiter with other planets to learn how large it is relative to the other planets. • REPORTS: Ten multimedia class reports, including facts, animations, videos and jokes about the planets and the solar system—all from a child's perspective.

TABLE 4-1 ▌ *(continued)*

	Fact Sheet
	• CLICKABLES: More than 200 "clickables" throughout the software to engage children and encourage exploration. In the classroom, for instance, kids click on the volcano to make it erupt, and click on Ms. Frizzle's dress to make the planets twirl.
	• GAMES: Fun games at each of the nine planets enable kids to earn tokens for the "Friz Finder," where they're exchanged for a clue to Ms. Frizzle's whereabouts. In these games, kids might catch the floating space boots or experience the effects of gravity on different planets.
	• ON-SCREEN HELP: Liz the Lizard guides children through the product, providing help if they need it.
	• STATE-OF-THE-ART MULTIMEDIA: Multimedia elements such as studio-quality character voices, sound and animation are used to make learning fun. Take the bus to Saturn or get out and explore the Moon to experience incredible 3D animations.
Special activities	• PLANET PICKER: Choose destinations anywhere in the solar system by clicking on the planet picker and flying to the selected planet. Users take a 3D trip to their destination, where they can get out and explore the planet's surface.
	• PROJECT PLANET: Kids exercise creativity by clicking on the classroom globe, which launches them into a fantastical world where they can create their own planets and special effects.
Age level	Kids ages 6–10.
Content development	Microsoft conducted hundreds of hours of usability research with children, educators and parents.
Format	CD-ROM only. Designed to be multimedia from the onset.

Source: Fact sheet provided by Microsoft Corporation.

See Figures 4-13 through 4-15 from Microsoft's edutainment program *How the Leopard Got His Spots*. Note the first image—a prototype screen eventually not used in the final product.

You can see that though edutainment stresses learning, it doesn't aim to become in integral part of school curricula. However, some programs are designed specifically to train and educate, as you will see in the next section.

FIGURE 4-13 ▌ *Prototype screen for* How the Leopard Got His Spots. *This was never used in the actual program.*

FIGURE 4-14 ▌ *This menu and the one in Figure 4-18,* How the Leopard Got His Spots, *are "Story Books." To hear how any word sounds, click on it once. Click twice on colored words to find out what they mean—pictures, video, and animations are also revealed to help explain the meaning.*

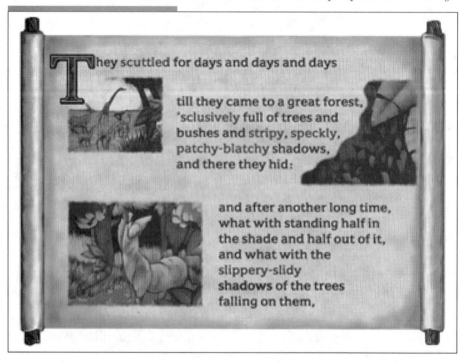

FIGURE 4-15 | *Clicking on the pictures allows the user to read along as the story is told. Clicking on P. J. the Bunny (not shown) gives the user Help.*

INSTRUCTIONAL INTERACTIVE PRODUCTS: CHANGING THE CLASSROOM

"When multimedia is utilized properly in education, the teacher's role changes significantly; the teacher is no longer the 'sage on the stage' who stands up and delivers information to students, but actively works with students to guide, facilitate, and support their academic experience."

—Helayne Waldman, instructor: Multimedia and Education, SFSU Multimedia Studies Program[20]

In 1990, fifteen states approved a change in the definition of *textbook* to make it include electronic media.[21] The edutainment products that Alex Shapiro has worked on, however, were created to supplement regular classroom curricula. As such, they would not be considered textbooks.

Purely instructional interactive titles, though, do serve as "textbooks." For example, a program that teaches how to type or one that covers a specific curriculum, such as geography, presents the material concretely. Such a program can be interactive in terms of the user having multiple choices, different ways of doing things, or answering a problem. However, such programs tend to be somewhat more rigid in their design than edutainment products and have fairly strict curriculum outlines. In edutainment programs, children have more control over what they might choose to do. In an instructional program, users follow an outline that says, "First you're going to learn this, and do these exercises, and then you're going to learn that and do *these* exercises." Also, each section usually ends in a test. In an edutainment program, such as *Magic School Bus,* the user can fly to any planet at any time. There is no testing, few instructional materials if any.

Alex Shapiro feels that instructional CD-ROMs greatly help one teach disabled children, because the children can set their own pace. Because teachers and computers can give individual attention, each student can learn at his or her own level.

One question comes up fairly often: Will the classroom ever become a place without a teacher? Some wonder if the teacher will be replaced by the monitor who merely watches over the students as they work with computers at their own pace. Can this kind of technology replace or change standard teaching?

That digital, interactive technology will change the classroom is pretty much a given. Conservatively, many classrooms will be "electronic" within ten years. Many colleges already offer telecourses, and some offer courses online. However, as with writers, teachers will not become anachronistic. If interactive multimedia is really used to enhance teaching, then it will allow instructors to better help those students who most need it. The instructor will, of course, have to learn the new technology to use it.

New technology could also allow students to participate more in the teaching process than before. Instructors may well learn a lot from their students.

There are potential downsides to the electronic classroom. With classes at many institutions already filled to capacity, administrators who feel that interactive technology will lessen the instructor's load may attempt to pack even more students into each class. In the ultimate interactive electronic classroom, the instructor might teach in front of a camera, with rows of monitors showing the faces of students from all over the world who have signed up electronically for the class. I wonder how many video monitors it will take to fill such a "classroom" to capacity.

However, as Shapiro has noted, a need definitely exists for educational interactive multimedia technology. In fact, many interactive programs already in use show positive results.

Multimedia Used for Instruction and Training

Task-oriented skills used to be acquired through the use of films and/or slide shows, memorizing text, and on-the-job training. Now, with the help of computer-based multimedia programs, people can learn how to do everything from repairing a faulty wire to performing gall bladder surgery. One of the largest and fastest-growing areas of interactive multimedia, such programs allow people to learn the basics of given tasks and apply them through simulations. For example, a program in electrical repair might have users find a faulty wire in a simulated house.

COMPUTER-BASED REHABILITATION

Computer programs are particularly helpful in rehabilitation: training someone who has been in an accident or suffered a major trauma to relearn processes usually taken for granted.

Lynn Gottlieb, the project manager for the Rehabilitation Learning Center (RLC) at Harborview Medical Center in Seattle, says she met her first computer when she was fifteen years old and immediately fell in love. "It was an Olivetti 101," Gottlieb remembers, "and I went to college and I was a math/computer-science major and I spent twenty-one years in what used to be called data processing and is now called information services industry starting as a grunt programmer and working my way up to being a director at the City of Seattle."[22]

Gottlieb held a number of other jobs that also prepared her for working with digital technology. She worked for US West and for Turner Broadcasting at the Good Will Games. In 1989, when she decided to do some volunteer work for the university hospital, she was assigned to work in the Department of Rehabilitation Medicine. There, she helped recreational therapists "transition" people back into society. "We would take people who were in rehab and have them do field trips and it was really wonderful. ... I enjoyed it, I learned a lot and I also ended up doing some work for the university as well."[23] Soon after her job at the university ended, Gottlieb found a job at the Rehabilitation Learning Center that combined her love of computers and information technology with her interest in rehabilitation.

Purpose of the RLC   The RLC is designed to help people with spinal cord injuries but not traumatic brain injuries. In other words, the RLC helps people who have no cognitive problems and whose brains are functioning as well after their injuries as they were before. The RLC aims to teach these patients skills while they are inpatients so that they learn to function once they are outpatients.

Depending on their level of injury, some patients will come from the trauma unit able to move their upper body, but some can move only their tongue and eyes. "It's like going back to being six months old again," Gottlieb says. "These people literally have to learn every single life skill they knew before; you cannot do anything the way you did it before a spinal cord injury."[24]

The Rehabilitation Learning Center helps people with spinal injuries learn the skills they need to get back into society without requiring a therapist constantly at their side: "The Rehabilitation Learning Center (RLC) at Harborview Medical Center (in Seattle) seeks to create a computer-based rehabilitation environment designed to educate and train individuals with acute or chronic spinal cord injuries and empower them with the knowledge necessary to make informed choices regarding life after spinal cord injury."[25]

Both Anthony Margherita, the principal investigator and project director for the RLC, and Gottlieb are already hard at work on two key components of the RLC. First, they are developing a multimedia information system. Second, they are establishing a network of computer workstations that support connection to the Internet, electronic mail, and digital instructional materials.

The Need for Interactive Programs   Gottlieb and Margherita point out that though the multimedia system will in no way replace the physical therapist, it will certainly augment therapy. For starters, the therapist will not have to start from ground zero: At the first meeting with the therapist, the patient will have already learned quite a bit from the multimedia system. Gottlieb refers to this as "preteaching":

> Patients have to be emotionally ready to receive therapy and learn skills. ... There are five transitional emotional stages involved in trauma recovery for the person dealing with a traumatic injury, very similar to those Elisabeth Kubler-Ross listed in her book *On Death and Dying:* denial and isolation, anger, bargaining, depression, and acceptance.[26] For example, you're going to be unable to teach someone going through the depression stage. We used to have nine months for inpatient therapy. Because of a change in the health-care providing systems since the early 1980s, we now have an average of four to four-and-a-half months to work with a patient. So, how can we speed up the learning curve but teach patients as much as we taught them fifteen years ago?[27]

The answer would appear to be the multimedia information system based on instructional materials designed to help the patients achieve "mobility independence."[28]

There are other reasons such an informational program is needed:

> Fifteen years ago, most of our patients, some 85 percent, were male, ages eighteen to thirty, who spoke English and were either college educated or graduates of high school. They were most likely to have been in, say, a rock-climbing or automobile accident. Now the population of rehab patients we get is younger, maybe fourteen to fifteen years old on average. This is a population that may not speak English as a native language: They may be Hispanic or Asian or from the Philippines. These may be people who are functionally illiterate in both our and their own native tongue.[29]

Through interactive multimedia, the patient can understand and learn through graphics, animation, and video. They can also learn at their own speed, and take in the basics faster than otherwise. Writers working on such a program must put themselves in the place of these patients, many of whom cannot speak or read English and thus would feel particularly frustrated working through a foreign language as well as injuries. The design and presentation of the material is therefore critical. Also, writers will need to do a lot of research, even if they already have backgrounds in long-term care. Of the program used for the RLC, Gottlieb says,

> This [program] is designed for people to start taking control of their own rehabilitation. We want to empower our clients: Empowerment means hope, and it allows the

clients to do for themselves. We cannot teach the skills [the clients] need to learn linearly to be truly effective. People come down from trauma center scared, frightened. Now, the first thing they're given is an adaptive device. It might be a microchip on their cheek or on their head, so they can manipulate a mouse, be it by head or tongue movements and there will be a computer in some form accessible to them.

Computers are used from the very beginning [of rehabilitation]. [Our clients] are shown how to log onto the computer.

This particular program is set up as one of a number of interactive modules. Patients can also go backward to reevaluate, they can go to a dictionary to look up words, and they can play edutainment games. Harborview originated this program, but many others are being designed.

Though Gottlieb manages the project, she considers herself a generalist, knowing a little bit about everything. She makes it clear that this program is only one part of an interactive training program that will include putting people on the Internet, allowing communication with others who have disabilities. There are also other advantages to being online, as she says: "On the Internet, no one knows you have a disability and nobody cares. Everyone is equal on the Internet. For the disabled, that is an incredibly empowering experience. So we work on getting [our clients] on there. The learning center will be put on the World Wide Web and items will be continually updated; everything from wheelchair information to new forms of therapy."

What Writers Need   For this kind of project, writers need a background in instructional design as well as technical- or speech-communications courses. A background in designing computer software or a computer system is also a plus, particularly because the various stages of design for computer systems and software resemble those for instructional multimedia:

1. The ability to see a problem
2. Deciding on a specific platform (Mac, IBM, kiosk), software, and hardware to be used
3. Getting the multimedia staff together
4. Working on a particular subject matter with experts and consultants who gather much of the necessary information
5. Working with the technical people to implement the information
6. Developing the different components of multimedia for this system (audio, video, animation, etc.)
7. Testing and bringing all the pieces together

As for the future of rehabilitative training using technology, Gottlieb says, "We will be able to utilize virtual reality to teach people how to maneuver a wheelchair, and, as technology improves, we'll be able to use better video and animation to teach all the necessary skills. As adaptive equipment improves, it will, in turn, be easier for people to learn how to use and to access computers and information. We'll still have to teach people how to function: how to bathe, eat, dress. But if they are unable to do this, we'll be able to teach them skills so they can direct others in their day-to-day care." In time, perhaps a combination of robotics and computer technology will allow even the most severely disabled to be more independent than ever before.

COMPUTER-MEDIATED LEARNING

CBE, CBI, CMI, CBT. These initials are often interchangeable in the world of computer-based interactive multimedia programs. Some have said that computer-based education (CBE) is more general in its concepts, while computer-based instruction (CBI), also called computer-managed or computer-mediated instruction (CMI), is more task specific. Here, I'll use CBE in regard to educational institutions such as schools and colleges and CBI for corporate instruction programs. Computer-based training (CBT) refers here to programs used in industry.

Learning Japanese on the Computer   Terry Weston, a language instructor at Bellevue Community College, has a background in business as well as Asia, where he has lived. While involved with the stock market in Tokyo, Weston began to work with computers and in desktop publishing. He's always been interested in how one can use emerging technology for education within an academic environment. For example, he took advantage of freeware on the Internet comprising Japanese word processing and dictionaries.

Weston feels that using computer-based education to teach subjects such as Japanese raises the level and the quality of learning. With advancements in technology, cross-disciplinary courses combining Japanese language, speech classes (small-group dynamics), and programming are now possible. The students could correspond frequently and easily via e-mail with students in Japan. Those engaged in such a course could also work with a group to create their own programs to benefit future students.

In Weston's current program, all authority and direction are turned over to the students, with Weston acting as a resource. The students working on these programs feel in control of the class and their learning.

"Lectures don't work," Weston says. "They don't get the language across. Projects work better if they are interactive."[30] In other words, a group may develop a food module in which different types of Japanese cuisine and restaurants can be explored, rated, and discussed. The goal is a food guide for other students. Weston hopes students create practical projects. For instance, one group did a guide of Seattle Center for Japanese students in Japanese.

"There are two ways to learn," Weston says. "One is to read and listen and use a pencil and a dictionary. The other is to go find someone who knows the answers to the questions you're interested in. This is interactive, and utilizing teams working on creating computer programs leads to group interaction as well as interactivity by the rest of the class with what the group has created."

Weston puts many lessons on the computer and presents them to the class, replacing overheads and slide shows and providing much more interactivity. An online dictionary helps students check what they write, looking up words.

Students can work on computer projects at school, put them on floppies, then take them home to work on them.

Though computer-mediated learning can speed things up, Weston feels it is still somewhat linear, because the students can't go wherever they want to go, only where the programmer wants them to go. For example, suppose a student comes across a Japanese word he doesn't know. He can highlight the word and press F6. The online dictionary provides the meaning of the word, the Japanese symbols or characters connected with it, and the digital audio lets the student know how to pronounce it. However, students cannot suddenly jump from this particular program to one on, say, Japanese food—they must first complete the lesson laid out before them.

Technology can work with any number of educational programs. The Internet, for example, is a great resource.

As Weston says,

> Suppose a student wants to know what the MTV music scene is like in Japan. He can find that out through a series of searches and then apply what he learns to a lesson. So, a number of layers: Japanese Music Scene—the language itself (a dictionary)—the pronunciation—there could be a hypertext layer [for] students interested in, say, music publishing or Japanese influence on their rock music scene—there might be a traditional Japanese instrument involved in a group and you can find out about the instrument itself.
>
> We shouldn't limit ourselves—you're not just learning about language, you're learning about a culture.
>
> One student did a brilliant presentation on Japanese comic books, utilizing *Power Point* along with audio interviews and sound effects.

Practical Steps   Here are ten steps to creating a simple program within the structure of a college or high-school course:

1. Work on the sociology of the group. When each group commits to togetherness and discipline and chooses their own name, a cohesion will take place.
2. Students discuss their different talents so they can put a production team together.
3. A proposal in the form of an outline is presented and the instructor gives feedback and suggestions.
4. A treatment is written, perhaps for each module.
5. Each group production team decides who's going to do what and who's responsible for what—one person is a content person, one is a programmer, another the layout artist.
6. The group submits in anecdotal form how the project is going. How have group meetings been going, has everyone in the group been able to meet, any disagreements?
7. Toolbook software is used: The metaphor for the project becomes a book, with each person in the group responsible for one part of the book. So, if there are six people in a group, there are six sections to the book;

if one section isn't done, it's obvious who didn't do the job. The group, not the teacher, then fires this person.

8. A storyboard is done showing what each screen will contain and what the links will be.
9. A flowchart is created.
10. A script for each module is written, each script containing at least a few short Japanese sentences (the dictionary might be used).

Suppose a group is working on a short story. At this point, the format can be a split page, half in English, half in Japanese, interspersed with visuals including both Japanese characters and images, either still or animated, that show what's happening in the story. As Weston puts it, "The teacher is no longer the sage on the stage—the teacher is now the guide on the side."

Computer-mediated learning frees up the students and affords them the opportunity to really learn themselves, which is what education is all about. Also, just learning one subject, such as Japanese, isn't enough anymore. Students need to have other skills, including computer literacy and teamwork.

COMPUTER-BASED TRAINING

A consultant in computer-based training and testing, Jim Benton has studied physics, electrical engineering, and math. He spent fourteen years as a technical trainer, mainly for industries heavily regulated by the government, such as chemical plants and refineries. His company, Multimedia CBT Consultants, creates interactive computer-based training modules geared specifically to enhance learning, work performance, communication, and management. The same software that delivers the training and testing modules can also deliver point-and-click access to critical procedures and diagrams.

Benton's program on learning how to do computer-based training begins with an introduction complete with animation and music: "Welcome to computer-based training. If you need help at any time, simply click on the question mark button."

Animation follows, showing a rocket taking off, complete with the sound of engines. Then, the program asks the most important question: "Why use computer-based training?"

More and more companies use CBT mainly because it saves them money: "Sometimes it's able to get the costs down to one or two dollars per person, which is way below what it would cost to have instructor-based training."[31] Also, it's available at the students' convenience rather than management's or an instructor's convenience. Companies also use CBT to comply with government regulations and to avoid liability.

Even so, "a lot of questions come in when a business starts considering computer-based training: What's the benefit, what's involved in the design, what equipment and software will they need?" Benton says.

In any type of computer-based program, the planning should be complete before the production begins. Benton agrees. "I see a lot of situations where the production is started before the planning is finished and people end up going down dead-end streets."

Another concern centers on the educational level of the employees. As Benton claims, "Particularly in an industrial environment, you can be dealing with employees who only function at a sixth-grade reading level. At that time, you may want all the text read to them, and that's an important factor. If however, you're dealing with a person who has a graduate-level education, they're going to be insulted to have that text read to them."

One must also choose the appropriate hardware and software to produce the program. In addition to graphic software, one needs text software to generate the story, as well as administrative software to generate and control download files and control animation.

Before undertaking a CBT project, the writer must do quite a bit of research. Often, the subject matter expert (SME) and the writer are the same person. If not, then an SME will definitely be needed. "A lot of times, particularly where liability or regulation is involved, you'll have to get a safety management person involved; it's people who have actual experience with the subject matter that are very important to the writing of a CBT program," says Benton.

The writer will also have to understand that icons or on-screen buttons will be used to generate the script. As Benton advises, "Realize that you are going to have to be as visual as possible, and understand that you will be working with graphics, text, and sound files and then pulling them all together into a cohesive if nonlinear form." CBTs should be cross-platformed; in other words, they should be able to run on both Macs and PCs. To be accessed very quickly, CBTs might also run on a local area network, or LAN (some training documents can be accessed in under three seconds). While working on the project, the writer must also note how the testing is going—what works and what doesn't. It would be very helpful if the writer used a program that automatically kept a record of the testing.

Writers should start with an outline. Benton always begins this way: "I have scenes in editable format, so I don't have to go back and redo screens later. Have everything on paper, pull together articles and written material. Then, talk to others on the production team: This is what I've got, what do you think of it?"

Writers need to work on the team and have meetings, but they also need a firm agenda in place. The SME should especially have his or her material down and have the approval of all the other people—and all conflicts out of the way, particularly where policy is involved—before production begins. Often, company policy will drive the information within a CBT program. An outdated policy can pose a real problem. Policy should be updated and approved by anyone who has anything to do with that subject and by the corporation or client.

The design should focus on the interactive aspects of the medium: the more interactivity, the greater the learner's grasp of the material. Also, as Benton argues, the medium presents certain responsibilities:

> Because the CBT is interactive, you need to have the user doing something besides just acting like a couch potato, just pressing a button on a control. So [at certain

points] a question will pop up, asking the user to remember what he's seen on the screen, requiring feedback. If the answer is wrong, the user is forced to get to the right answer. Particularly where safety is involved, you can never have the user walk away and say, "Well I never did get the right answer shown to me," because you'll be in violation of regulations and expose yourself to a great deal of liability.

During the course of a CBT program, students might also encounter a trap—going off on a tangent and losing track of where they were. Writers of CBT programs need to maintain a fair amount of linearity, because students must be aware of what they skipped or didn't learn.

Many people do not have a large amount of memory in their computer, so CBT developers must keep memory requirements down. Files that use less memory play better and faster. One should always conserve as much memory as possible.

Authoring software pulls the graphics, text, sound, video, and testing files together. The software should be powerful, but also easy to use. Similarly, hardware must support the software used.

Economy drives CBT. It is, again, a way to cut costs while maintaining a highly trained workforce that feels empowered by the tools the computer provides. Later in this chapter, you'll see the creation of such programs in greater detail.

COMPUTER-MANAGED INSTRUCTION

Steven Conrad is the Director for Business Development at MediaPro, Inc., in Seattle. With a background in finance and the computer sciences, he has worked in the computer field for over fourteen years. Though he has served in sales and marketing for a variety of software companies, his technical proficiency has greatly benefited his most recent work. In 1992, Conrad and others created MediaPro, which develops high-end educational materials for corporations. Along with the realization of interactive technology, Conrad's interest in education served as a major incentive in the development of the company.

Computers can now "manage" as well as monitor the educational process by gathering statistics, giving reports on what people have taken, what they haven't taken, and what their progress has been through different activities.

CMI monitors the educational process for mainly "hard" or measurable skills, such as how a worker learns to operate a computer system; that is, teaching someone how to use a computer by using a computer in an interactive way. In other words, the CMI MediaPro, in large part, measures skills that enable one to accomplish a specific task or series of tasks, such as processing sales orders or analyzing budgets. CMI takes users through a process of how to accomplish a particular task in a reasonable manner that's cost effective for the company; it also gives workers any additional skills they need. Using CMI has proven to be a cost effective and practical alternative to the more traditional ways of teaching skills.

FIGURE 4-16 | *Sample screen from one of MediaPro's Computer-Mediated Learning Programs.*

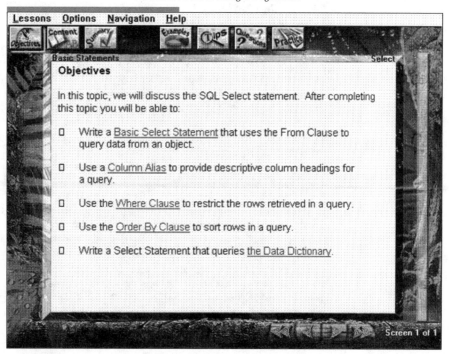

"What are you doing now?" Conrad will ask his clients—

Let's measure the results, and if we can put a CMI program in place we can look at the outcome of it and see what's the difference, how much time it took, how much did it cost.

We try to speculate on new technology—but we try not to second guess. When we first started, 2X CD-ROMs were $500, a decent 16-bit sound card was $300—we said that's our market ... then we felt maybe it required too much, so we took a step back—took some interactivity out—we hit the market a year and a half later and CD-ROMs were now $150—so the market caught up with us. If we would have stayed on course and stuck with our gut feel on where the technology would be, we would've been right on target—even a little ahead of the market.

[This taught us to] go with your gut, read everything you can get your hands on; you need to make a stab and go for it. The market moves so fast, I thought the market would take two years to catch up with what we were initially doing—it took one.[32]

The writer's role on the kind of projects MediaPro works on can take several different avenues, as Conrad explains.

A lot of times, we go into a company and they have existing training material. In other words, we go to a company and the company may be teaching the same class every week fifty times a year—very boring for the instructors to teach the same thing over and over—and the students are inconvenienced. So we'll take a course like that and we'll put it on the computer, in an interactive fashion. People can take it whenever they want to, and instructors can move on to do more higher-end, higher-value things and get away from the basics.

We have technical writers and instructional designers. Hopefully if you have the qualities of both, that's the best for us—but you definitely need some kind of instructional-design background on how to present this material. You'd be amazed at how many corporations don't have any clearly defined objectives within their content. I mean, Basic Instructional Design 101—what are the objectives, what are the goals? Or, a company might have the objectives but the content doesn't match. They need to know how to achieve the objectives. There will be problems if you have someone who is, say, a great word processor teaching word processing but he or she doesn't have a background in technical design or instruction. What you end up with is a hodgepodge of material varying in quality.

So, the first thing we would do from a technical-writing and instructional-design background is look at their material and decide if it's sound from an instructional standpoint: Do they have objectives, do the objectives match the content, how do you test to make sure you've achieved objectives, how do you certify that they're competent in the subject matter we're dealing with? So that's the first task.

The second task is how do we want to present this material? We utilize different media elements—so you may have a graphic artist with you or someone experienced in media enhancement who might say, "Well, look at this area here, this would be great for a video clip, there could be some great graphics you could do here, this type of interaction. We can do a drag interaction here, we can do a click/touch on interaction." Basically, from a high level, you determine what fits where.

The main thing to remember: *The content will dictate the flow and the interaction.* We don't want linear presentations, people don't like the linear presentation aspect in training. People learn in different modes, and we need to account for that. The question is, how do you do that and still keep a structured form and approach to the materials? If you let people fly all over the place and go anywhere they want to, studies have shown, they get very confused. They get lost. But if people are sitting there with just a page forward and page backward on the screen and all you allow them to do is just walk through the material in a very predetermined fashion, people get very bored, people don't feel they have control over the material, and they learn less.

An idea that comes up again and again in all types of interactive multimedia is that the user must be engaged enough to stay interested and, in the case of CBT, to keep working with the program. By the same token, the program must also be easily understood. As Conrad puts it,

The user likes to feel they're in control. Also, the user likes to have some overall structure in place. I may want to hop around, I may want to look at different things, but I want to have some kind of [obvious] framework to deal with. ... I don't want to get lost. Confused people don't learn anything. If you're confused, you spend your time battling the interface and you're not getting the content. ... We need to give people control, we need to have people have the ability to—as their learning styles dictate—jump from subject to subject but within a somewhat defined context so they don't get lost. We need to keep media active for them so we don't present the same thing in the same way all the time so they get bored with it. They have to be interactive, they have to be doing something, and it's got to be entertaining. This is the

MTV generation, we can't have static objects sitting on the screen like we used to. So this is a very great challenge—presenting content. We do some courses that go on for days; so how do you present something that keeps someone's attention for so long and presents them with the ability to go into it from different aspects and that's the really key challenge?

We will sit around the table and have all personnel meet, and we have debates that sometimes last for days concerning the material [see the section on brainstorming in Chapter 6]. Even if we decide on something, as we go forward, it will be refined, I guarantee it.

This is a collaborative process; we need our people to work together. I'd never have a programmer create the interface, but you need the programmer there because he knows what's technically possible. What you have is interface married to content that's married to interaction, and they all have to work together. Interface cannot be an obstacle to the content; you need to make it intuitive and free flowing, and it can be difficult to do.

In many cases, according to Conrad, the content *is* the interface. Different content will take on different interfaces.

You need to look at every project and say, "What is the content, what are you going to present?" That will basically help us determine what the interface looks like. And though you look at each project individually, you don't have to reinvent the wheel every time, but be careful not to shoehorn content into interface. For recent projects, we have not had a "previous" and "next" button on the screen—that says "linear content" to me.

Technical writers are then looking to work in, for lack of a better term, sound bites [see quicktalk in Chapter 8]. The approach that we've taken ... for the writer is look at your content and group related material into sound bites. For example, if we're teaching someone how to use a word-processing system, and we come to how to do search and replace, the basics will be covered, but then [we need to] allow users the option of going different directions with it. We start with a basic concept: Here's what we're going to cover, here's how it's used most times. The user then has the option to go into more detail or into different areas.

Now, suppose you have a sales course. You're basically teaching a soft skill: How would the user manage a call? Well, we go over basic concepts on how to do that and then we break it down into any number of areas: How will the user deal with a type A personality? ... The end result is to have the user tested. A certain level of competency needs to be reached. It's the same [with harder skills like] the internal operation of a database: How do you tune and set up a database? How will you impart that knowledge to a person in a way that allows them to do their job? They can be focusing on different things: They might be focusing on security or on tuning a database. And so the users are allowed to drill down through the content to the levels they feel that they need to be competent in their job. We then test to make sure they know what they're doing. The program asks, "If you have this situation, do you know how to solve it?" If you press "Yes," the program says "OK—prove it. Show us how you solve it and walk us through it." Based on how the users walk through it, we give them feedback. "This is how you did—you took a left turn here, you probably should have taken a right, for this reason. You went down this path ... that was a solution, wasn't the best solution." It isn't necessarily whether it's right or wrong, it's what the *best* answer [is]. This is something you can do today with computers that would have been very difficult to do without them, a few years ago.

> Some companies test, some don't—but the users are responsible for their knowledge. And, if the users know they will be tested, they'll pay more attention. They'll go through many more paths and they'll repeat paths—so you'll find a free-flowing approach to content [italics mine].

MediaPro makes use of authoring tools such as *Authorware, Icon Author,* and *Toolbook.* The developers lean toward the icon-based authoring tools, because they find them more productive than others.

Interface and content structure will lead the production team into a storyboard and/or a writing template. As Conrad states,

> At this point, you need to know the amount of content to be presented on the screen and the different interactions. So we'll create a word template in *Word* and set the fonts as well as the width of content. We always give students the option of presenting both text and audio on the screen at the same time. Some people want to turn off the text and just listen to it, but most people like to see and hear at the same time. Also, people like to go back and review. This limits us in terms of how much on-screen text and audio we can use. When we write we need to be cognizant of those little sound bites and say, "Well, this is what we're covering here; this is what we're covering next."
>
> Templates actually go to programmers. ... It's the writer's job to put that content into an organization and the programmers just take that content and put it in. Ninety percent of content delivery, what we're going to present when, is done by the writers. That means, the writers need to be aware of several things. [For instance,] are we presenting material in a course that refers to previous material? A student may run across a term from an earlier part of the program, so we may have a list of terms, a glossary, and the writer needs to keep track of that. All technical words and words that relate to content presented should be "hot" words—words that you can click on and get a definition of what that word is. We don't define words in the content, we just use them. If a student doesn't know what the word means, he then has the option of clicking on the word and having a definition presented to him. The people who know the word don't have to wade through all the text describing it. ... We give the student the ability to jump around. So "jump words" can be blue, underlined words in our particular course, much like on the Internet, and so if ... something really catches my eye and I say, "Oh that's what I really wanted to learn—I've learned some basics, that's how I really want to apply it," it's another lesson. The student can click on that; it'll jump him back to that lesson. And the students need an obvious way to return, which is part of the interface.

Computer-based training and instruction are burgeoning fields, with entire textbooks devoted to them. The concepts and visions of these areas still offer new and exciting ways to train workers and students in all industries and disciplines.

Kiosks and Homepages

THE INFORMATIONAL KIOSK

Certain institutions, shopping malls, and public information centers have begun to use informational *kiosks,* or small interactive pavilions. Recently, however, it's been felt that Internet "Homepages" are more easily and less expensively created, updated, and accessed.

Jim Shuman is the Director of the Faculty Multimedia Resource Center at the Northwest Center for Emerging Technologies at Bellevue Community College. One of Shuman's projects, an informational kiosk for the college, was intended to provide students with access to information about courses and programs, services, faculty, and current events. The platform used to develop the title was a Macintosh Quadra 7100, and the actual kiosks were to be PC 486 computers with touch screens.

In such projects, writers and designers work together on the program. Shuman comments on what kind of work a writer might expect on such a project.

> The need for highly skilled writers and designers is more critical in an information kiosk than many other multimedia applications. The kiosk is a way to obtain information, and in many cases the kiosk is located in a public place. Therefore, the challenge for the designer is to develop an interface that will attract attention and make it easy for the user to navigate to the desired information. Often, the challenge for the writer is to *condense information* in a way that will not burden the user by having him/her sort through a lot of data, while making sure all of the important information is included.
>
> In most ways, the development of an information kiosk is similar to other multimedia projects. Special considerations have to do with location of the kiosk and the equipment used for the kiosk. The location is important because the purpose is to give the user access to information. The equipment issues involve security, the use of touch screens, and whether or not to have sound, keyboards, and printing [italics mine].[33]

Anyone interested in writing this type of multimedia program should have certain skills, as Shuman states: "Writing skills are critical to multimedia, especially in information kiosks. Users do not want to spend a great deal of time searching for the desired information. In addition, they do not want to read screens full of text. Therefore, the writer must be adept at assuming the role of the user to determine the level of writing that would work with the intended audience."[34]

To expand on Shuman's thought, here are the skills I consider necessary to write interactive multimedia scripts:

1. The ability to both understand the intended audience and to put themselves in the audience's place
2. The ability to distill large amounts of information into a concise presentation without losing critical data
3. The ability to work with others or to be, as Shuman puts it, a "team player"
4. The ability to communicate well with the other personnel throughout the development of a project

There has been a phenomenal growth in the use of digital information kiosks. As the cost of equipment comes down, more and more organizations and companies will use this way to disseminate information.

"Kiosks will evolve from delivering information to dispensing items such as airline, theater, and sports tickets; and providing for registration in college classes. In addition, many of the services provided by physical kiosks will gravitate to cyberspace as the Internet and especially homepages take on the look and feel of a kiosk."[35]

HOMEPAGES

Homepages are informational electronic programs found on the Internet. They differ from CD-ROM or kiosk-based interactive multimedia programs only because homepages use a different delivery system, the Internet.

Homepages most often refer to a set of linked documents that contain text, graphics, sound, and/or animation as well as *hypertext*—written words presented so that the user can jump from topic to topic following a series of annotations and cross-references. Recently, developers have built on hypertext to include images and audio material. This expanded format became known as *hypermedia*.

Homepages are stored on the same or different servers where they can be linked to one another. The **World Wide Web** (WWW or Web) refers to the body of homepages that currently run on the Internet. As such, the Web is an Internet information service based on hypertext technology. Allowing users to access literally any type of Internet resource, the Web gathers Internet resources from all over the globe and organizes them into menu pages or screens. Essentially, the Web attempts to organize all the information on the Net as a set of hypertext or linked documents. The WWW is an Internet client/server application: The user gets to a homepage that offers a range of choices for exploring the Web. The homepage will have a variety of linked words or images that one can expand on (think of footnotes in a book).[36]

Developing a Homepage   Rhonda Davis, an information specialist at Bellevue Community College, was the Content Coordinator for the college homepage. Her tasks involved the following:

1. The determination of content
2. The "look" and "feel" of the layouts
3. Giving direction to the artist or artists, as well as meeting with the artist and revising work
4. Gathering, editing, and writing content
5. Applying **HTML** (Hypertext Mark-up Language) to files
6. Transferring files to a server
7. Assembling the main pages, writing the "linking verbiage," and placing graphics
8. Linking files to the main pages
9. "Tweaking" both file content and graphic look
10. Updating the page with new information and features

With a background in journalism, Davis formerly worked on the *Seattle Times Community Newspaper* as a photographer and feature writer. Becoming involved with the creation and design of a homepage and working in the field of multimedia was something new. "[Homepages] can be thought of as 'interactive brochures.' They are innovative because, unlike a kiosk, they can be accessed anywhere a computer, modem, and **browser** can be found. Unlike a 2D brochure, which must be mailed or retrieved in person, the homepage provides immediate access to information and can include multimedia 'bells and whistles.'"[37] These "bells and whistles" include the graphic interfaces as well as the use of animation, video, and sound.

"Internet browsers, such as Netscape and Mosaic ["*Windows* for the Net"] make homepages possible. Browsers ... allow access to all the Internet functions, such as e-mail, file transfer protocol, etc. Homepages make access to the Internet more functional and carefree, much like graphical interfaces have made computers less intimidating to the technophobic," says Davis.

Homepages are providing wonderful opportunities for educational and other institutions. For example, students entering a college or university site can obtain much more than just text-based information about a particular program or course. They can also post e-mail to or even have an online "chat session" with an instructor or advisor for further information.

Homepages and Kiosks Compared   "Information kiosks have a similar look and feel to the homepage in that they contain 'clickable graphics,' which lead to other documents," Davis says. However, some bypass the kiosk completely, putting their information directly on homepages. In fact, kiosks might well be considered the eight-track tape players of the multimedia world. The information on a kiosk is static and located only at the kiosk itself. This means one must update its information on-site. Further, one cannot link the kiosk to other kiosks. Homepages, on the other hand, can be accessed by anyone with a computer and the proper equipment from anywhere in the world. Also, the content of homepages can be continually and quickly updated from remote locations and can be linked to other pages with similar content. Essentially, because of such versatility, the homepage is usurping the informational kiosk as the ultimate interactive information center.

"The kiosk of the future," Davis says, "will probably be a computer running a browser locked in to a Homepage—another link on the World Wide Web."

Working on the Web   A writer working on the Web needs to remember the following important points:

1. The writer is addressing a worldwide audience.
2. The writer has to be both graphically and technically literate (as in all multimedia writing).
3. The writer must be able to determine the most appropriate medium for presenting information.

4. The writer must be particularly specific and succinct, because users require immediate and understandable information.

As Davis puts it, there must be "a balance of solid, concise information and attractive graphics." As noted before, the main thing to keep in mind is that *the only difference between writing for a homepage and writing for a CD-ROM is the delivery system.*

What's terrific about homepages is that writers can receive immediate feedback by posting their e-mail address on their homepages. Davis notes that this has positive as well as negative aspects: "All the world is your critic!" She continues, "While the homepage is an exciting medium because it can be ever changing, it puts an extra burden on the publisher/writer because [he or she will have] to update information more frequently." Technical aids make such administration easier.

"In its present form, the World Wide Web of linked homepages is the great equalizer. It is an artist's playground where anyone with a computer can gain worldwide exposure for their writing, photos, video, or artwork. Many artists have homepages displaying their work to a worldwide audience. It is fertile ground for writers and audiences," she claims. However, she also cautions that "future regulations may hamper this spontaneity."

One might consider the homepage as multimedia distilled to its essentials: a user-friendly menu consisting of text, pictures, sound, animation, and/or video. For that reason, Davis's college homepage will be used as a template for multimedia navigation in Chapter 10.

Documentary Programs

"The documentary film is one of the most complex kinds of films to make. It requires a special kind of discipline and intelligence to make it work: To manage to capture real people and real events on film and do it well is a difficult task."

— Hal B. Wallis, letter to the author

If you think it's difficult to write and design a documentary film or video, "You ain't seen nothin' yet." In linear documentaries, one must take hours of footage and cut it down to the bare bones. Even an epic documentary series such as *The Civil War* had enough footage left over to be used in another, wonderful, one-hour documentary, *Songs of the Civil War.* However, interactive multimedia offers the user a lot more information than documentaries do. Developers also need to provide pathways and, in most cases, make sure the piece still makes sense. For example, in a historical piece, the user should be able to jump around in time. Remember, the users won't have to go linearly from, say, 1860 through 1865, as viewers must do in *The Civil War.*

With my background in documentary filmmaking, I'm glad to see a number of powerful and well-done examples of interactive multimedia documentaries (sometimes referred to as **infotainment**). Medio Multimedia's *Vietnam* gives the user a powerful, well-crafted, and thorough history of the war. *PC* magazine calls Graphix Zone's *Bob Dylan: Highway 61 Interactive* "a lovingly crafted tribute to Bob Dylan's career. The interface—a sort of beat-generation coffee house/cafe—is original, and it represents the best of this genre of CD."[38]

Haight-Ashbury in the Sixties!, another fine, in-depth interactive multimedia documentary, is the first CD-ROM title produced, published, and released by Rockument, Inc. The company focuses on producing and publishing interactive media titles on the cultural impact of rock music as well as the music's roots and foundations. Rockument's team of Tony Bove and Cheryl Rhodes have already produced several CD-ROMs for Random House and the Voyager Company. With strong backgrounds in New Media, Bove and Rhodes have been writing about computers since 1976. Prior to founding Rockument, Bove was the editorial director and Rhodes the managing editor of the newsletter division of Hypermedia Communications, Inc. For the past five years, they have also edited the *Macromedia User Journal* for multimedia developers. Bove has also been a contributing editor for *NewMedia* magazine and, with Rhodes, has written over seventeen computer books, including the recent book/CD-ROM package, *The Official Macromedia Director Toolkit* (Random House/Hypermedia). They have also written a number of books on emerging technologies, including the bestselling *The Art of Desktop Publishing* (Bantam, 1986).

Both Bove and Rhodes have always enjoyed working in and writing about emerging technologies. With *Haight-Ashbury in the Sixties!* they have wedded their love of new technology with their love of the music and spirit of a special time.

To the majority of you under the age of thirty-five or forty, a lot of references I'll be making will probably mean little. For example, when I purchased the *Haight-Ashbury* CD-ROM, the salesman at Egghead Software asked me, "Who or what is Haight-Ashbury?" As such, I've decided to give a concise history of the period. For those who do know all about the sixties, skip ahead to the next subsection.

A SHORT HISTORY OF HAIGHT-ASHBURY

Like the East Village in New York City, Cambridge in Boston, and the Sunset Strip in L.A., Haight-Ashbury was a place where artists congregated during the middle and late 1960s. The Haight had been a blue-collar district that bordered the ghetto, but rents were cheap and many of the old Victorian houses and mansions were lovely.

The San Francisco sound, which came out of the Haight area (among others), began as a combination of folk, blues, jazz, and British rock known as the Mersey Beat. Groups like The Byrds had already shown that folk-rock was a viable alternative music, but the Haight, not far from Berkeley, site of the Free Speech Movement begun in 1964, was politicized to a certain extent as well as artistic. With the addition of psychedelic drugs like LSD (still legal in the early and mid-1960s) a new type of music and lifestyle emerged from the area, personified by such groups as The Warlocks (later The Grateful Dead), The Great Society, Jefferson Airplane, and Country Joe and the Fish. One can say it all started in the Haight: the pseudo-Edwardian style, Art Nouveau cum psychedelic posters, and street theater (actually, it all started in 1965 in Nevada with a group called The Charlatans, but that's another story).

The Haight was one of the main sites during the so-called 1967 summer of love and, in fact, became a spot the tour buses would pass (one hippie with a sense of irony used to run alongside the buses holding up a mirror to the passengers). By the early 1970s, the Haight had grown dangerous, and peace and love were replaced by street crime, heroin, homelessness, and later crack and street gangs. Two excellent books on the era are *It Was Twenty Years Ago Today* by Derek Taylor (New York: Simon & Schuster, 1987) and Joel Selvin's much less nostalgic *Summer of Love* (New York: Plume Books, 1995).

HAIGHT-ASHBURY ON CD-ROM

What It's Like   *Haight-Ashbury in the Sixties!* begins with a montage of stills and music from the era. You click and a menu appears that impels you to either "TURN ON, TUNE IN, or DROP OUT." Around this main screen are various hidden icons for the navigation menu that pop up when you move your mouse pointer to that part of the screen (see Figures 4-17 and 4-18).

The play icon is a revolving yin-yang symbol on the top center of the screen. It indicates that the show is running. If you click on this icon, the show will stop playing at the end of the particular scene you're watching. In the right upper corner of the screen is a watch icon that you can click on to view a time line. It shows you the year the material you are watching occurred and also allows you to jump from one year to another nonlinearly. Below the time-line

FIGURE 4-17 ▌ *Introductory screen for* Haight-Ashbury in the Sixties.

FIGURE 4-18 ▌ *Navigation menu for* Haight-Ashbury in the Sixties.

icon is a pointing right hand that can move you forward scene by scene each time you click on it. A quit button sits in the lower right corner. At the bottom center of the screen is the menu button, a miniature of the main menu screen that, if clicked, takes you back to the main menu. Lower corner left is the help button, which opens the help windows for you. Above that is a pointing left hand that takes you back to the previous scene, and above that you can click on the credits button, which brings up the credits for the images and sounds you are currently taking in.

Throughout the program, a moving or blinking object may appear. Essentially, this is a reference button. If you click on it, you visit a tangent, a part of the program that gives you more information without your losing your place.

The main menu is laid out as follows:

"TURN ON" plays the show "The Rise and Fall of the Haight-Ashbury" in linear format.

"DROP OUT" gives you an opportunity to play a game in which you have just arrived in Haight-Ashbury in the late sixties and your goal is to gain enlightenment.

"TUNE IN" takes you to a menu that offers you the following choices:

- Oracle: This is a reference section where you can read articles and view artwork from the underground newspaper, *The San Francisco Oracle,* for the years 1966 through 1968.
- Music: You can listen to music of the era while observing animation and edited scenes from the "turn on" show in music-video style.
- Video: You can watch video clips, including a variety of interviews, from two television documentaries: *It Was Twenty Years Ago Today* and *The Hippie Temptation.*
- Credits: This features biographies and available works of the artists, filmmakers, musicians, and writers involved with the program.
- Topics: Here you can find where to select a specific topic, such as politics, and view the available material.
- Roll your own show: You can choose from some 150 scenes and narrations and place the material in any order you'd like, in essence creating your own mini-documentary.

How It Got Started   Allen Cohen based the script for this program on a live 1980s slide show he performed, using material collected from more than thirty photographers. Cohen had served as editor of the *San Francisco Oracle,* one of the first "underground" newspapers, had helped organize the Human Be-in, and had been a major figure in the San Francisco poetry scene.

Cohen combined his idea for a multimedia slide show with an imaginary interactive documentary that he wanted to create. The project was conceived as a CD-ROM program in 1990, when the major participants held a meeting to define it. Final production began four years later, after several prototypes had been made and major licensing agreements signed (an important part of any visual medium that uses well-known images or music). With these agreements signed, Rockument could secure an advance against sales from Compton's

NewMedia in exchange for distribution rights, not unlike what many independent producers do with films and videos. The CD-ROM was released on July 1, 1995.

"In simplest terms," Tony Bove states, "we wanted to create a story that would run for one to two hours from beginning to end without interruptions or the need to interact, yet still allow the user to have interactive control: pause and play a tangent (which might have a short video clip to play, an image to examine, or a text to read), move forward or backward in the story, jump to different periods in the story, and so on."[39] (See Figure 4-19).

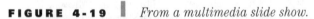

FIGURE 4-19   *From a multimedia slide show.*

Development The writing staff at Rockument took the initial script to a series of meetings, periodically refining it and sharing copies of the **working drafts**[40] with artists, animators, sound editors, the director, and the producer. This allowed the other personnel to work on different sections of the script, make annotations, and report any changes back to the project editor, who would then make up a new draft and deliver copies to everyone. Bove points out that with digital technology, such as electronic documents and e-mail, the process of rewriting and retooling the script neither takes much time nor wastes paper. It also has the added benefit of keeping developers current.

As with most documentaries, linear or nonlinear, research for this particular piece was ongoing. The staff continually looked for specific images to accompany the written text, such as pictures and video clips of the march on the Pentagon and Grateful Dead footage. Research for the project, of course, benefited from Allen Cohen's personal experiences with the people and events of the Haight during the late 1960s. Also, several people who had heard of the project contacted Rockument to offer material for possible inclusion in the program. "This was going on up to the last minute!" Bove states, "It was nearly impossible to turn off the spigot, and the project grew to fill two CD-ROM discs before it was finished."[41]

Bove mentions that along with the pivotal research and the material provided by Allen Cohen, three other major steps were involved in putting the Haight-Ashbury piece together:

> The first step was to identify the big pieces of the final product, such as the story itself, the images, the video clips that would be interesting to use as tangents, the music, and the organizing metaphor for the interactive experience [metaphors are discussed in detail in Chapter 7].
>
> The second step was to digitize everything that was already "in the can," such as photos, finished art, video clips from archives, and every graphic image that could be used for promotional and advertising purposes. Existing material could then be used in experimental ways while creating the new material.
>
> The third step was to create the new material needed specifically for CD-ROM navigation, menus, and whatever else is needed to cue the user that interactivity is possible. New material, such as video clips for an introducer who welcomes the user to the CD-ROM, were also created to augment the existing material.[42]

Concurrently with these steps, the entire story's narration and music were recorded, digitized, and finally **subsampled** for use in the title.

Rockument aims this product at two markets: those who remember the sixties, particularly the San Francisco scene, and those too young to remember but who want to know what the era was really all about. As Bove explains this, he also expresses the satisfaction of producing an interactive documentary:

> It is often said that today's hackers are descendants of the original hippies, and that the computer industry was built by ex-hippies (Steve Jobs, Mitch Kapor, and many others are examples). Certainly there is a "free-speech" attitude in today's Web society, and the wizards of computer graphics were certainly influenced by the sixties-era light shows that started in Haight-Ashbury.
>
> Because Haight-Ashbury in the sixties is one of the most distorted and misunderstood periods in the twentieth century, we have tried to present the period as a living experience, as a primary, multisensorial experience that will allow viewers to see it as if they were hippies on Haight Street during the Summer of Love. So our audience expands from those who were there and want to experience it again, to those who are too young and want to know what it was really like. Future generations will have the opportunity to have this more immediate experience of the times, as will students and historians.[43] (See Figures 4-20 and 4-21.)

Rebirth: An Independent Project

In 1994, Bruce Wolcott, a designer, a 3D modeler, and formerly the media production coordinator at the Pacific Science Center Foundation in Seattle, presented his final project in his class, "Writing for New Media." For his prototype, *Rebirth,* he used slides and narration to portray an interactive multimedia piece documenting and dramatizing the history and myths of Tibet. Wolcott soon got together with other innovative and creative people within the field of digital

FIGURE 4-20 *These are original images created exclusively for* Haight-Ashbury in the Sixties! *by the artist Alton Kelley.*

technology and began to create the actual CD-ROM presentation of the project. The best way to describe what a project like this entails, particularly an independent project, is to let Wolcott relate the project's history in an essay written

FIGURE 4-21 ▌ *Here are a couple of scenes from the White Rabbit animation sequence. Win the Haight-Ashbury game, and you can see the whole thing!*

specifically for this textbook, "The Rebirth Project: Brief History of an Independently Developed Interactive Multimedia Presentation." Here follow the first pages of the essay.[44]

THE REBIRTH PROJECT: DEVELOPMENT AND HISTORY OF AN IDEA

Developing an idea outside the mainstream production process has advantages and disadvantages. For this project, Seattle provides a wealth of technical resources as well as a solid base of Tibetan scholarship, from which we've been able to draw through people's good will. Because we're not working under the imperatives of a fully-financed project, we've had the freedom to expand our contacts and scope. This has enabled Rebirth to grow in an "organic" way, albeit more slowly than in a strictly commercial setting.

The Rebirth Project evolved from conversations among several people, dealing with two related main ideas. A series of discussions evolved around John Wieczorek's restoration of Tibetan sacred art for the Sakya Monastery in Seattle, and his idea to create a CD-ROM on the traditional Tibetan board game of Rebirth. Simultaneously, Bruce Wolcott was involved with the Bellevue Community College Media Program, and had created a proposal for a CD-ROM project on Tibet, with an emphasis on Tibet's spiritual leader, the Dalai Lama.

In the initial discussions, it was assumed that we would combine the two ideas into a single CD-ROM title. It was quickly decided that for aesthetic and technical reasons, the project would benefit from a dual treatment in two companion CD-ROM's. Further discussions explored the possibility of an on-line implementation as well. In the first CD-ROM, *Rebirth: Quest for Ancient Wisdom,* traditional Tibet along with its artwork, religion, and perspectives, will be presented in a 3D gaming environment, where people can participate first hand in this virtual representation of their historic world. In the second CD-ROM, *Rebirth: The Homeland,* issues surrounding the 14th Dalai Lama as a world leader, current politics, geography, and other aspects of Tibetan history and culture will be portrayed in a combination of encyclopedia and documentary styles. A last component for the project includes implementation of a website presence on the Internet called *Rebirth: Virtual Tibet*. This will provide a multimedia venue for sharing ideas on topics concerning Tibet, and will also serve as a springboard for marketing the CD-ROM products to a wider market.

The original participants met to develop these ideas further and to expand our human resource network. [Writers, artists, educators, and other consultants were then brought in.] ... As our ideas formalized, the need for visual content became apparent. By now, our resource network had grown to include several talented photographers who'd each documented various aspects of Tibet and Tibetan culture. Photo CDs were pressed of over 150 images from three local photographers, Russell Johnson, Jon Garfunkel, and Marco Mascarin. We began to plot out the structure of our 3D gaming environment, which we plan to develop in the "MYST" tradition. In this case, the mystery and allure of that environment is based on an actual ancient culture, with all its beauty and multiplicity. We considered our potential market as well—which we see expanding from a "niche" audience with interests specific to Tibet, to individuals interested in this topic on the basis of education curriculum, eastern philosophy, travel, or art appreciation.

The Rebirth project, with its broad scope of information, and diversity of participants, requires an approach that can handle a high level of complexity. In order to do that, we have used concepts from information architecture as well as from new "virtual worlds" technologies.

THE REBIRTH PROJECT AS A PROCESS OF "WORLD BUILDING"

During planning for the Rebirth project, it became apparent that our subject, the history and culture of Tibet, would require an approach that was different from a traditional script-writing process. Tibet has a cultural heritage reaching back in time for thousands of years, an elaborate weave of religious beliefs, self-governance, life patterns, artwork, music, language, architecture, and stories. Because of Tibet's location within a ring of mountain ranges, its civilization was able to develop in relative isolation from the rest of the world until the 20th century. Thus, Tibetan society evolved its own distinct view of the world, which we are seeking to recreate in the Rebirth project. This interpretation will come through the experiences of Westerners in Tibet, as well as from the Tibetans themselves. In order to portray the complexity of the Tibetan world view, we have chosen to utilize four aspects of information architecture—world building, use of metaphor, multiple pathways to content, and information design economy.

Conclusion

It has probably become obvious by now that no one person creates an interactive multimedia program. Certainly, such programs rely on the combined talents of a number of people, much as a motion picture or television show does, despite what the idiotic "auteur" theory says; i.e. that the director is the "author" of the film.

The next chapter will give you an in-depth look at the personnel in a multimedia production team and how each expert enriches the virtual world being created.

ENDNOTES

1. Theodor Holm Nelson, "Virtual World Without End," in *Cyberarts: Exploring Art and Technology,* ed. Linda Jacobson (San Francisco: Miller Freeman, 1992), 161.
2. Paul Delany and George P. Landow, *Hypermedia and Literary Studies* (Cambridge: The MIT Press, 1994), 3. See also p. 55.
3. Daniel Tynan, "Enhanced CDs: The Sound of Things to Come?" *CD-ROM Today,* August 1995, 30.
4. Ibid., 34.
5. Ibid., 33.
6. All Miller quotes taken from Drew Miller, interview with the author, Sept. 22, 1995.
7. Al Lowe, interview with the author, July 1995.
8. Ibid.
9. Lorelei Shannon, interview with the author, July 1995.
10. Sierra On-Line Press Kit: *Q & A with Phantasmagoria Designer Roberta Williams,* by permission of Sierra On-Line. It is interesting to note that, recently, a number of interactive movies have, in fact, been put into general release. Even before the release of the awful *Mr. Payback, I'm Your Man,* dubbed an "Interfilm" by its creators, opened a few years ago as the first theatrical showing of a live-action interactive film. See William Grimes' article in the *New York Times,* "When the Film Audience Controls the Plot," for the week of December 18, 1992.
11. Ibid. For instructional or educational computer-based programs, "chapters" are referred to as *modules.*
12. All Worley quotes taken from Robin Worley, interview with the author, July 1995.
13. Howard Gardner, *Multiple Intelligences: The Theory in Practice* (New York: HarperCollins, 1993), 14.
14. Ibid.
15. Ibid., 9. I encourage you to read more on MI; a summary cannot do it justice.
16. Richard A. Lanham, *The Electronic Word* (Chicago: University of Chicago Press, 1993), 16–17.
17. Ibid., 124.
18. Bruce Barcott, "Second Thoughts on the Virtual Life," *The Seattle Weekly,* July 19, 1995, 17.
19. All Shapiro quotes taken from Alex Shapiro, interview with the author, June 29, 1995.
20. Helayne Waldman, interview with the author, March 1994.
21. Trip Hawkins, "State of the Media," in *Cyberarts: Exploring Art and Technology,* ed. Linda Jacobson (San Francisco: Miller, Freeman, 1992), 18.
22. Lynn Gottlieb, interview with the author, July 1995.
23. Ibid.
24. Ibid.
25. *The Rehabilitation Learning Center Executive Summary,* by permission of Anthony Margherita, Principal Investigator/Project Director, 1.
26. Elisabeth Kubler-Ross, *On Death and Dying* (New York: Macmillan, 1969).
27. Gottlieb, interview with the author.
28. *The Rehabilitation Learning Center Executive Summary,* 7.
29. All Gottlieb quotes taken from Gottlieb, interview with the author.
30. All Weston quotes taken from Terry Weston, interview with the author, January 30, 1996.
31. All Benton quotes taken from Jim Benton, interview with the author, February 6, 1996.
32. All Conrad quotes taken from Steven Conrad, interview with the author, February 8, 1996.

33. Jim Shuman, interview with the author, September 18, 1995.
34. Ibid.
35. Ibid.
36. Harley Hahn and Rick Stout, *The Internet Complete Reference* (Berkeley, CA: Osborne McGraw-Hill, 1994), 495–512.
37. All Davis quotes taken from Rhonda Davis, interview with the author, October 8, 1995.
38. "The Top 100 CD-ROMS," *PC* magazine, June 27, 1995, 142.
39. Tony Bove, interview with the author, October 3, 1995.
40. A working draft, according to Tony Bove, consists of callouts for images (using PhotoCD ID numbers and descriptive names), music loops (filenames with designations for different sampling rates), and tangents with either high-resolution images or digital video movies (filenames with indicators).
41. Bove, interview with the author.
42. Ibid.
43. Ibid.
44. "The Rebirth Project: Brief history of an independently developed interactive multimedia presentation," submitted by members of The Rebirth Project, copyright © 1995 (Rand McDonald, Amanda Moore, John Wieczorek, and Bruce Wolcott), 1–3.

A Guide for the
New Developer

5

The Multimedia Production Team

Who Does What, and Where the Writer Fits in with the Group

"Producing a communication-effective multimedia program is not easy, even though technology has made the physical aspects relatively simple. The tough part is mental— reasoning, planning, accomplishing. It takes in-depth knowledge, superior cinematic skills, artistic achievement, and verve. In the aggregate, such attributes are best found in the multimedia team."

— S. M. Shelton, "Multimedia"

There was a time when hiring a "writer" was the last thing any multimedia producer thought about. Fortunately that's been changing. "I have a couple of clients who now realize they have to bring writers on from the very start," Frank Catalano writes.

But there's a lot of confusion about the type of writer, and I think that's an important distinction to make. Ideally, you hire writers who understand interactivity intuitively. But that's rare. So you go with those who understand how to *tell a lot of story in a brief amount of time* [italics mine], episodically—perhaps TV or radio drama writers. And you augment that with writers who know how to create a rich world and tell the "internal story" of character motivation, etc.—short story or novel writers.

Companies that choose to tack on a writer late in development are making a mistake, since the creative synergy a writer brings to the process can help meld the product concept, or at the very least make it richer. That is, if the writer understands the potential and limits of the medium. Writers who say "let me just write and leave me alone" won't work in this industry. As more and more software products become content-based, good writers are critical to differentiate the products in the marketplace.[1]

The Members

Like productions in film and video, an interactive multimedia project depends on a team: who they are, how well they work together, what their specialties are. Different projects require different teams. Here is a list of the members of a generic production team:

1. *Project manager* is the equivalent of the **producer** on a film. The project manager does just about everything: coordinating schedules, finding resources, hiring people, and keeping an eye on the design, the development (making sure it follows the design), and the budget.

2. The *creative* or *design director* is the equivalent of a director for film. Many times, the project manager will take on this position as well. The creative director has a "vision" of the project in terms of its look, consistency, and ultimate effectiveness as multimedia.

3. *Content experts* are consultants who know the field the project is dealing with.

4. *Writers* (you knew I'd get to them) follow the manager and director's instructions to give shape to the project by putting all raw data into words. Writing duties may be divided up between content writers, who work with the experts, and scriptwriters, who write the narration and dialog, making sure that the tone fits the project.

5. *Graphic designers* and/or *animators* do everything from original storyboards to designing icons, deciding on the look of the piece, and creating characters, working with both the director and writers.

6. *Sound designers* work with actors, narrators, composers, and musicians and must be familiar with MIDI and digital sound recording and editing.

7. *Videographer* or *Cinematographer* is the person who shoots the images, though most multimedia projects use video, not film. Often an entire video production team will be hired.

8. *Interface Designers* and *Programmers* have excellent technical backgrounds. Designers put all the pieces into a digital format. Programmers make use of authoring programs to write the computer and software programs that will allow the multimedia project to work.[2]

Working Well Together

Members of the production team have to work together and need to understand the different roles of other members on the team. The hope is that the team will work well together: "A lot depends on synergy," Alex Shapiro says. "If you're creating a complete script in isolation that you're going to show to people, then [the writer] should include as much visual information as possible. Also, what's really different about writing for CD-ROM is that, since the technology is so new, teamwork is essential. So being able to work with people is essential. Many writers do work in isolation, and to suddenly find yourself working on a team can be a bit of a shock."[3]

For example, you might have worked all night writing a skit or sketch for a project. You bring it into the office bright and early, hand out copies to the team, but then somebody tells you it won't work, that it's technologically impossible to carry off, or it has to be two minutes shorter. Shapiro continues, "And you're thinking to yourself, 'My God! They want me to convey X amount of information and have it be thirty seconds long?' And in a weird way that's where you're your most creative, because you have to work within the technological constraints and still convey the same emotion and information that you would as if you had no restraints. And yet the technological restraints are stiff."[4]

Check and Balance: Manager and Creative Director

Al Lowe suggests that to keep a project manageable, the best approach is to follow the movie industry's model of having both a producer and a director, or a manager and a creative director.

> We have two people who have different interests, who fight each other, as a form of check and balance. My feeling is, you have a producer and a director and usually, in our business, the director is also the writer. You have the producer and you have the director and the two go toe-to-toe: One's responsible for keeping the project on budget and on time and up to quality and the other person is responsible for pushing the technology and pushing the story and getting as much as they can and getting it as best as they possibly can. The writer, the director, they're not worried about the money; they're worried about the game and the experience. ... To me it seems, that's a good idea. You have the two guys who fight each other and it ends up [leveling or balancing things out]. When one person's in charge, it's tough, because that person has split interests. You've got to bring the project in on some kind of budget, or else you don't get to play anymore. To me [working in this field] is like having this ultimate recess, where you can go and play and have this wonderful time and you can do all these great things and really have fun doing all this stuff—but don't screw up! Because if you screw up, well, suddenly they throw you out of the sandbox and you don't get to play anymore.[5]

Lowe used as an example the film *Waterworld,* which Kevin Costner starred in, directed, and produced. As Lowe says,

> The major problem with *Waterworld* is that Kevin Costner didn't have anybody on board to tell him "no." You know, you've spent a hundred mil, and it isn't working, and you don't want to go and throw it all away, so you put another twenty mil in to see if it works, and then another twenty mil, and so on. And that's how projects end up out of control, and we've had those here, it's happened to us. But, typically those people [who allow the budget to go out of control] don't last, because the whole idea of this business is, it *is* a business; you've got to make money, and the people who do it as an art form and produce projects that are beautiful and wonderful and have a million-dollar budget with a potential sale of thirty thousand or something [are in trouble]. There's no council of the arts that's going to come in and pull you out. You've just got to turn a profit on these games, and so Sierra's been fortunate that way, and, again, I think we balance [the creative with the business side] as well as anybody. We'd all like to spend all the money on every project and never ship it until

it was perfect, until you couldn't add any other possible thing to it. On the other hand, if you miss Christmas [at least in the gaming business—Ed.] you're dead! So, you've always got those twin swords hanging over your head: money and deadlines.[6]

More on Teams

THE REBIRTH TEAM

Even when it comes to an independent project, such as *Rebirth,* you still have a team with specific jobs and duties that must be taken seriously.

> The Rebirth Project is an example of a group of people voluntarily organizing around a subject of common interest, and working together to develop that idea into a marketable digital media product. In this case, the project initiators all have previous experience in various aspects of media production and computer programming. The subject of common interest is the culture and history of Tibet. We're looking to use the latest digital technologies to tell the story of that country, its plight, and its people. Our intent is to build a project architecture and human resource base that will enable us to launch this project when full funding becomes available.
>
> Amanda Moore [a media producer], through her involvement with Northwest Cyberartists and ShadowCatcher Entertainment, met Brian Karr (software engineer), John Wieczorek (simulation software engineer and practitioner of Tibetan Buddhism), Bruce Wolcott (visual designer and 3D modeler), Russell Johnson (photographer, co-author of *Kailas: The Sacred Mountain of Tibet*), and Rand McDonald (media designer, software engineer) in the Fall of 1994.
>
> Two writers, Marco Mascarin and Kimberly Ludlow, were brought on board to begin converting the concepts into a "story web" of characters and events. The Tibetan artist, Dhawa Dhondup provided consultation and drawings for use in the 3D environment. Jon Garfunkel, founder of the *Tibet Education Network,* offered input on school curriculum applications for the project. John Wieczorek completed a World Wide Web site to house the initial offerings of the Rebirth game, with 108 realms of possible states of existence, ranging from the lowest hells to highest heavens of the Tibetan Buddhist cosmology. This site also includes general information about the Rebirth CD-ROM, Tibetan Buddhism and a bibliography of media resources.[7]

Note that there are at least three subject matter experts involved in the project at many levels.

SUBJECT MATTER EXPERTS

Kiosks and instructional pieces present unique problems and require some special personnel. For instance, the first people involved in the Rehabilitation Learning Center project were instructional designers and subject matter experts—doctors, therapists, and people who have had traumatic injuries. In other words, the people integrally involved in the subject matter are the first ones involved (and they will stay involved throughout the entire project).

Essentially, they brainstorm to stimulate and illuminate the subject, then they decide exactly what needs to be covered and what will actually go into the program. Instructional designers have to be good communicators and, more than anyone involved in the project, have to work well on a team. For a project like this, there isn't necessarily reams of text, but there is still a definite script and story to be followed. The instructional designers are responsible for the *way* the project is written, but not necessarily *what* is written, unless they are also the subject matter experts. The main personnel involved in the production of the RLC's multimedia program include the following:

Principal Investigator/Project Director: Anthony Margherita
Project Manager: Lynn Gottlieb
Technical Communications: David Farkas
Multimedia Development: Terry Swanson
Media Communications: Chris James

For this particular project, there were also two members of the team (one a rehabilitative counseling consultant) who focused on educational methodologies, as well as consultants for occupational therapy, speech therapy, and physical therapy. Every such project involves its own specialists and consultants. The writer must distill what the consultants bring to a project into a coherent form that others can then adapt for nonlinear, interactive presentation.

Obviously, before one begins to write the actual script, there has to be some preproduction planning. This planning has a number of distinct steps, as you will see in Chapter 6.

E N D N O T E S

1. Frank Catalano, interview with the author, September 2, 1995.
2. For a more detailed description of the variety of people involved on a production team, I refer you to both Apple Computer's *Multimedia Demystified,* published by Random House, and Erik Holsinger's *How Multimedia Works,* published by Ziff-Davis Press. The first book is, of course, aimed at owners of Apple Computers, but both books give thorough and well-written accounts of the people and jobs involved in making a multimedia program work.
3. Alex Shapiro, interview with the author, June 29, 1995.
4. Ibid.
5. Al Lowe, interview with the author, August 1995.
6. Ibid.
7. Rand McDonald, Amanda Moore, John Wieczorek, and Bruce Wolcott, "The Rebirth Project, Brief History of an Independently Developed Interactive Multimedia Presentation," 1995.

6

From the Idea to the Content Outline

Six Steps Leading to the Actual Writing of the Script

In writing an effective multimedia script for any project, there are several points the writer has to know and understand before even beginning to write the treatment:

- The *purpose* of the program, or a way to make sure users know what they will accomplish with each action
- The various *goals* users will have for each section of the program
- The actual *procedure,* or the various things users need to know in order to reach the goals
- The *time* required for users to reach various destinations or goals
- *Feedback,* so that users know if they are doing the correct thing or traveling down the right path; the writer often comes up with where the feedback will be available
- *Options,* in the event a user becomes stuck

Once these objectives are met, the writing can proceed. (Goals will be discussed in detail in the next chapter. Procedure, required time, feedback, and options will all be discussed later on as well.)

If you are doing a work-for-hire project—in other words, a company has hired you to produce a multimedia program or work on a team as a writer—then once you know the purpose, goals, procedures, time, feedback, and options, you need to next find out the *budget* and the *delivery dates.*

The writer must deal with six considerations during preproduction:

- The Idea
- The Audience
- Brainstorming

- Goals and Objectives
- The Treatment
- The Content Outline

In this chapter, I'll describe these six points in detail. In the next, I'll go over the use of metaphors and world building, which usually take place during actual production.

The Idea

Every good multimedia project starts with an idea or a **terminal objective:** what it is you want your project to do, what you want it to tell the user, etc. "I want to tell people about ... " "We need to train people how to ... " "Wouldn't it be great if we had a multimedia package that could ... " For CBT programs, the terminal objective determines what the users will be able to do when the course is completed; that is, what they take with them from the program.

The Audience

The central consideration for the overall design of any multimedia project is its intended audience. To develop a learning program, for example, one needs to know what knowledge the user starts out with, or what the required entry-level skills are. For all interactive multimedia programs, you need to ask: How will people use the product? And, perhaps most important, how will the product sustain the attention of a diverse audience?

For example, the Bellevue Community College Homepage is aimed at students and prospective students. With other projects, engaging the audience might be more complicated.

Writing about The *Rebirth* Project, the CD ROM program dealing with Tibet, Bruce Wolcott says,

> Tibet is a subject that can be approached from many perspectives. It is a good topic for educational issues concerning geology, language, architecture, anthropology, human rights, natural sciences, medicine, and history, among others. From an aesthetic standpoint, Tibetan civilization has evolved a rich tradition of sacred art, music, metalwork, and sculpture. Tibet is also a land of mystery, with vast mountainous landscapes, evocative architecture, myths, legends, and practitioners of advanced mind sciences who've explored the nature of human consciousness. Although much of the culture of Tibet is now in exile, due to the Chinese occupation of their country, there is an extensive network of Tibetan support groups all over the world, who are in contact with each other via fax, computer networks, and newsletters. We want the Rebirth project to attract people who seek to experience Tibet from any or all of these viewpoints.
>
> Our strategy to reach these various audiences is to divide the project into three major sections with close stylistic and information links to one another: 1) a CD

ROM entitled *Rebirth: Quest for Ancient Wisdom,* 2) a companion CD ROM called *Rebirth: The Tibetan Homeland,* and 3) eventual implementation of *Rebirth: OnLine*—a presentation site on the Internet with connections to an extended Tibetan information community. If you remember, the audience is one of the key issues a writer needs to understand once the subject or idea of the piece has been stated. Will the piece you're writing be for children or adults? How your program will look and what information it will contain is determined primarily by your audience—those who will be using your product. An interactive piece on *Moby Dick* could be packaged for either children or adults, but if it was specifically for children, it would be a different product than if it was to be marketed to a more adult audience. Likewise a program about the brain will be very different if produced for a group of doctors than it will if produced for a group of elementary school age children. The same is true of any program: teaching a subject to adults is different than teaching children. You may decide that the audience is "general"—that no specific audience is being targeted. If you decide to go for a general audience, it is a good idea to make sure that you keep your message simple enough that anyone can understand it.[1]

WRITING FOR CHILDREN

One major audience issue at Splash Studios is the violence seen in many interactive programs. "We want these programs to teach positive values," Robin Worley says, "and we're picking stories to base our titles on that have a positive message for kids." She continues,

> Violence is out! There won't be any violence in our stories. You're not going to see Mighty Morphin Power Rangers karate chop monsters. There is, however, a dialog we keep going with our writers. The subject of censorship does come up, and even though all of our writers have written for children, there are still differences of opinion as far as what's appropriate. It's definitely a concern, and we talk about certain lines in the dialog that might be offensive to some people—so it's a continuous dialog that we have, in order to make sure everyone's OK with the [way in which we present] the positive messages that we're sending to kids.[2]

It's interesting to note here that according to Liquid Mercury Soup's online Interactive Index, the two-week sales figure from Walmart for the *Mortal Kombat* videogame rated PG was 28,000 units, while for the M-rated edition of the game, the two-week sales figure was almost double: 40,000 units.

The products Splash creates are aimed at children ages six to twelve. However, a twelve-year-old will find certain challenges much less difficult than a six-year-old. By including three levels of complexity, developers have produced a CD ROM that appeals to different age groups. At installation, the user simply types his or her age, and the program provides the appropriate challenges.

DEALING WITH VIOLENCE

Multimedia created specifically for children is intended for the most part to teach them positive values while entertaining them. Interactive movies such as *Phantasmagoria,* however, may use content too intense for children. Lorelei

Shannon describes how she as a writer dealt with the issue of violence, specifically how the writers have planned to put a blocking system into *Phantasmagoria II* that parents can initiate to stop children from watching the program.

> Basically, what I would do is that, when I would come to a scene that was going to have sexual content or violent content, I would write two versions of it. A PG level—I would describe it: this is what happens, this is what you see. Then I would have a whole separate interactive branch at the R level, and describe that as well: this is what you'll see. Sometimes, certain scenes would merely be truncated: sections of scenes would be removed. But, more often than not, the scenes [would be] completely rewritten.
>
> The story of *Phantasmagoria II* is very adult in its content and concept. It's sort of "Jacob's Ladder" type of really sophisticated horror, and it's hard to carry that off in the more soft-peddled version. We don't have a lot of overtly graphic violence. I prefer to imply things, but what we're implying is pretty awful.[3]

GRAPHIC HORROR OR NOT?

This is another creative decision, particularly when it comes to violence or horror: Do you show it graphically or just imply it? There are two schools of thought on this, which Stephen King has eloquently discussed.

> Bill Nolan was speaking as a screenwriter when he offered the example of the big bug behind the door, but the point applies to all media. What's behind the door or lurking at the top of the stairs is never as frightening as the door or the staircase itself. And because of this, comes the paradox: the artistic work of horror is almost always a disappointment. It is the classic no-win situation. You can scare people with the unknown for a long, long time ... but sooner or later, as in poker, you have to turn your down cards up. You have to open the door and show the audience what's behind it. And if what happens to be behind it is a bug, not ten but a hundred feet tall, the audience heaves a sigh of relief (or utters a scream of relief) and thinks, "A bug a hundred feet tall is pretty horrible, but I can deal with that. I was afraid it might be a *thousand* feet tall." ... There is and always has been a school of horror writers (I am not among them) who believe that the way to beat this rap is to never open the door at all. ... My own disapproval of this method—we'll let the door bulge but we'll never open it—comes from the belief that it is playing to tie rather than to win. ... Consequently, I'd rather yank the door open at some point. ... And if the audience screams with laughter rather than terror, if they see the zipper running up the monster's back, then you just gotta go back to the drawing board and try it again.[4]

Actually, not opening the door at times is pretty darn scary. Here's one example King uses. In *The Haunting*, directed by Robert Wise, you never actually see the ghosts but are truly frightened throughout. There is, however, something to be said for opening the door wide: *Alien* is still considered one of the best horror films ever made, and the believability of the alien itself has a lot to do with that. But what happens if *Alien* has to be repackaged for a "General Audience"?

"In multimedia, I would prefer to just target my market and aim straight for that market," Lorelei Shannon says, voicing sentiments agreed on by many writers of multimedia. "For various business reasons we are going for the PG and R thing, but this game really is sort of an R-level game, and I do feel it is somewhat diluted by being at the PG level."[5]

Roberta Williams, who came up with the idea of *Phantasmagoria,* offers her views as well. "Violence for violence sake is bad. But, violence that benefits a certain story is unavoidable. I think there are all kinds of stories to be told, and sometimes violence is a necessary factor in telling those stories. You can't eliminate it from real life, and you can't eliminate it from certain stories. It has its part in society—if for no other reason than to remind people of a certain darkness in humanity that we must always battle."[6]

Harlan Ellison put it well when talking about television violence during the late 1960s:

> It would be simple to make an artistic case for violence. All great art from Beowulf to Faulkner's *Intruder In The Dust* has demonstrated that violence is often what results in moments of stress, when people under tension must seek release. ... So then, if violence is *necessary* to the freedom of creating art, what is it about TV violence that has all the tippy-toe types running scared? ... What it is, of course, is what George Clayton Johnson, the videowriter, said it was ... "gratuitous" violence. ... It is a death onscreen that no one cares about.[7]

In other words, zapping a bunch of ghouls in *Doom* or tearing out the heart of a fighter in *Mortal Kombat* is gratuitous. The issue of violence in all media, including new digital media, is not to be taken lightly. It is an ethical choice that all drama writers must face at some point.

The violence in *Phantasmagoria* affects both the heroine and the user. In fact, it probably affects the "audience" more than if it were a motion picture simply because home interactive multimedia is so intimate. You feel as if you're there, you feel as if you know the people getting hurt and, ultimately, you feel as if the violence matters. Also, it is you, as the user, who makes the choices that determine just what violence might befall a character.

Brainstorming

Brainstorming, sometimes called "free association," is an exercise most writers have probably done by themselves, perhaps without even knowing it. In brainstorming, one approaches a subject from every conceivable angle, writing down ideas as they come. During an interactive multimedia project, brainstorming often occurs in a group of writers, designers, and directors all working together to think up ideas and jot them down.

In multimedia, brainstorming sessions are fairly ongoing, with the first session easily taking two or three days. Later, when the last Diet Coke is finished, and everyone's quieted down, the ideas are gone over and the best ones kept. Some will be tossed out because they're too expensive to do, some because they don't fit the tone of the piece, some because they cannot be technically pulled off, and some because they're just plain loopy. But you'll be amazed at how much good material can come out of a brainstorming session.

Goals and Objectives

As a writer, you will need to know your goals and objectives. What do you want the user to learn, find out, etc.? Exactly what is the ultimate message of the project? What specific steps will the user need to take to achieve the goal you're going to create? What do you want the user to experience, learn, find out, and bring away from the product? Whatever the answers to these questions, the important thing to remember is *goals are reached, objectives are learned.*

The *goal* is the ultimate message of the project. Here are the goals of some of the projects discussed so far: "The user will learn how to function after injury." "The user will be able to list the planets of the solar system." and "The user will find the object of his quest."

The *objectives* are the specific steps users must do to achieve the goal. These objectives should be written as specifically as possible, not just for the eventual user, but for yourself as the writer. Well-stated objectives will help you gather the necessary background material and will become, in essence, the blueprint for actual project development.

Chris James, the department chair of the Media Communication and Technology Program at Bellevue Community College, puts objectives into a "CABD" format: Conditions, Audience, Behavior, and Degree.[8] For example, suppose you are creating a program for first aid and CPR. You might write the objectives as follows:

1. C = Conditions: "Given a situation in which a person has suddenly passed out ... "
2. A = Audience: " ... the student ... "
3. B = Behavior: " ... will be able to show how CPR should be applied to the stricken person ... "
4. D = Degree: " ... with 100 percent accuracy."

Goals and objectives are usually written into the treatment, because they play a direct role in the "look and feel" of the final interactive multimedia project.

The Treatment

According to Tony Bove, one of the creators of the Haight-Ashbury program, "The process of writing and editing a script for an interactive documentary starts with the same steps you would take to write any script for any type of film: with a 'treatment' that describes the goal of the writing project and summarizes the topic, theme, and characters [if any]. After that, the designated writer puts together the first draft of the script, [describing] images and possibly even some 'stage directions' [as in 'animation occurs here'] to be used with the words."[9]

Again, the *treatment* is the written summary of what one wants the final multimedia product to look like and how the user will interact with the product. A present-tense, narrative version of the program, the treatment also contains ideas about production standards, the general tone of the piece, and how the scenes and menus will look. The treatment determines how the script will be written and how the **navigation,** or how the user moves from one point in a program to another, will work (see Chapter 11 for more on navigation).

A *detailed treatment* should contain the following information:

1. A cover page, citing the name of the project, the writer, and the date of the treatment.
2. The elements of production, including
   a. the project type
   b. the audience
   c. technical material (equipment, special effects, animation, archival footage, etc.)
   d. a synopsis of content (written in the present tense), and even proposed locations and talent (sex, age, look, etc.)[10]

The treatment also determines the "flavor" of the program. Is the program to be neutral in its presentation or is it trying to sell a product or an idea? Is is to be serious or humorous? Corporate? Informative? Writers must choose the program's flavor early, because this decision determines how the script itself will be written and how the navigation through the program or product will work.

You can make the treatment visual through the use of **storyboards.** I shall discuss these in detail in Chapter 9.

Once you have made all decisions about the idea, the audience, the treatment, and the goals and objectives of a piece, you should take one more step before producing the actual script. You need to create a content outline.

The Content Outline

The **content outline** is a specific list of what will actually be included in the project. Through this list, the writer can tell the rest of the team not only what the production is about, but how it can best be crafted in terms of its goals and objectives. This enables, for instance, production people to craft a project and people who do the "authoring" to program the computer and CD ROM. Multimedia authoring personnel in particular must be closely involved in all aspects of the project.

As you know, the subject matter expert (SME) is the person who knows about the topic being presented: the equivalent of a creative consultant on a film or a television series. For example, Bruce Catton might serve as the consultant on a series about the American Civil War. The SME or content specialist could also be the writer, the person requesting or producing the program, or a research assistant hired to help the writer. However, it's usually not the production staff. As Chris James writes, "the production staff usually has plenty to do without spending time researching the 'History of the Spanish American War' or 'Forklift Safety.' "[11]

The content outline is much more detailed than one for a book, motion picture, or television show. It has to list *everything* that needs be included in the program. It could also indicate what media format might be needed for each portion of the product. Here's an example:

OUTLINE: KORRY PRODUCTIONS, LTD. VIDEO AND FILMS
An Interactive Multimedia Catalog

I. Introduction—Animation of Korry logo—to be utilized as metaphor [more later on metaphors], followed by full-motion video of company president Elle MacPherson
   A. Quick clips from various Korry films & videos
   B. Welcome from the company president
      1. Proud of past Korry achievements & awards
         a. text list
      2. New selection of Korry products for '95
         a. graphics of new videos
      3. We're a company interested in history and fantasy
      4. "Welcome to our Interactive Korry Catalog!"
II. How to Use the Interactive Korry Catalog: (Elle's narration w/graphic-animation sequence)
   A. Brief description of multimedia navigation
      1. Korry logo as menu device
      2. Click-on buttons
         a. take you to different sections of catalog
         b. click "end" to bring you back to Korry logo/menu (or chapter index)
      3. Click on graphic images and/or photos from new videos
         a. takes you to full-motion scenes from each video or film available
         b. click "end" to bring you back to Korry logo/menu
   B. How to order videos (audio sequence, with graphic support)
      1. Click on "price" of item selected to access order form
         a. note that item is already in order form per your selection
         b. select "quantity" and postage cost in order form
         c. click on "next" to return to menu for next selection
      2. Continue for each video selected
      3. Select "method of payment"
      4. Send order form via fax number

You continue the outline process and include every fact, idea, and concept that you want to include in the production. Don't take shortcuts because it seems too detailed to include a certain idea. Remember—*this is where you are capturing your ideas on paper* and if an idea is left out of the content outline, you may find it left out of the final multimedia product.

Also, remember that you are dealing with a *nonlinear* program, not a linear script. Therefore, you will have subsections that can be entered and exited at any time. Each example given in the above sample outline is its own interactive sequence with its own media and graphic support.

The Project "Bible"

Once you have all the ideas down in the content outline, you have a blueprint from which the script can be written. At this point in development, you should create a "bible" for your production, particularly for a dramatic piece. Television series always use these bibles, which list the characters, the characters' attributes and relationships, the location, the mood, the history, etc. A bible for a multimedia project is a bit different. It can, of course, include all the items just listed, but it must also present every aspect of the piece. In other words, sound effects, graphics, animation style (if any), music, style of icons, and tools available to the user must all appear in the project bible. The project bible, sometimes known as the *backstory*, is particularly important for the world-building step of your project. It is also a good idea to have a more detailed content outline in the bible—a map of how characters, environments, objects, and situations are going to relate within the navigation structure.[12]

Creative Differences

There are still major problems between the creative and the investment end of the business. Investors want to see a fast return on a project. With multimedia, such results may be difficult to achieve.

While this text was going to print, Splash Studios experienced the mass firing of fourteen of its twenty-one full-time employees, including Patrick Ford and Jack Turk, two former Microsoft executives who founded Splash in 1994.

Phoenix Partners, a Seattle venture-capital firm and majority owner in Splash, made the decision to "streamline" the company after negotiations with another firm broke down. This other venture-capital firm would have brought in the five million dollars necessary to continue current projects. According to the *Seattle Times,* this tumult "exemplifies a fundamental tension between the venture-capital firms that invest in multimedia companies and the creative visions of the founders of those companies."[13] The article goes on to state that "Greg Roach, CEO of Seattle-based multimedia company HyperBole Studios, said an unresolvable conflict exists between a company trying to create products and grow within an industry, and a venture capital company that wants immediate cash returns on its investments."[14] Such conflicts will continue to plague the multimedia industry for the foreseeable future and will, by their very nature, impact the writers.

ENDNOTES

1. Bruce Wolcott, "World Building and the Use of Metaphor," pp. 4–6, copyright 1995 by Bruce Wolcott. All Rights Reserved, by permission of the author.
2. Robin Worley, interview with the author, July 1995.
3. Lorelei Shannon, interview with the author, July 1995.
4. Stephen King, *Danse Macabre* (New York: Berkley Books, 1981), 111–113.
5. Shannon, interview with the author.
6. Sierra On-Line Press Kit: *Q & A with Phantasmagoria Designer Roberta Williams.*
7. Harlan Ellison, *The Glass Teat* (New York: Pyramid Books, 1975), 32–33.
8. Chris James, "The Development Process for Interactive Multimedia Products," paper for Media/CIS 223, January 1994 (by permission of the author).
9. Tony Bove, interview with the author, October 3, 1995.
10. Carol J. Anderson and Mark D. Veljikov, *Creating Interactive Multimedia* (Glenville, IL: Scott, Foresman, 1990), 129.
11. James, "The Development Process."
12. Many thanks to Chris James, Department Chair, Media Communication and Technology Department, BCC, for use of his material for this section.
13. Leyla Kokmen, "Fledgling firm navigates uncertain seas," *Seattle Times,* April 13, 1996.
14. Ibid.

7

World Building and Metaphors

Before I discuss creating the story, dialog, and characters for an interactive multimedia script, you need to learn about the use of metaphors and world building.

The Use of Metaphors

According to Webster's, a *metaphor* is the application of a word or phrase to an object or concept that it does not literally denote. Neil Postman wrote that "metaphors create the content of our culture."[1] Just look at some earlier cultures' gods, goddesses, and demons. Often, these merely represented abstract concepts, as Aphrodite was love, Persephone the changing of seasons, etc. Statues, drawings, and paintings of such entities gave such concepts a form that people could recognize. In Judeo-Christian cultures, "a fortress is our God" is a metaphor that connotes the strength of faith and belief.

TIME

Circular Time One single concept that all cultures have created metaphors for is *time*. Heraclitus, an early Greek philosopher, felt that time was like a river, flowing endlessly through the universe. For many of the ancients, the river of time eventually emptied into a sea of time from which yet another river began, perhaps that very river from which the journey started or the ultimate circular view of time.

For centuries, people looked on time as circular, in concert with the rhythms not only of nature, but of the heavens themselves:

> The repetitive motions associated with breathing, with the beating of the heart, and with the daily sleep patterns are all examples of the clock-work rhythms called cyclic time.
>
> It was noticed that the sun would die every evening and then would be reborn the following morning. ... The same held true for the motions of the moon and the stars.[2]

Birth, life, death, and rebirth became inseparable from the four seasons, a metaphor for the cyclical nature of time. Father Time became the ultimate metaphor. He begins the year a baby and leaves an aged old man with a scythe, a symbol of death.

"O, call back yesterday, bid time return!" Shakespeare writes. But there was no way to return to the time that had passed—that is, until the medium of film arrived. As you will recall, one of the earliest proposed multimedia programs was a "time machine" that would at least give the illusion of breaking the constraints of time.

New Notions of Time   With the Industrial Revolution, the idea of time began to change: "Therefore, after the Industrial Revolution the idea of change in one's life and in one's world came to be seen as natural and necessary."[3] Further,

> Since the Industrial Revolution, humanity has become increasingly alienated from the soil and from the seasons. The "simple life," with its rituals and rhythms connected to agricultural cycles, has been largely abandoned in the western world. The traditional notions of renewal and harmony have been replaced by a drive toward expansion and development. For the first time, people must deal with a rapidly changing culture in which values and traditions are shed whenever they do not fit emerging economic and social frameworks. ... The meaning of time has changed in both religious and scientific cosmological models. The universe is no longer seen as static and clock-work; the "city of man" is no longer considered to be permanent. Time is now viewed as dynamic rather than static, as historical rather than ignorable.[4]

New metaphors became necessary for this new outlook on time. For instance, the pocket watch, so often used as a metaphor for the circular nature of time, was replaced by digital numbers, yellow and green points blinking forever into the future. I've even seen a pocket watch that, when you clicked open its case, revealed a digital clock inside with red numbers on a jet-black background. Ironically, philosophers have called digital time *linear,* as opposed to circular or cyclical, even though digital technology is usually associated with the nonlinear.

One might argue that, until the electronic revolution, the metaphors used for time had not changed. But now, digital technology, along with all the new forms of communication it helped create, has changed people's outlook on time and the circular or cyclical nature of life. Today, there are new metaphors for a rapidly changing human culture.

For awhile, as Neil Postman states, television became the all-encompassing metaphor for twentieth-century life. Suddenly, newspapers and magazines look like television screens. And then, before people could even begin to get comfortable with this new metaphor, another one replaced it. Television images were beginning to look more and more like computer screens, as in the use of icons on CNN's news shows. In any case, you can see the importance of metaphors to life and culture.

THE NEED FOR METAPHORS IN MULTIMEDIA

For an interactive multimedia project, the metaphor or metaphors used can provide a strong foundation for a product. The metaphors can also help make interaction for the user comfortable and engaging.

Blended Space   According to Tim Rohrer, "Any well designed interface takes on the tool perspective and allows for positive feedback and feeling from the interface as if it were an extension of the user's body. This has the effect of creating what Mark Turner and Gilles Fauconnier [two important metaphor/ cognitive-science researchers] call a blended space."[5]

Rohrer uses the phrase *land yacht* as an example. "According to Turner and Fauconnier, when we hear 'land yacht' we take some of what we know about yachting, blend it with some of what we know about the situational context—the speaker is talking about a car—and come up with an understanding of the new meaningful expression. A well-designed graphical interface creates a similar blended space between our bodies and the interface's metaphorical ground." Another example is *Microsoft Office*.

"The payoff," according to Rohrer, is that "by creating a blended space the [users forget] that there is any conceptual distance between themselves and the computer." In essence, the computer "becomes an extension of the arm in the same way a well balanced hammer is when we do carpentry." When this happens, productivity is maximized. Thus, the computer becomes a comfortable tool while interactivity gives the user more control. Rohrer continues, "As one of my friends ... puts it: 'It's about playing video games at work. We're just trying to make work more fun and more satisfying.' The payoff of fun is productivity; the payoff of the blended space created by a good interface is that people can be absorbed in their work, not in tweaking the tool." The payoff for the writer of multimedia is that the user is immediately comfortable, if not familiar, with the program, and is therefore more easily engaged.

Graphics and other visual material are extremely important to interactive multimedia. Rohrer says,

> Graphics aren't necessary; but using them is awfully smart ... for we humans devote an enormous portion of our brain to processing visual information. Eventually we may see more kinesthetic and aural metaphors in interface design as well, as our brains have large subsystems for processing these modalities as well. ... We will

continue to see systems that take advantage of all three primary modalities (multimedia interfaces). ... Yes, metaphors are necessary. ... Metaphor is one of the central organizing principles of cognition (perception and awareness). Metaphors are not optional features of interface design because they are not optional features of cognition. As we refine our interfaces, we will refine our metaphors.

Baseball   Metaphors allow writers to make complex ideas in multimedia comprehensible. A well-chosen central metaphor can serve as a framework for several interrelated ideas and events. For example, in *Baseball,* Ken Burns uses the game of baseball as a metaphor for U.S. culture during the nineteenth and twentieth centuries. In fact, in certain episodes, baseball becomes a metaphor for the end of segregation in all aspects of American life. Bruce Wolcott points out that baseball can "provide a central story for describing (our culture)."[6] He points to related phrases and expressions such as *being out in left field, striking out,* and *pitching an idea.* He takes it even further, as Burns did, when he states, "The rise to fame and fortune based on competition and individual achievement as played out on the baseball diamond also represents part of the North American story."[7] In these ways, the game of baseball can become the central metaphor for the game of life in the United States.

A *Rebirth* Metaphor   Finding central metaphors for interactive multimedia projects could be as easy as using a control panel for a drag-racing game or using a haunted house and all its rooms for an interactive ghost story. Complex projects may require research as well as trial and error. For example,

> Finding a central metaphor for the Tibetan people requires uncovering central themes in their culture. ... In developing ... the Rebirth project, core metaphors were needed to represent the religious character of Tibet. One of these central metaphors is the circumambulation about a sacred place to cultivate one's spiritual nature and gain religious merit. In every Tibetan village there is a form of shrine called a *"chorten"* which people walk around as a form of prayer. In Western Tibet there is a sacred mountain named Kailas, which is a destination for many Tibetan Buddhist practitioners as well as pilgrims from other religious disciplines. The mountain is both a physical location as well as the mythical Mt. Meru which is said to extend from the deepest hell realms to the highest heaven, and as such represents a spiritual symbol of the path towards enlightenment. As a metaphor, the story of a journey to a sacred location and its exploration works both as a storytelling vehicle, and as a way of understanding many levels of Tibetan culture.
>
> Associated with the religious pilgrimage is the symbol of the *mandala,* a circle which encloses a diversity of deities and representations around a central location. The mandala is used as an instrument of meditation among Tibetan Buddhists, and is said to aid in balancing and harmonizing the mind. From an information design standpoint the mandala works as a captivating visual design, and also as a means of incorporating many diverse subjects around a common theme.[8]

Thus, the mandala, which turns into Mt. Meru in the opening of *Rebirth,* becomes a perfect metaphor for the culture, religion, and myths of Tibet, the subject explored in the CD-ROM.

World Building

THE "TALKIES" STAGE

Frank Catalano considers interactive multimedia to still be in the "talkies" stage of its development. In other words, this new medium is about where films were in the late 1920s, when sound was first introduced. Almost overnight, the art, technique, and craft of filmmaking changed, and it took the better part of the next decade for motion pictures to reach the level of sophistication silent cinema had achieved by 1927.

Catalano doesn't expect this stage of multimedia to end

until the standard, home configuration of a multimedia PC (Windows or Mac) is robust enough to handle real-time, full-motion video, CD-quality audio, and has a very fast **broadband** network (either Internet or cable) connection. ... The bottom line is, it's much tougher telling interactive stories when the most common hardware platform may not effectively be able to deliver what a writer wants to say—in other words, the technology gets in the way of the story telling. And gets in the way of what the personal computer can do that books, movies, comics, radio, and video can't do very effectively—simultaneously allow the consumer to interact with the story, change the story, and immerse themselves in the story—in effect, making the consumer an extension of the storyteller.[9]

MOVING FORWARD

Then what must the writer of interactive multimedia concentrate on to make New Media stories engaging? Catalano states that what is required, and what will be required, is for writers to "build fully developed universes—worlds—as well as story lines for those worlds. It's not unlike the development a science-fiction or fantasy writer has to do to create an internally consistent universe, or the backstory or "bible" a TV writer has to create for a series. Much, if not most, of what is created may never make it into the story [or be noticed by the user. Ed.]. But it provides the depth required for rich stories, and now the depth required as the consumer partners with the author."[10]

HOW TO BUILD A WORLD

The creation of the world users will find themselves in is called *world building*. Writing about *Rebirth*, Wolcott describes in detail the use of new digital multimedia technologies to recreate a virtual world of Tibet. He explores the process of world building, by which users can trek through the Himalayas, hear music, see sacred art, interact with Tibetan characters, and learn Tibetan Buddhist perspectives.

[The] task of world building or perceptual design is very similar to constructing a home. You need an architecture which describes the overall look and feel, an engineering plan which will provide the code to allow people to navigate in the environment, project direction to ensure that all the parts of production are coordinated, and specialized skills to supply needed detail work.

Part of this building process includes the implementation of an interactive script, which must take into account the potentials and limitations of current multimedia technologies. Underlying this structure is a core of content providers who provide raw materials for completing the intended project. In the *Rebirth* project, these include Tibetan scholars, photographers, videographers, writers, historians, artists, musicians, performers, and curriculum developers. You can think of this part of the world making process as a living web of resources and consultants whose material will be integrated into the final project. [You are, in effect, creating a culture of the mind—Ed.]

Another important design consideration is the implementation of a world database so that all materials used in the program can be traced and catalogued. You can think of this as a library where the names and works of all the participants are organized for future reference. This is important for three reasons: 1) as a multimedia bibliography so that sources can be identified and accessed, 2) as a legal template so that copyright and other legal issues can be openly referenced, and 3) to enable an "open architecture" so that every individual object can be changed or replaced as necessary. Our intent in *Rebirth* is to provide an electronic pathway so that every object, text sequence, photography, sound, video clip, and graphic can be traced to its origin.

In a 3D representation of a Tibetan monastery, for example, a *thanka* (wall painting) will be referenced by the building and wall where it is located in the digital environment. The *thanka*'s creator, and copyright ownership will also be indicated to allow easy access to media resources. This information will be available to the end user at the click of a mouse within the monastery environment. Because the *thanka* is an independent object within the virtual world, it can be modified, removed, or replaced at any time. This object interdependence throughout the world will provide flexibility for future growth or revision of the existing model.[11]

Wolcott goes on to note that world building is collaborative and can be organic, particularly in a self-financed project without the demands and deadlines of a fully financed one:

"World Building," he writes, "at its most fundamental level, is a highly social, collaborative endeavor. The number of interrelated tasks are too numerous and diverse for one person to manage."[12]

FIVE COMPONENTS OF REBIRTH

Wolcott cites the five main components or sections of *Rebirth* (see Figure 7-1).

1. *Database component:* The foundation of the project, this is where the record of each part of the world being created is kept. Here, the text, graphics, video, and sound files wait to be called up by the program. Other information stored here includes bibliographies and human resources. It is also where online connections are stored and updated. I've found the database important for access to and economy of space.

2. *Content component:* Integrally involved in this component, the writer works with what Wolcott calls a "network of knowledge." Historians,

FIGURE 7-1 ▌ *World building at its most fundamental level is a highly collaborative endeavor. The number of interrelated tasks are too numerous and diverse for one person to manage. This diagram shows the various layers of organization within the* Rebirth *world structure. Each of these layers represents a unique view of the information in the final product. The arrow running through these views indicates that they are all closely integrated and mutually dependent.*

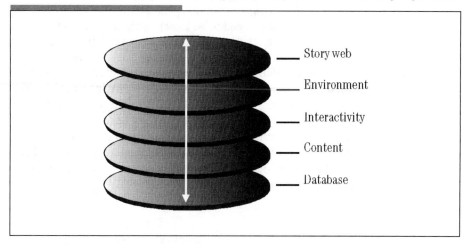

scholars, researchers, documentarians, and curriculum developers all might work with the writer to insure that information in the program is accurate and accessible, and reflects the desired viewpoint.

3. *Interactivity component:* The computer programmer supplies the code that integrates all aspects of the project; the code is the glue that binds the created world together. These days, those writers who can program stand in the best position. New Media needs "creative programmers," those who can both write and "author." The programmer integrates media, maintains a database, enables the user to navigate and interact with the environment, and provides a window into the Internet. Programming is the heart of any project. *"The core of programming talent that builds this code is closely involved with the design process to insure that the world and story web develops in a way that is technically feasible,* and within the budget of available computer memory resources."[13] [italics mine].

4. *Environmental component:* Wolcott calls this component the "equivalent to a stage in a theater—the place where all the action takes place. As in theater, the environment is concerned with set design, staging, lighting, timing, and presenting events in a way that sustains an audience's participation. This is also where the interface resides, which provides tools for users to interact with information resources in the program. Graphic consistency, a look and feel, mood, geography, architecture, sound effects, music, and use of actors and voice talent are important issues here."

5. *Story-web component:* In this component, essentially the outcome of the design, the scripted action is woven into the created world and its environment.

> One can think of storytelling as that part of information architecture that structures events through time. The story web differs from traditional scriptwriting in that it provides viewers multiple paths of action [or layers] at various moments in their experience—they can choose which pathways to follow within a set of different possibilities. *Good stories are still the prime ingredient for sustaining and holding an audience's attention.* The trick here is that they need to be closely integrated with strengths and limitations of the current click and point interactive multimedia technology. [Italics mine.]

Frank Catalano feels that for some undetermined time, there will need to be what he calls a "couch-potato mode" in interactive storytelling. "In other words, consumers will want a safe, familiar way to get through the story-world, using a mostly linear story. But as they become more comfortable, they can use the tools the writer has created to extend the story in their own way, discovering new things the author has developed as part of the backstory."[14]

The following chapter will discuss story development, character development, and dialog.

E N D N O T E S

1. Neill Postman, *Amusing Ourselves to Death* (New York: Penguin Books, 1985), 15.
2. Paul Halpern, *Time Journeys* (New York: McGraw-Hill, 1990), 1–2.
3. Ibid., 29.
4. Ibid., 50–51.
5. Tim Rohrer, "A Brief Paper on Metaphor Generation," Internet, April 1995 (by permission of the author). Subsequent Rohrer quotes from this source.
6. "The Rebirth Project: Brief history of an independently developed interactive multimedia presentation," submitted by members of The Rebirth Project, copyright © 1995 (Rand McDonald, Amanda Moore, John Wieczorek, and Bruce Wolcott), 1–3.
7. Ibid.
8. Ibid.
9. Frank Catalano, interview with the author, September 2, 1995.
10. Ibid.
11. Wolcott, "The Rebirth Project," 1–3.
12. Ibid., 8.
13. Ibid., 9. Subsequent Wolcott quotes from p. 9.
14. Catalano, interview with the author.

Nonlinear Script Writing

Story, Character, and Structure

"There is a common misconception that to write for interactive (multimedia), a writer must first become a computer expert. A writer need not understand the inner workings of a computer to write for interactive any more than a screenwriter needs to understand the inner workings of a 35mm camera to write a film script. What's really required is an understanding of how interactive technology effects story structure."
— Brian Sawyer and John Vourlis,
Screenwriting Structures for New Media

There are certain "basics" in the art of storytelling that one cannot ignore, such as the following: The main character must change, the story should have "peaks" and "lulls," and "plot points" and "cuts" need to come at specific parts of a story. How does one apply such "basics" to a nonlinear, interactive medium?

Story Development

PRIORITIES

Aristotle listed six elements of drama for playwrights, from most important to least:

1. Fable or Plot: what Aristotle referred to as the action. "All human happiness or misery takes the form of action; the end for which we live is a certain kind of activity, not a quality. ... So that it is the action in [a play], i.e. its Fable or Plot, that is the end and purpose of [the play]."[1]
2. Character

3. Theme or thought (the moral lesson, what the point is, the human element)
4. Music or Melody (in Greek drama, the pacing or rhythm of a piece)
5. Diction, meaning the style and the kind of language used
6. Spectacle, or the staging or setting of the story. Interestingly, Aristotle says, "The Spectacle, though an attraction, is the least artistic of all the parts, and has the least to do with the art of poetry. The tragic effect is quite possible without a public performance and actors; and besides, the getting-up of the Spectacle is more a matter for the costumier than the poet."[2]

During Shakespeare's time, character replaced plot as the main element. Today, with digital special effects, and with motion pictures routinely budgeted at fifty million dollars, spectacle has moved to the top of the list. And so it is with interactive multimedia.

Agents and marketing people note that audiences love spectacle. If people didn't, then why would the *Batman* and the *Die Hard* movies be so successful? Even so, smaller movies that focus on story and characters can also prosper, given a chance. Though spectacle remains high on the list of priorities for multimedia programs, it may not stay there for long. One simple reason for the change is that, as fun as *Doom* might be, anyone with a modicum of intelligence will eventually get bored zapping the monsters. The user will want the story to continue, the plot to go somewhere:

> Story is where we all begin. Forget all the crap intellectual critics (a contradiction in terms) spew at us. If you don't care about the story, if you're not hooked, screw the rest. Critics didn't begin wondering what the symbolism was in *The Little Engine That Could*. They weren't fascinated by the alliterative wordplay.
>
> They were like the rest of us—they were rooting for the train to get the toys over the mountain.
>
> Now we progress from that point, obviously, but this much is still true: narrative is only a piece of string, and it's where you choose to cut it that's essential.
>
> Where *you* choose to cut it. I might pick a piece farther along, or earlier. No one is right. There is no right way to tell a story, only your way.
>
> And I'm glad it's a mystery, because if the computer schmucks ever figure it out, then anyone will write wonderful stories, and if anybody can, nobody will.
>
> And that, folks, we don't want. We want our storytellers. Somebody's got to keep us alive through the dangerous night when the flames are flickering and the wolves howl. That's all, by the by, that storytellers do.
>
> Not a bad occupation, truth to tell.[3]

In most interactive multimedia pieces, even many CBT programs, there is a story, and story, as William Goldman writes, is where it all begins. Note in particular Goldman's comparison of narrative to string. I think it very interesting that Goldman wrote, "Where *you* choose to cut it," because in the interactive world, the writer will have to decide on a number of points where the user can decide to "cut the string." Writing for such a medium, in which the audience doesn't just interact with the story but actually chooses where a story goes, is challenging to say the least.

PLOT AND STORY COMPARED

Before I go further, you should clearly understand the meanings of *plot* and *story* as they apply to scripts. The plot is a basic element of good screenplay structure. If you look in most dictionaries under *plot* you'll be told "see *story*," which doesn't help you very much, because when you look up *story* it says, "see *plot*."

For our purposes, the definitions are as follows: The **plot** is the plan of action of a story—the terminal objective. The **story** is the actual telling of an event, or what happens. In interactive multimedia, the story contains the activities used to move the user toward an objective. For example, the plot of *Frankenstein* is "A man creates life from nonlife." The story of *Frankenstein* is "An undead being is created who longs for love and feels alone and hated." In *Phantasmagoria,* the plot concerns a young woman trying to get out of a house of horror. The story involves the various doors she might open and the awful things she might encounter.

To put it another way, plot is usually the structure of a screenplay, particularly interactive screenplays. The plot is made up of scenes, challenges, crises, etc., that move the story, or telling of the event, along.

Al Lowe from Sierra On-Line here talks about the challenges involved in creating plot and story for a program:

Now, *Freddy Pharkus Frontier Pharmacist* was something very different. I'd just taken a class in plot, and I decided I wanted to do something with plot, and I did a product that was very plot driven. I mean I had a specific series of puzzles that had to be solved. If you are plot driven, then the sequence of puzzles and the sequence of presentations is much more critical, whereas the [*Leisure Suit*] *Larry* games tend to be less plot driven. There's a flimsy excuse for a premise, but yet the games tend to be much rounder (in terms of character and interaction). I don't have to limit you, the user. You don't have to do certain things, whereas with Freddy, I was forced to keep you in this little line so you ended up doing, solving these puzzles like beads on a string (what would be "problem solving" in CBT programs). We actually had a game variable (something that makes you interact) that was the puzzle: It went from one to twenty-seven. And you had to do the different parts of the puzzle in that sequence, because otherwise the plot made no sense. There were a few things you could do out of order, but in general, there was a specific goal.

Plot driven then means more of a straight path is followed, whereas premise driven or weaker or less plot allows you to be more free-form or round. When you play *Larry VI* you have this ability to do anything and go anywhere almost in any order, except for the last girl. With the final girl Larry meets, you had to have solved the other eight girls below in order to satisfy her. She wanted all eight things, but you needed to finish [every girl] down below before you did the last one. [Italics mine.]

I've played at both ends of the randomness I talked about, I did them right in a row. *Freddy* had great plots, and I loved the way it advanced, and I was giving people peaks and valleys and peaks and valleys, but there's only one way to play that game. To a certain extent, *Phantasmagoria* is the same way. You can get through it, but you go back and play it a second time, and it's going to be about the same game, whereas some of the games we used to do years ago were much more random; they didn't have any story particularly but [it was a lot of fun].

[Multimedia] encyclopedias are looser or more random in that way; you can move around [the program] more freely, whereas with true storylines, you're more boxed in. I think this is one of the things that the movie guys have failed terribly at: They love those plots and they love the intricacies and they love the inner layers and weaving of all those things and that's great, except in our medium that limits you to that very strict beads-on-a-string kind of pattern.[4]

Essentially, the writer and creator of multimedia must remember another Aristotelian rule of drama: Causality and integration, or the synthesis of incidents, give form to the drama as a whole. Every pathway writers create for a user must have a reason for being there and, as difficult as it may seem, each alternate scene must still follow the scene that precedes it. One way to keep a program moving logically, no matter which direction the user might choose to go, is through strong characters. As always, your plot and story are propelled forward by the power of your characters.

Character Development

> "What is character but the determination of incident? What is incident but the illustration of character?"
>
> — Henry James

> "Story is something that happens to characters you care about."
>
> — Raymond Chandler

Do you have a favorite character from *Myst, Under a Killing Moon, Doom?* Some of you may think the main character of *Mortal Kombat* is pretty cool. What do you remember about her, though, other than the fact that she either beat the stuffing out of monstrous competitors or was herself a victim who had her head pulled off?

THE NEED FOR GOOD CHARACTERIZATION

In any medium, characters need drive, must elicit sympathy, and require obstacles to overcome. This is simply good storytelling. As one writer and musician said, "Let's face it—writing a story without characters is like writing music without the notes."[5] Even in a program like *Myst,* a good deal of the fun is figuring out who the characters are and what they did.

The creation of characters and their development definitely has a long way to go in interactive multimedia. In fact, with the present available technology, character development in this medium can seem a nearly impossible task. However, character will become more and more important to interactive multimedia as time goes on. In the meantime, character is still an integral part of just about any type of program one creates. "People—characters—are the true substance of all fiction, most nonfiction, all drama, and a lot of poetry ranging from the *Iliad* to Robert Lowell," William Sloane writes in *The Craft of Writing.*

"There is no such entity as a piece of fiction that is devoid of human beings or personifications; by the nature of ourselves and our lives there cannot be any such fiction. People *are* the story and the whole story."[6]

In Ray Bradbury's powerful short story, "There Will Come Soft Rains," a mechanical house continues to function even after the people who lived there have long gone. As the house begins to deteriorate, its mechanisms slowly break down. One of the saddest stories you're likely to read, it's all about a *character:* the mechanical house itself, a personification of humanity in the twenty-first century. You should remember that even in a linear medium, writers use their characters' personality traits for an emotional or a dramatic purpose.

Lorelei Shannon, a writer at Sierra On-Line, considers her double degree in literature and fine arts beneficial, allowing her to create and design stories and characters with detailed descriptions, which the artists and graphic designers can use to execute the concepts. Shannon worked on the successful *King's Quest VII*, which she codesigned with Roberta Williams. At the time of this writing, she was working hard on designing *Phantasmagoria II.*

> When you're creating characters that are going to be animated, so that the art can be drawn, you have to spend a considerable amount of time on what the visual representation of that character is going to be or look like. If you're using live actors, again the considerations are the same, though not as severe, because you're able to capture facial expressions [which] can give a lot of character. How [characters] sound is equally important. If the response of a character is purely a facial expression, the writer had better put it in the script.[7]

GET TO KNOW YOUR CHARACTERS

Basically, you should write the biographies of all your major characters. Even if most of this information—the characters' likes and dislikes, where they come from—never appears in the finished program, the fact that you know these characters will make a big difference. It all boils down to the three P's of character development: each character's *professional life* (what he or she does for a living), *personal life* (married or single, and why), and *private life* (hobbies, interests, fetishes, whatever).

A character, particularly in multimedia, should display action. The old rule for film and television (and, for that matter, all good literature) truly applies here: Show, don't tell. In other words, don't have a character say, "Boy, am I angry!" Show the character being angry. Have her slam her fist on a desk or throw a book against a wall. For example, when a member of the press asked John F. Kennedy how he felt about a difficult steelworkers' strike, the president picked a book off his desk and threw it against the wall.

Think of it this way. A man can say something about himself—how liberal he is, how he loves animals, how he thinks children are cute. Now, all of this could be true, but people judge what a person really thinks, who a person really is, by his or her actions. If a man says he's liberal but then moves away when an African-American family moves in next door, then obviously his action speaks volumes and shows that what he's said is, essentially, untrue. If a woman says she loves animals but displays fear when a dog runs over to her, or if she says she finds children cute but then visibly glares at a child who is laughing loudly, then her actions belie her words.

The methods that produce good characters in fiction, television, and movies also work for multimedia. As such, the writer needs to know and understand the following basic points about the character before the script-writing process begins:

1. What does the character need or want to achieve? In other words, what *drives* the character toward what end (the terminal objective)?
2. How does a character view the world? A character's *point of view* must be clear, as well as his or her circumstances.
3. What are the character's *attitudes*? Is the character extremely intelligent? Is he a whiner? Does she view life negatively or optimistically?

HAVE YOUR CHARACTER CHANGE

In film and literature, your main character or characters need to *change*. Even James Bond, a somewhat flat character, changed in some way at the end of each book.

In Brian de Palma's *The Untouchables,* Elliott Ness provides an example of a character who changes dramatically. Ness, an upholder of justice and the law, becomes as hardened and murderous as the gangsters he has been pursuing during the film, going so far as to throw Frank Nitti off a roof for killing his friend. The innocent, naive lawman becomes a cynical, hard-boiled murderer by the end of the film.

To show a character changing is much trickier in multimedia, though you could, for example, show your characters learning as they perform various tasks and go on various quests, building a scenario on past knowledge. One might considered the main challenge for multimedia writers to be creating characters as full as those found in linear media. The way to do this, perhaps, is not by profound changes (impossible in some programs) but subtle ones, showing a character slowly gain knowledge and expertise. Even Leisure Suit Larry becomes much more proficient in picking up women! In a CBT program, a similar development involves tracking the learning growth of users—the "characters" here. As the user learns more, the program delivers more sophisticated learning episodes using all the different layers of available tools.

NEW EMPHASIS ON CHARACTERS

As noted earlier, as the technology improves, writing for character development and the creation of worlds will receive more attention. Lowe agrees: "It's been easy with us, because our technology has improved between each of the games so, in a sense, we keep layering on top of layers, and we're building this big base of technology as we go through the story. In the first *Larry,* we were dealing with 160 pixels; Larry's nose was the size of New England. Now that the platforms are more stable, I think the technology will become less of an issue and the stories and the game play and the interactivity and game experience will become more important."[8]

Already, character development has improved exponentially from that in the early games of the 1980s:

"There's quite a bit of character development in *Phantas II,*" Lorelei Shannon says. "There was a certain amount of character development in *King's Quest VII,* but of course we had the advantage of having characters that had been through seven other games, so people knew them. As far as limiting the dialog, that is very true, and I've had to learn to work around that—Roberta smacked me around quite a bit on that—not really—but she did teach me how to be very concise with it—I look at it as a challenge, I mean, I can go home and be verbose in my novel if I want to—it really doesn't bother me."[9] She continues,

> Basically, [you tackle this problem] the same way you would in a novel, only at least with my game ... the end result is several different possible changes. [The character] definitely changes, but you decide how he changes through your game playing and your handling of the character. It actually takes more time than planning and writing a novel because you're working on a [series of linked parts] with multiple pathways. It's very time consuming. By the time I'm done with one of these [scripts] I have a stack of paper—anywhere five to seven hundred pages [as opposed to a screenplay: only one page for each minute of screen time]. But of course, that's including everything: the character sheets because we have to be consistent—in case someone else comes along and decides to do *Phantasmagoria III* with my characters, they'll need the sheet—just like a Disney character, we'll have the photographs of the person and their characteristics.
>
> The earlier games I designed were for animated characters, and you had to be very very specific. With *Phantasmagoria,* basically what I tried to do was include definite subtext that's not overtly obvious and trust the actor to carry it off. We're in the process of casting now, and I've never done it before, and I'm very excited about it, and we're hoping to get some really good talent—this is very psychological horror and we're going to need good actors to pull it off.
>
> For *Phantasmagoria I,* Sierra hired an outside director who was a movie director named Peter Maris. *Phantas I* was entirely **blue screen**; our new game is 75 percent real location so it won't be as hard—I [spoke to] all the actors on *Phantas I,* and one of the things they all said was how bizarre it was working with a blue screen—they'd be halfway through one very emotional scene and the director would interrupt and say, "Excuse me, you're head is partway through the wall."
>
> I have a real feeling this technology will merge with all different kinds of entertainment—I think that movies, television, computer games are eventually going to start intertwining more and more and start creating more and different types of entertainment that will be very mainstream, and I'd really like to be a part of that. It's already starting with games like *Johnnie Mnemonic* where, at night, they actually filmed the game on the actual movie set ... . *Casper*'s another good indication of where this technology might be heading—the computer-generated characters were amazing, and Casper was on screen I heard for like forty minutes, and that's the lead character of the movie and he's not real—that's astonishing![10]

Whether animated, computer-generated, or portrayed by a "live" actor, the physical description of a character is still something the writer has to know and describe. For example, in both the film and the book *To Kill a Mockingbird,* Atticus Finch, a gentle lawyer, is described in Lincolnesque terms. In the screenplay for *The Wild Bunch,* arguably one of the greatest American westerns ever made, Pike Bishop, the gang's leader, is described as a "not unhandsome" man with a thoughtful, weather-beaten face who is "afraid of nothing—except the changes in himself and those around him."[11] The screenwriters Sam Peckinpah (who also directed) and Walon Green also describe Pike as "walking with a limp, always slightly in pain."[12] The audience, besides having sympathy for this relic of a bygone era, is left to wonder just how he got the limp (a scene now restored to the "Director's Cut" version of the film).

To continue this example, the setting of *The Wild Bunch* also enhances the characters. The original ads for the film contained the following phrases: "Unchanged men in a changing time" and "Out of step, out of place, and dangerously out of time." Most people can easily visualize the American West. That the movie takes place in 1914 and shows motorcars and electric lights on the newly paved streets of towns graphically demonstrates just how "out of time" the "Bunch" is.

In multimedia, writers may have a harder time than in other media, creating characters who are walking, talking clichés, mostly because there is so little time and space to round the character out. That's why biographies, even if 98 percent of them don't appear in the finished program, are so important. Such biographies can greatly help the writer avoid clichés. It could be as simple as changing gender: If a character is supposed to be a policeman, try creating a policewoman. The author Irwin R. Blacker has a wonderful formula for dealing with clichés. He argues that if one must use clichés, and from what I've seen they're often unavoidable in multimedia, one should at least make them different:

> Not the hero who holds his liquor well,
>   but the one who doesn't.
> Not the soldier who is all courage,
>   but the one who overcomes fear.
> Not the sweet girl next door,
>   but the bitch.
> Not the whore with the heart of gold,
>   but a venal slut.
> Not the frail poet,
>   but the one who was a football star.
> Not the obsequious black servant,
>   but a Malcolm X.[13]

DIALOG

Dialog can express a lot about a character. Because of the nature of multimedia, writers have even less time to say something than they would in a "linear" motion picture. I like using the term **quicktalk** for dialog and narration in multimedia. Quicktalk is not that far removed from screenplay "reel talk" or "movie talk." Those of you in the film business might have heard the term before, though it's more of an academic term employed by screenwriting instructors. What it all comes down to is this: In a movie or television show, people do not speak or talk as they would in real life. Just listen to the dialog in any motion picture. People don't hesitate, they don't say "ah" or "um" or pause to collect their thoughts. There just isn't enough time! A screenwriter will have anywhere from 26 to 120 minutes to have the characters do and say everything they must to make the film work. So, in a teleplay I did for a PBS film about alcohol and drug abuse in middle school, I had dialog like this:

SARA: Roxanne? Do you ever think about the future?
ROXANNE: I never really think about it. It's just too scary.
SARA: *(gently)*
What are you scared of, Roxanne?
(Roxanne just shakes her head.)
SARA: It's all right. All of us have fears.
NICOLE: Yeah, I worry if people will hate me because I hang around with certain kids ...
SIMON: I'm not scared; just bored. I get depressed. Every day's the same. Sometimes, I can't even get up in the morning.

Compare this dialog with what it's based on—the transcript of an interview I conducted with middle-school students:

FEMALE STUDENT: I get scared by peer pressure, um, by parents and teachers getting on my, like, on my back. All that danger about getting kidnapped and stuff ...
MALE STUDENT: I'm not, like, you know, scared. I'm just bored. People are depressed at school because it's so ... I mean, there's nothing really new that happens, you go to classes and do the same thing and, um, like, you are so bored out of your minds, that you don't even ... I mean it's hard to, like, you know, get up in the morning when you know the same thing's gonna happen every day, but I mean, I can get up if I know something new will happen, but if it's just a normal day, people just come to school, it's like ... I dunno ...

As you can see, you have to shorten what people say, making crisp, clipped sentences that are actually more "reel" than "real." Even in documentaries, footage is often edited so you won't hear people stumbling or stuttering.

Here's another example to show the difference between "real talk" and "reel talk." In the early 1980s, the television miniseries *Blind Ambition* aired. Based on John Dean's book about the fall of the Nixon presidency, it starred Martin Sheen as John Dean and Rip Torn as Richard Nixon. At some point, the director or the writer decided to have the actors use the sort of wording that their characters had used on the infamous tapes. Suddenly, Sheen and Torn went from crisp, powerful, intense dialog to something resembling the following:

DEAN: We have to make ... you know ... make it, um, all, you know ...
NIXON: Oh, yeah. Um, like, make it seem, um seem ... as you were saying. It wouldn't be good for the, ah, um, the President, to ah, um ...
DEAN: No, but we'd have to take care of, um, that other thing, ah ...
NIXON: Oh, um, yeah. That's right.

The change from "reel" to "real" talk was sudden, reducing for many the tension and intensity. The comedy show *Saturday Night Live* repeated the scene in a sketch, this time with Buck Henry as John Dean and Dan Ackroyd as Nixon. In the sketch, Nixon is telling his daughter Tricia that the whole Watergate thing was a joke, that both he and Dean were well aware they were being bugged. Then, there's a flashback: Dean and Nixon struggle not to laugh as they speak into a large microphone. Suddenly, Nixon scrawls something down on paper and holds it up so Dean and the audience can see what it says: "Let's talk in incomplete sentences!" At that point, the two begin to speak directly from the transcripts of the tapes, which sounds almost as silly as it did in the original miniseries.

In multimedia, writers don't even have time to use movie or reel talk. They must express dialog in an even more abbreviated form: sound bites. Hence, the term *quicktalk*.

In a review of Terrence Malick's film *Badlands,* John Simon writes that dialog can function in three ways: First, it can faithfully record how people talk, conveying a cultural climate. Second, it can also elicit sympathy for the speaker, as well as make the speaker seem more realistic. Finally, dialog can portray a character, revealing the speaker's innermost psychic mechanisms.[14]

Writers may find these three functions hard to apply to quicktalk, but it can be done. Even in the children's CD-ROM *Magic School Bus,* everything each person on the bus says shows something about both their character and their state of mind. Even so, the writer of multimedia must always keep in mind that dialog must remain minimal.

"A lot of information is graphic oriented," Alex Shapiro states. "Even when you're thinking of a storyline, you have to think of it in visual ways—so a screenwriter is at a little bit of an advantage because he or she is somebody who is used to thinking in visual terms. When you write dialog, it should be short for technological reasons as well as user-interest reasons. People who work on a computer expect to click—if dialog goes on too long, they'll get bored. The technology can't carry that amount of information."[15] Of course, this is changing.

As Shapiro says, users will get bored if the dialog goes on for too long. As Robert Gelman and Kenneth Melville state, "For the most part, dialog that expresses character depth and motivation requires a pace and verbosity that players find, frankly, frustrating. They want clues. They want path choices. They want information."[16]

Always remember that the most important character in any interactive multimedia program is the user.

Storytelling is still important, it just needs to proceed from the player's [or user's] actions and explorations. Not from a rigid, pre-digested, linear, writer-as-god mindset.

Make players earn plot surprises and character payoffs through their own cleverness and hard work. [Italics mine.][17]

Structure

"Writing for the screen has nothing to do with mechanics and everything to do with character, story, and structure—structure, structure, structure."

— Richard Brooks

Along with interesting characters and good but concise dialog, a multimedia piece must have *structure*. Even though users have choices about which route to take, each scene must remain integral to the main story. Each scene also needs a strong line of dramatic action. Think of a sturdy tree with many branches. Each branch must be strong or else it will wither away. In multimedia, the main story is the tree, the branches are the various pathways the user can choose. In the multimedia tree, though, some of the branches might well connect with one another.

PLOT POINTS

Remember the discussion about plot? Well, plot *is* a story's structure, the basic idea of a piece. A plot is composed of scenes, which usually involve a crisis or conflict. Where this crisis occurs during a scene is called a **plot point** or crisis point. This conflict or incident should propel the story forward and the user toward choosing a pathway. Examples of plot points are numerous. In the movie *Frankenstein,* the doctor's assistant gives him the wrong brain to put inside the monster. In the CD-ROM program *Phantasmagoria,* one plot point takes place when Don encourages Adrienne to explore the strange house they have moved into. In both cases, this crisis or plot point in the story requires an action and/or a decision by the main characters—in *Phantasmagoria,* by the user as well.

Within any nonlinear, interactive piece, writers should make certain to choose crisis points well. These places, where the action and story can diverge, can destroy the flow and intensity of the program if they occur at the wrong time or place. The same is true when one places a crisis point where none is needed. With interactive technology, the writer may often feel the urge to script a crisis point every few seconds. Remember, the places where the user can choose to interact with the program serve in a way second only to the actual story.

In multimedia, the user becomes intimately involved with the plot or crisis points. In *Phantasmagoria,* for example, users decide what path the heroine should take. Should the heroine take the wrong path and be killed, the intimacy of the program makes her "death" that much more harrowing for users.

FUN

So, it is up to the writer to come up with a story line and plot points to keep the user engaged, entertained. Lorelei Shannon feels that the one word that the writer really has to keep in mind is *fun.*

"Think of *FUN* in huge glowing capital letters," she says. "So many games I've seen have ended up being merely interesting because I think their developers got too involved in one aspect of them—in the graphics, or story, or some individual aspect—and forgot the fun and forgot the fact that this is still a game. They're not interactive movies yet; they are games and they're meant to be entertaining and fun and keep you involved for hours. When you start to design a particular scenario or puzzle, think to yourself, 'Well, will this actually be fun? It may be cool but is it fun?' "[18]

Challenges

There are frustrations besides the limitations of the technology that writers will encounter. As Shannon states,

> Budgets are very frustrating. Being a writer, I can think up infinite numbers of strange and exotic situations which we can't afford to develop—we either have to build a set, find a set, or create it in 3D—all of which is very expensive—it's limiting in that respect at this point. Once we start getting big budgets like *Waterworld* had—even Kevin's lunch money would be good at this point—we'll be able to do a lot more. [Right now] it's a little bit limiting. In the world of the novel, there's nothing I can't conceive of and put to paper, and here I have to rein myself in a little bit.[19]

The point is to see these obstacles as challenges that writers can overcome through their imaginations. So remember, sometimes, simple is best and less is more. If you can't build an entire Otherworldly town, then decide how to get the "idea" of the town across to the user. If your producers can't afford a lot of special effects, think of other interesting ways to move the story and the user ahead. Sometimes I wish that someone would encourage video, multimedia, and film producers to completely forget about special effects just once. It can really be amazing how much a writer can convey to an audience without a video toaster (a generator of special effects, created by New Tek).

There have been some odd, strange, and abortive attempts at interactive movie making, such as *Mr. Payback*. However, as Lorelei Shannon points out, we are at the very edge of a multimedia entertainment explosion. Things are so new that there will necessarily be some, in Shannon's words, "real woofers coming out."[20] It will be up to the writers to make use of their imaginations and take multimedia entertainment beyond the "talkies" stage.

ENDNOTES

1. Aristotle, *On Poetics,* in *Great Books of the Western World* (Chicago: Encyclopedia Britannica, 1952), 684.
2. Ibid., p. 1450a.
3. William Goldman, *Hype and Glory* (New York: Villard Books, 1990), 163–164. Goldman's statement that "if the computer schmucks ever figure it out, then anyone will write wonderful stories, and if anybody can, nobody will" is true up to a point. I think there's a difference between a writer and someone who interacts with a narrative. Many people now own Hi8 video cameras that can give you broadcast- or near-broadcast-quality video. However, there's a big difference between a tourist or even a hopeful young director with a video camera and a Vilmos Zigmond. It is the craft of writing that will always be important and I believe, at least for the foreseeable future, that if a software is developed that can "mimic" a writer's style, it will still seem mechanical at best to the sharp-eyed editors. At least, I hope it will.
4. Al Lowe, interview with the author, August 1995.
5. Leslie Johnson-Evers, interview with the author, September 12, 1995.
6. William Sloane, *The Craft of Writing* (New York: W. W. Norton & Co., 1979) 74–75.
7. Lorelei Shannon, interview with the author, July 1995.
8. Lowe, interview with the author.
9. Shannon, interview with the author.
10. Ibid.
11. Syd Field, *The Screenwriter's Workbook* (New York: Dell, 1984), 81.
12. Ibid., 82.
13. Irwin R. Blacker, *The Elements of Screenwriting: A Guide for Film and Television Writing* (New York: Collier Books, 1986), 42.
14. John Simon, *Reverse Angle: A Decade of American Films* (New York: Clarkson N. Potter, 1982), 147–184.
15. Alex Shapiro, interview with the author, June 29, 1995.
16. Robert Gelman and Kenneth Melville, "On the Trail of the Interactive Grail," *Interactivity* magazine, January 1996, 58.
17. Ibid.
18. Shannon, interview with the author.
19. Ibid.
20. Ibid.

9

Script Formatting and Prototypes
Treatment + Content Outline = Script

"Writing for film and television and [writing for multimedia] isn't the same at all," Al Lowe states. He ways the latter is "interactive writing. ... My rule is—always go in the direction of more interactivity. The less you have people sitting back and watching and not participating the better; the more participation the happier the consumer tends to be."[1]

To be *interactive*, a project must enable the user to navigate within a multimedia environment by interrupting, directing, and selecting any number of pathways. As such, the script for an interactive multimedia program is not the traditional script or screenplay, but what Chris James calls "the nonlinear content and presentation of all the material you wish to convey in the multimedia presentation."[2] In other words, a multimedia script is not just dialog and action, but a written narrative describing how the user will interact with the program. The finished script for a multimedia piece will describe both character and user actions and tasks as well as the details of the created world.

To make such a script, James suggests writers think of the following equation:

$$\text{Treatment} + \text{Content Outline} = \text{SCRIPT}$$

In the treatment, the script writer shows how the script and graphics will "look and feel," while the content outline shows what the script and graphics will actually "say." The actual script writing process includes not only narration and/or dialog, but also all text for graphic portions of the project, an outline of other media that might be used, and text for video and audio sequences.

Script Formatting

Multimedia is so new that no "official" script format has yet surfaced. Most multimedia companies use basic screenplay formatting, which is also used for feature-length motion pictures, as well as many one-hour (or longer) television shows. As you will recall, a full-length screenplay runs about 120 pages, with each page covering a minute of film time. This, of course, is not true for multimedia scripts, which often include descriptions more detailed and longer than those found in traditional screenplays. Also, multimedia scripts might have chapter or module headings, as opposed to scene or segment headings:

> A couple of notes on script formatting: *Try using standard screenplay format* with scene numbers keyed to the design flow chart. Include a lot of ... design description, including interface and graphics utilization at appropriate places within the script. This helps the production folks understand the ... context and motivation of the dramatic action, and gives them a better sense of the final screen presentation and dynamics of the product. Be sure to italicize that material so the production manager and the director don't associate it with anything they have to budget and shoot. [Italics mine.][3]

RULES OF FORMATTING

The following rules apply to both film screenplays and multimedia scripts making use of screenplay formatting. Note that computer-based interactive programs (CBT, CMI, etc.) are done screen by screen (see Jim Benton's series of screens for his program on CBT in Chapter 10).

A line at the head of each scene will specify and describe the location, note whether it is an interior or exterior shot, and indicate the time of day during which the scene is meant to take place. For example,

EXT. A LARGE HOUSE - EVENING

would be the way you would write out an exterior shot of a large house during the evening. If you were to begin with an interior shot, the heading would read,

INT. A LARGE HOUSE - EVENING

Descriptions of action are single-spaced and run from margin to margin while double-spacing separates descriptions and dialog.

The first time a character's name is used, it should be written in all CAPS. For example,

INT. CLASSROOM C222 - MORNING

APRIL DANCER, a young attractive woman about 28 years of age, takes her seat in the back row of the classroom. There are some twenty other students in the class. JAY GARRICK, a slim young man with glasses, sits next to April and can't take his eyes off her.

Do *not* put a character's name in all caps in a description or action sequence once you have already done so (note: "sits next to April."). When you are showing who is speaking dialog, then the character's name is also in all caps and centered over the dialog. For example,

JAY
(clears his throat)
Um, is this History 101?

April gives him an odd look, then turns her attention back to the blackboard.

As you can see, dialog is always single-spaced and set in a column about three to three-and-a-half inches wide at the center of the page. All transitions are marked by double-spacing.

In final drafts of scripts, a scene that extends for several pages is marked "CONTINUED" in the upper-left corner of each page until the scene ends. In multimedia, speeches cannot be particularly long. However, if they extend beyond one page, "(MORE)" should appear centered at the bottom of the first page. On the following page, the name of the character speaking must be printed again (all caps) followed by "(cont'd)". For example:

JAY
Um, is this History 101?

April gives him an odd look, then turns her attention back to the blackboard. The classroom becomes silent as another person enters. The teacher, MRS. MCPHERSON, a young-looking thirty-year-old with long brown hair, enters the room and begins to speak.

MCPHERSON
My name is Mrs. McPherson. This is a special
history class. We'll be able to actually experience
events.

She picks up a piece of chalk, stops speaking.

(CONTINUED)

Now, let's continue with the classroom as our main menu and metaphor for what follows. Within the classroom, there might be hot spots: places the user can click on and find various items or clues. These *hot spots* should be noted in your script as follows:

CONTINUED: [from previous page]

Hot Spots:

- the blackboard, the door next to the blackboard, the clock on the wall, the globe.

CLICK ON THE BLACKBOARD

only after Mrs. McPherson has stopped speaking. Various years and dates appear on the blackboard when you CLICK ON it, which you can do whenever you come back to this main menu.

CLICK ON THE CLOCK

anytime after clicking on the blackboard. The hands move quickly backward and the face of the clock is replaced with a kind of swirling galaxylike image. You will then find yourself back in the year you highlighted by clicking on the blackboard. A smaller version of the clock then appears on the lower-right corner of the screen, letting you know how much time is left in this particular historical era.

CLICK ON THE GLOBE

anytime after clicking on a year on the blackboard. This transports you to a particular part of the world. However, until you click on the clock, which remains suspended in space, you will remain at the chosen location in the present time.

It is easy to see that in a multimedia script it may take five, ten, or more pages for the writer to script each particular place and era the students can travel to. These locations, in turn, may have numerous hot spots, which take the user down different **pathway**s or **branches**. The minute-a-page rule for film scripts obviously does not work here.

Generally, you should use one font only when scripting, mainly because it makes the script easier to read. Most companies use the "Courier New" or "Times Roman" font with a size of twelve points.

The more you script, the more natural the format will seem. You can use the examples in this book as templates for your script. Fortunately, there are many script and screen-writing software packages available (see Appendix D), costing anywhere from $80 to $200. Though no specific script-writing software exists for interactive multimedia, regular screenwriting software can be amended easily enough to provide for descriptions of hot spots and click-on directions.

SAMPLE SCRIPT

The following pages present the first three pages of Sierra On-Line's *Phantasmagoria II: A Puzzle of Flesh*. Note the formatting: Camera direction is in **Bold** (see glossary for specific terms), descriptions are printed pretty much margin to margin, and dialog is centered. Notice also the variations from regular screenplay formatting: quote marks used for dialog and more camera directions than usual. Also, the writer has indented descriptions slightly and printed the locations in bold and a larger font size.

I tend to stick to a more traditional screenplay format (no quote marks with dialog, locations printed screenplay style, with no bold lettering for camera placement, editing instructions, or locations), but slight variations in formatting are the norm these days in multimedia. However, there's every reason to believe that this will change and a single multimedia script format will come into wide use.

CHAPTER 1 SCRIPT

MENTAL HOSPITAL: CORRIDORS (Opening Cartoon)

FLASH IN:
TO THE MENTAL HOSPITAL CORRIDORS, SHOT OF DOUBLE HOSPITAL DOORS.
With an overly loud CRASH, the doors bang open and a Dr. Marek and the orderlies
wheel in Curtis on a cart.

ANGLE CHANGE:
THE CAMERA SWINGS UP SO THAT IT IS POINTING AT THE CEILING.
Extremely bright ceiling lights are flashing past, far too quickly. The camera is shaking
and rocking. This is supposed to be Curtis's POV from the gurney. We HEAR distorted
voices in the background. Some of what they are saying is understandable:

> DR. MAREK:
> (offscreen; voice
> distorted and cold)
> " … severe psychotic episode. Keep
> your hands away from his mouth!"

> ORDERLY 1:
> (offscreen; urgent tone)
> " … Jesus Christ, look at him!"

> DR. MAREK:
> (offscreen)
> " … potential for violence … watch him!"

ANGLE CHANGE:
THE CAMERA ABRUPTLY SWINGS AROUND, REVERSING ITSELF SO THAT IT IS NOW LOOKING
DOWN AT CURTIS ON THE GURNEY.
DR. MAREK is there, walking alongside the gurney, talking to Curtis. His voice is so
distorted that we can't understand what he is saying. ORDERLY 1 and ORDERLY 2 are
pushing the gurney. Curtis is FLOPPING AROUND wildly, looking around him in
absolute terror. He SCREAMS, over and over. Orderly 2 is trying to hold him down. Dr.
Marek tightens the straps holding Curtis down until he can hardly move. He takes a big
rubber bit out of his pocket, and jams it into Curtis's mouth, despite the fact Curtis is
thrashing his head back and forth and trying to get away from him.

PULL BACK:
TO A LONG SHOT OF THE CORRIDOR.
We see that OTHER MENTAL PATIENTS are in the hallway, grabbing at Curtis as he is
wheeled past, gibbering nonsense. The camera FOLLOWS HIM down the hall, shaking,
as if handheld. The gurney seems to be going way too fast. The RATWOMAN pops up
and sticks her face in Curtis's.

CUT TO CLOSE-UP:
OF THE RATWOMAN AND CURTIS.
She pops up right next to his head as he is wheeled by, and hisses into his face.

> RATWOMAN:
> (horribly gleeful)
> "Freak!"

PULL BACK:
TO LONG SHOT OF CORRIDOR AGAIN. CAMERA IS ONCE AGAIN FOLLOWING CURTIS DOWN THE HALL.
The cart CRASHES through a pair of DOUBLE DOORS. The camera follows the cart into the ELECTROSHOCK ROOM.

MENTAL HOSPITAL: ELECTROSHOCK ROOM (Opening Cartoon)

CUT TO:
LONG SHOT OF ELECTROSHOCK ROOM. WE CAN SEE ALL SORTS OF OLD, SCARY, SKANKY MEDICAL EQUIPMENT.

NOTE:
THIS WHOLE SEQUENCE SHOULD BE DISTORTED AND STRANGE, AS IF SEEN THROUGH CURTIS'S DRUGGED AND PSYCHOTIC EYES.

CUT TO CLOSE-UP:
OF DR. MAREK'S FACE. IT APPEARS DISTORTED AND SCARY.
Dr. M speaks to Curtis reassuringly, but his eyes are cold and betray a horrible hidden glee.

> DR. MAREK:
> (falsely reassuring;
> voice distorted)
> "Can you hear me? Curtis, you're having a psychotic episode.
> We're going to help you."

PULL BACK:
TO MEDIUM SHOT WHICH INCLUDES DR. MAREK AND CURTIS.
Dr. M jams a huge HYPODERMIC NEEDLE into Curtis's shoulder. Curtis goes limp, but his eyes still cut around in terror.

PULL BACK:
TO LONG SHOT OF ELECTROSHOCK ROOM.
Orderly 1 and Orderly 2 unstrap Curtis from the gurney and toss him onto the electroshock table. They strap him down. Dr. Marek applies the electrodes to his body, and shoves the bit even further into his mouth. Dr. Marek sets the level on the dials of

the electroshock machine, then reaches for the lever. A tiny SMILE plays on his mouth as he pulls the lever. Curtis bucks and convulses on the table. He lets out a horrible, inhuman WHINE, then sags back down onto the table. The switch is pulled again, and this time when Curtis convulses, he bites the bit in half. He is still making that horrible noise.

CUT TO CLOSE-UP:
OF DR. MAREK'S AND ORDERLY 1'S FACES. THEY APPEAR DISTORTED AND MONSTERISH.

ZOOM IN TO CLOSE-UP
OF CURTIS ON THE TABLE AS THE SWITCH IS PULLED A THIRD TIME. WE END UP ON A CLOSE-UP OF HIS FACE.
His face starts to STRETCH and RUN like wax from a candle. His wail escalates to a piercing SCREAM. The screen goes BLACK.

BRING UP TITLES

FADE TO:
CURTIS'S BEDROOM AFTER TITLES.

CURTIS'S APARTMENT: BEDROOM
(End of Opening; Start of Game Play)

CURTIS IS SLEEPING IN HIS BED. SUNLIGHT IS FILTERING THROUGH THE BLINDS AND STRIPING ACROSS HIS FACE AND BODY.
A SUBTITLE appears across the screen. It says "ONE YEAR LATER." The subtitle FADES away. Curtis begins to wake up. He rubs his eyes, and sits up in bed. He rubs his face, and gets entirely out of bed. The player now has control.

Hot Spots:
The nightstand drawer, the dresser drawer, the dresser mirror, the photograph of Curtis's parents in the nightstand drawer, the door to the living room

NOTE: NO hot spots will appear in the apartment (except for the dresser) before Curtis gets dressed. We don't want to have to film him doing everything twice.

Click on the Dresser
   Before getting dressed: Click on the dresser drawer gets Curtis opening the drawer, and pulling out a T-shirt and jeans. He walks into the BATHROOM. We get some kind of TIME FADE, and he comes out of the bathroom, dressed, rubbing a TOWEL on his hair. He tosses the towel into the bathroom. The player now has control of him.

   After getting dressed: No hot spot.

Click on the Nightstand Drawer
   Anytime: Click on the nightstand drawer gets Curtis opening the drawer. There are a number of things he CANNOT take in the drawer, such as CONDOMS, a PING-PONG

BALL, and a RUBBER RAT. The PHOTOGRAPH OF CURTIS'S PARENTS is in the drawer, unless he has already taken it. That has a hot spot.

While looking for wallet: Curtis will open the nightstand drawer and mutter that his keys are not in there. He will shut it again.

> CURTIS:
> (muttering to himself)
> "Hmm … no wallet."

Click on Photograph in Nightstand Drawer
   Anytime: Click on the photograph in the drawer gets Curtis to take the photograph. He looks at it with an enigmatic expression. Then it goes into INVENTORY.

OTHER FORMATS

Along with the screenplay format, multimedia writers can also adapt a **split page format,** used often for television and video productions. One side of the page contains the visual information under the title "VIDEO" while the other side contains all "AUDIO" or "TEXT" material. Though the writer can focus equally on both the visual material and the dialog with this format, descriptions tend to be shorter than in the screenplay format and visual imagery tends to lose its impact on the reader.

There is also a **teleplay** or **video format,** used often for shows such as television sit-coms, that tends to present a lot of visual information. For instance, a scene will usually begin with the scene number, and then a "Visual Overview" of what the viewer is seeing. Besides the screenplay, the teleplay format is the one most often used by multimedia writers.

Sketch Prototypes

Writers have many tools for scripting a multimedia piece that also help other designers and personnel picture the final program. *Sketch prototypes,* which include storyboards, are the least expensive way to visualize a project. They also help writers develop more interaction and user-friendly programs, as well as explore alternatives regarding hot spots, pathways, and story development. Finally, sketch prototypes can also allow writers to test how well the program will work, letting them see if the user will both understand the story and be able to move around in the program.

Such prototypes help the entire production team understand just what the **interface** between user and program will look like. Interface is the method by which the user interacts with the screen; that is, what objects the user will be able to click on, etc.

KINDS OF SKETCH PROTOTYPES

There are three kinds of sketch prototypes, each created with a different objective in mind.

Fixed prototypes can be text, drawings, or menus. They let one know if the user can understand the material and how one part of the program relates to another.

Sequential prototypes generally show one path through a particular program and where it connects with other paths. Such prototypes can show one if users can follow the program, what they can expect to occur in the course of following a specific pathway, and whether the points where the path could diverge make sense.

Interactive prototypes can tell one if users will interact well with the multimedia program; that is, if users will be able to understand certain tasks within the program and complete them. Interactive prototypes help writers see how and when available tools can be used.

All prototypes allow the writer, as well as the entire team, to get feedback quickly and early on in the preproduction phase. Usually, a multimedia production team will use prototypes often and extensively. For example, many prototypes were tested for *Haight-Ashbury in the Sixties*. "The first five prototypes," the creator Tony Bove writes, "were short demonstrations of the different elements of the CD-ROM, including the metaphor for presenting the information. These were used to secure licenses for music from record companies, and licenses for images and words from over one hundred other content providers. The many prototypes made thereafter were used for internal testing, then customer testing, and finally for demonstrating at CD-ROM-related conferences and seminars."[4]

Here follow some of the best kinds of prototypes. Most can be done quickly, are inexpensive, and are fairly easy to create.

STORYBOARDS

Storyboards are essentially an attempt to indicate by drawings the shots in a motion picture. Storyboards have always greatly helped production workers plan and design the film production, as well as see the director's style. Storyboards are particularly helpful for animation and action scenes. However, storyboards also help such personnel as set designers, cinematographers, and actors understand just where the camera is to be placed and exactly what the camera lens will see.

Storyboards were used extensively first by the Disney company, mainly to prevent mistakes in the actual animation process. Sixty years ago, Walt Disney would call "story meetings" where the film his studio was working on could be told from start to finish in graphic form. Disney himself said that, to create a good storyboard, one had to "think in terms of pictures. That's how we tell our stories, not with words."[5] Later, Alfred Hitchcock always used storyboards to know exactly what each scene in his film would look like.

In multimedia, storyboards not only indicate what an animated or video portion of a program might be, but also serve as a series of sketch prototypes or models for the entire program. Storyboards are particularly important for computer-generated animation projects. As in a film or video, the storyboard *shows* the story that will appear in the final animation. It also communicates what is to be done; what kind of shots, drawings, and animations are to be used; and what the hot spots will do.

Fundamentals   In "The Process of Storyboarding," James Spies and Andrea Blake list five fundamentals of creating a storyboard:

1. Understand that *organization* is one of the main reasons for creating a storyboard.
2. Decide how complex and detailed your storyboard should be—does it need a few pages of sketches or will literally hundreds of thousands of highly detailed drawings be necessary?
3. Include all the necessary information in your storyboards. Many storyboards for live-action pieces show the angle, light direction, and direction of action. Others simply show that you cut from a Medium to a Close Shot.
4. Select the graphic format for the storyboard that best fits your objectives—will you need text along with a storyboard to completely convey what you are trying to do?
5. Once your storyboard is completed and authorized, DON'T FORGET TO USE IT IN THE CREATION OF YOUR PROGRAM![6]

Storyboards are important tools for all genres of interactive multimedia. Jim Benton states that in working on computer-based training, the storyboarding process will continue right up to the production level. Storyboarding will help one delineate what the text and graphics will be.

For his CBT screens, Jim Benton uses a particular template. He "pours" text into a box on the left-hand side of the screen. Graphics appear on the right, with control buttons in the lower-right corner. "From our studies, people start off reading at the upper left hand corner of the screen, read down, look at the graphics on right hand side, and then they go right to the buttons."[7]

Graphics   Graphics do not necessarily have to be drawn—they can just as easily be noted on the storyboard. In fact, storyboard pictures in general need not be elaborate. Stick figures are fine, though some storyboards, such as those for *Raiders of the Lost Ark,* are elaborate enough to have been produced and sold as picture books. However, as noted, the sketches need to indicate the basic design of a shot as seen through the camera's eye. Though you don't have to draw every shot in your program, you might select ten to twenty of the most important shots. You should number them to correlate with the shots in the final shooting script. If you have a moving or zoom shot in mind or if any sort of special effects are indicated, you need to describe them to the side or below the picture.

Formatting   There are many types of script/storyboard formatting. Those writing for video or advertising use their own format. They divide the page into three sections from left to right: VIDEO, STORYBOARD, and AUDIO (see Figure 9-1). The video section describes exactly what the viewer will be seeing. The storyboard should match what the text in the video section says, and the audio shows all sounds, including narration, sound effects, and dialog.

In the past few years, some companies have begun employing slight variations on traditional formats, gearing them for multimedia. For example, a few writers and designers use a small column on the right for User Opportunities, while two-thirds of the page is taken up by Descriptions of Visuals and Audio, all single-spaced. The bottom of the page might then contain a drawing of what the screen for this particular scene might look like. Conversely, as you can see in Figure 9-2, some people employ a format whereby the upper-right part of the page has about a third taken up by a storyboard "screen."

With any prototype, including storyboards and even scripts, writers shouldn't become too attached to any one idea or scenario. None of it should be considered written in stone. The process of creating a multimedia program should be as flexible as the medium itself. By using prototypes, writers ensure that the final product will work well, make sense, and present a story in an interesting and engaging way. Here are some storyboards from Splash's *Piper,* a children's interactive CD-ROM version of "The Pied Piper." (See Figures 9-3 through 9-5.)

DRAWINGS AND ARTWORK

Along with your storyboard, you might want to work with an artist to create *drawings* to show how each character and environment might appear. As with your storyboard, don't worry about your drawings being wonderful artistic creations. They serve merely to communicate your ideas visually.

Again, be prepared to have drawings nixed, changed, or incorporated into something else. Remember, you're working in a collaborative medium. Even the detailed drawings of "The Hecatomb," the main antagonist in *Phantasmagoria II* (Figures 9-6 through 9-8), went through numerous transformations before a final image was decided on.

FIGURE 9-1 ▌ *Video or ad script format.*

Client _____ KODAK _____ Length_____ Date _____

Product_____ KODAK FILM _____ Job No. _____

Title_____ "KODAK WAS THERE"_____ Commercial No. _____ Rev. No. _____

VIDEO:		AUDIO:

FADE UP TO:
FOOTAGE OF JOHN F.
KENNEDY AT PODIUM
GIVING HIS INAUGURAL
SPEECH

JFK: " ... let the
word go forth, from
this time and place,
to friend and foe
alike, that the torch
has been passed to a
new generation of
Americans."

IMAGE OF JFK AT
PODIUM <u>STILLS</u>

SOUND OF CHEERING
CROWD <u>FADES OUT</u>

WHITE BORDER FORMS
AROUND IMAGE, AREA
AROUND BORDER GOES
BLACK

ANNCR. (VO): Kodak
was there.

WORDS "KODAK WAS
THERE" <u>SUPERED</u> OVER
IMAGE—IMAGE <u>FADES
OUT</u>—WORDS REMAIN.

FIGURE 9-2 *A script format geared specifically for multimedia.*

Screen No. ____
Next Screen ____

- [ ] Audio
  1. ____
  2. ____
  3. ____
- [x] Animation
  1. Map will zoom
  2. ____
  3. ____
- [ ] Graphic
  1. ____
  2. ____
  3. ____
  4. ____
  5. ____
- [ ] Video
- [ ] Stills
- [x] VR
- [x] Other ICONS
- [ ] MAP

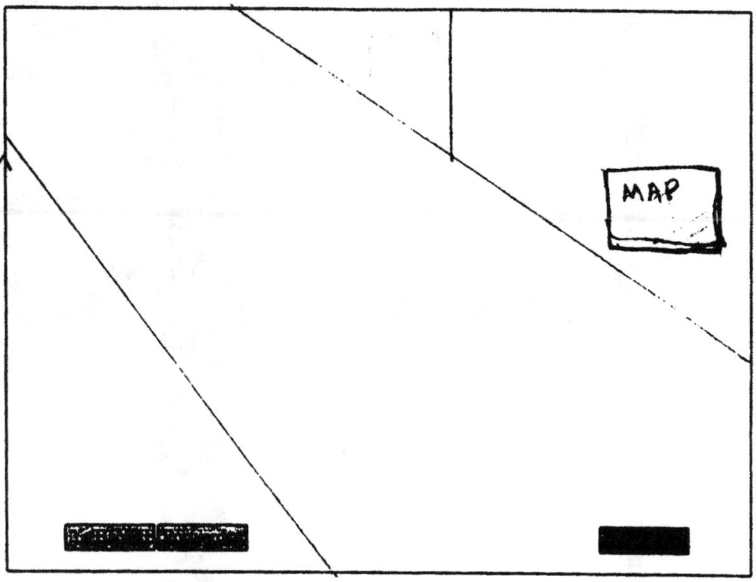

AUDIO/SCRIPT ____

chairs eye view

VISUAL VR tour of Hallway stitched together with tour elevators + outside + to cafeteria

NOTES MAP ICON accesses Map of any area in VR tour
EYE ICON accesses other VR tours - branching

FEED BACK ____

BRANCHING

Field 1 to:____	Field 4 to:____	Field 7 to:____	Field 10 to:____	Field 13 to:____
Field 2 to:____	Field 5 to:____	Field 8 to:____	Field 11 to:____	Field 14 to:____
Field 3 to:____	Field 6 to:____	Field 9 to:____	Field 12 to:____	Field 15 to:____

FIGURE 9-3 *The rats hear the Piper's music.*

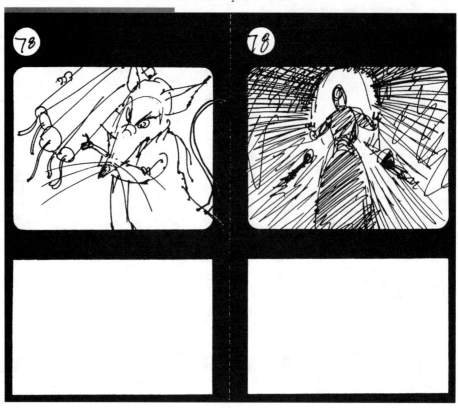

FIGURE 9-4 *Image #78 on storyboard as seen in the final product of* Piper.

FIGURE 9-5   *Townspeople hear and see explosion.*

FIGURE 9-6   *A prototype for Hetacomb, the antagonist of Phantasmagoria II.*

FIGURE 9-7   *Close-up—Hetacomb prototype sketch.*

FIGURE 9-8 | *More prototypes of malevolent creatures from* Phantasmagoria II.

Other Creative Prototypes

There are many other kinds of prototypes you can create. For example, puppets, models, and three-dimensional mapping can greatly help you show visually how the interfacing within a program will work. You can make and modify the puppets and models yourself, or use a variety of toys, action figures, and dioramas to give people a feel for both the interface and the landscape of the computerized world to be created. These types of working dioramas or working models can greatly enhance flowcharts, storyboards, and drawings.

PROTOTYPE ANIMATION

Animatics   With **animatics,** the writer and designer can give an idea how the visuals—animation or live action—might work within a multimedia program. Animatics are relatively inexpensive and easy to do. Simply pin your drawings, storyboards, or photographs to a wall or lay them flat. Set up a video camera (an inexpensive home video camera will suffice). Shut off all fluorescent lights and direct one or two incandescent lights at the images. Then, shoot the drawings in sequence. A few moments will do. You can zoom in or pan over the image to achieve an illusion of motion. Likewise, you can zoom in on hot spots. Since you'll be shooting in order, you should not have to edit. Finally, you can enrich the prototype by adding sound: music, narration, dialog, and sound effects.

Flipbooks   The flipbook is another easy way to show visually how transitions will work. You don't have to be a great artist to make a flipbook work; you can use stick figures to show the movement of characters or objects within a program.

Think of the flipbook as an interactive storyboard. The users can go as fast or as slow as they like, stopping occasionally to observe one specific storyboard or still. Get a package of three-by-five index cards (which tend to be uniform and have a "flippable" stiffness), draw a simple figure, and on each succeeding card make sure the figures at least move their arms and legs slightly. Clip the cards together, flip them, and there's your scene (see diagrams Figures 9-9 and 9-10).

Computer Animation   There are two types of computer animation: 2D and 3D. The former is your basic Saturday morning cartoon—flat drawings. The latter comprises a fully rendered three-dimensional effect, as with software such as *3D Studio*.

Even with special tools, computer animation is very time consuming. However, you can use tools such as hypercard or hyperstudio (for the Mac), *Toolbook* (for Windows), or *Macromedia Director* to move objects from one part of the screen to another (in *Director* you can do more).

Essentially you choose an object, such as a drawing that you've scanned into the computer. In *Toolbook,* you click on Recorder, select whatever it is you want to move, and move the object a little, then let it go, and continue in this way. The software will record the path you're moving your figure on. Stop recording, save as a script—you won't get arms and legs moving, no full-motion animation; the entire figure will move across the screen, but it will give viewers a

FIGURE 9-9 | *Bouncing Ball small cards for flipbook.*

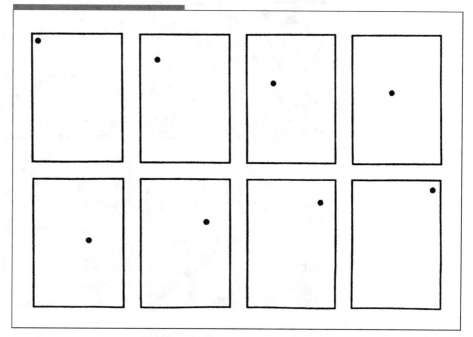

FIGURE 9-10   *"Light at the End of the Tunnel" cards for a flipbook by Matt Robkin.*

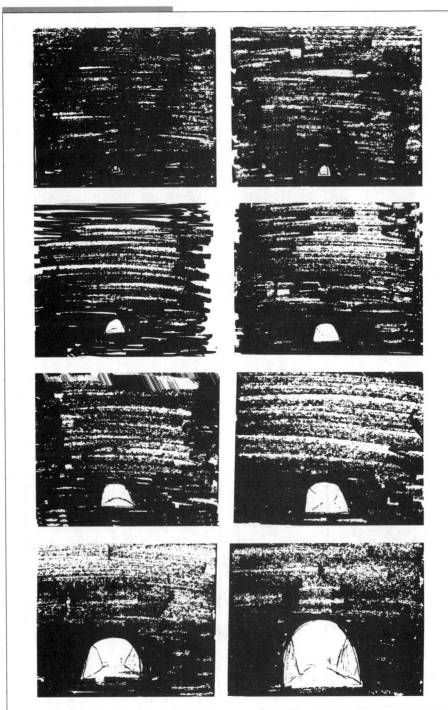

good idea of what parts of the program and interface might look like. In *Director* (for Windows and the Mac), along with simple prototype animations, you can also do full-motion animation.

TAPE/SLIDE PROTOTYPES

You can, of course, give a powerful presentation by using a series of 35mm slides with a projector and a tape recorder for sound effects, music, and narration. You can also use a software tool such as Microsoft's *PowerPoint* and project your digitized slide show. The *PowerPoint* presentation will take more time (you have to scan each photo or drawing into the computer), but it will be more effective.

You can be as creative as you'd like in creating prototypes. One group of students pitching a proposed multimedia program used a VHS camera to videotape drawings, live action, and animation. They then used a twenty-seven-inch television set hooked up to a VCR. On the bottom of the TV, they had attached a piece of cardboard with buttons and icons on it. One student stood at the television set, pressing the drawn buttons. Another student, sitting in the second row of the classroom, had the VCR controller and would pause the tape each time the fake button was pushed. This gave viewers a good idea of just how the program might work.

Conclusion

Now you've seen how script formatting works. You have also learned about the prototypes that during the preproduction and production process, allow the entire production team to understand the "look" of the program. They are also used for pitch sessions, when the producers are attempting a presale of the project or are trying to hook up with potential investors. In the final analysis, prototypes, even the most elementary and primitive ones, add a powerful dimension to the presentation of any multimedia program.

ENDNOTES

1. Al Lowe, interview with the author, August 1995.
2. Chris James, "The Development Process for Interactive Multimedia Products," paper for Media/CIS 223, January 1994 (by permission of the author), 1–3.
3. Robert Gelman and Kenneth Melville, "On the Trail of the Interactive Grail," *Interactivity* magazine, January 1996, 59.
4. Tony Bove, interview with the author, October 3, 1995.
5. James L. Sipes and Andrea Liv Blake, "The Process of Storyboarding," *PC Graphics and Video* magazine, March 1995, 36.
6. Ibid., 36–39.
7. Jim Benton, interview with the author, February 6, 1996.

10

Navigation for Interactive Multimedia

Before production based on the script can even start the writer must lay out the individual screen components as a navigational plan.

Once writers actually begin the writing process, they must determine the pathways the users can take and what kind of metaphor to use for a screen menu. At this point in production, the design team begins to choose icons and symbols for the "buttons," "page turners," and "links" by which the user moves from one part of the program to another.

Navigation Basics

Though navigation has been mentioned several times in this text, in the strictest sense it is a process not done by the developers but by the users. The navigation plan determines how users will find their way through the interactive pathways. The writer works on this plan with the designer and the programmer or author. It is always a good idea to create a navigation or flowchart, though some writers, such as Lorelei Shannon at Sierra On-Line, make use of three-by-five index cards:

> I'll have them stuck all over the walls and all over the ceiling and on my desk when I run out of room. Sometimes, I'll have to keep track of my notes on the computer too, but it really helps me if I have something physical to keep in my hand that I can say, "Well, if he goes there then he can do either this or that," and literally see it on the wall. I know Roberta [Williams, a cofounder of Sierra On-Line] likes to design with really big pieces of paper: She draws things out on a big map. Now, everybody does it a little differently, but I think most of us use some sort of visual aid. Once, we were trying to block out a scene that was really difficult, and we had a number of characters to interact with, so we had a lot of little action figures on the table.[1]

Navigation depends in part on the type of program. For example, CBT navigation has to allow the user to move *backward* as well as forward in case the user wants to reread or recheck something. The format should provide *consistency* as the learner moves from one screen to the next. For a CBT program, the chosen font should be easy to read, and both font and background should be the same on each screen. The CBT user must know where to find everything on the screen and should have control of navigation.

AUTHORING AND WRITING

Writing out and planning navigation can be the most time consuming of the pre-production processes. The use of metaphors can greatly help and enhance a navigational chart. They provide the best way to get into the variety of sections of a program. Once the user is at a location, writers can also use the stand-bys of "Forward," "Backward," "Help," and "Exit" buttons. In computer-based programs, these buttons are often all users need for navigation.

Once again, the process by which a multimedia product is made truly interactive is called *authoring,* which is not the same as "writing." Authoring involves *all* media (audio, video, graphics, etc.) in creating a program. An author in this sense puts the material into the computer, developing the **nodes** (the information screens or segments thereof) that the writer thought up, as well as physically creating the various *pathways* (links from screen to screen). All this is done with various **authoring tools**, **applications** or **programs** that allow one to write software combining text, graphics, video, and audio for playback and interaction.[2] The computer applications used to create the graphic elements and the links are also referred to as **authoring programs**. So remember, authoring isn't writing, it's programming and media management.

HELPING THE USER

The whole purpose of multimedia is to let the user control how he or she interacts with the program. The writer often helps to select the best media to achieve good navigation. These media include

- Full-Motion Video
- Animation
- Sound and F/X
- Graphics
- Text
- Voices

How does a user interact with a multimedia product? A series of on-screen *buttons, page turners,* or other graphic representations allow the user to click on them and travel through the program in a nonlinear manner. There's usually a title page and/or a main menu (making use of the main metaphor), a request-help page, a view-the-tutorial section, an exit-to-other menu, a select-a-topic icon, a way to view various material, and, for training and educational programs, a take-a-test button. Finally, there is a button or icon that will allow the user to exit the program. True interactive multimedia is a unique art in that it allows different users to travel down entirely different pathways from those used by other users. The pathway chosen could be based on interest, needs, desires, and point of view.

Flowcharts

The mapping of the various pathways and sections of a program and how they are linked is called a **flowchart**. Think of navigational flowcharts as the blueprints for an interactive multimedia program.

The easiest way to show the difference between an interactive multimedia program and a linear show is with flowcharts. Suppose you want to do a video on preparedness for an earthquake. There might be seven major sections:

1. The introduction
2. What to have on hand (water, radio, flashlight, etc.)
3. What to do if a quake hits and you're outside
4. What to do if a quake hits and you're indoors
5. First aid for people injured during a quake
6. Aftershocks
7. What to do after an earthquake has occurred

A flowchart of such a linear program might look like Figure 10-1, which shows the first four sections.

FIGURE 10-1 | *Sample flowchart for a video (linear) on earthquake preparedness.*

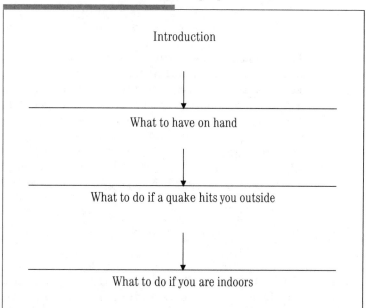

For an interactive multimedia program, though, you would add more choices and allow the user much more control. For example, you might still provide an introductory module or section. From there, you might offer the user the choice of one of two modules: "History of Regional Quakes" or "Locations of Fault Lines." Each of these modules might then move on to one of four other modules: "What to Have on Hand," "Finding Emergency Equipment," "Emergency Broadcasting," and "Emergency Phone Numbers." The user can choose one specific module and then jump to yet another set of modules ("What to Do Outside," "What to Do Inside," "First Aid," "CPR"). The modules "First Aid" and "CPR" might go off into completely different directions, actually taking you out of the main loop of the earthquake preparedness program. Also, the flowchart for the more interactive piece (Figure 10-2) looks like a Christmas tree as opposed to a stack of boxes. The modules of the two flowcharts are "linked" by a series of lines or arrows.

TYPES OF LINKING

One can link the components of a multimedia program together in many ways. Instead of trying to describe them all in context, I'll discuss each separately.

Linear Linking   Multimedia does not always have to be nonlinear. In most if not all programs, some segments are linear. Often, multimedia training programs need such segments because they provide the best way to present content and ensure user understanding. For example, a program on training the disabled to function better on their own may have a variety of segments the user may watch (such as how to get in and out of a wheelchair, or how to arrange an apartment so everything is easy to get to), but each segment will be linear. Indeed, the process of getting in and out of a wheelchair must be linearly explained; the user can't suddenly leap from step one to step five.

Next Page/Previous Page   These on-screen buttons allow the user to move ahead in a program or return and review a previous page, be it text or menu screens. Once the user has returned to the first node within a linear chain, the Previous Page button disappears and the user cannot go back any further in the program.

Return or Main Menu   This button allows the user to return to the first page of a program. This "escape hatch" button, as the multimedia instructor Chris James calls it, is usually available on every page or node of the program.

Help   Another escape hatch button, this should immediately take the user to a segment that has instructions on how to function and navigate in the current section of the program.

Decision/Crisis or Plot Points   Discussed in some detail in Chapter 9, these should be reviewed because they are the points where the multimedia program truly becomes interactive. At each plot point, the user can enter a new topic or

FIGURE 10-2 | *Sample flowchart for a multimedia (nonlinear) program on earthquake preparedness.*

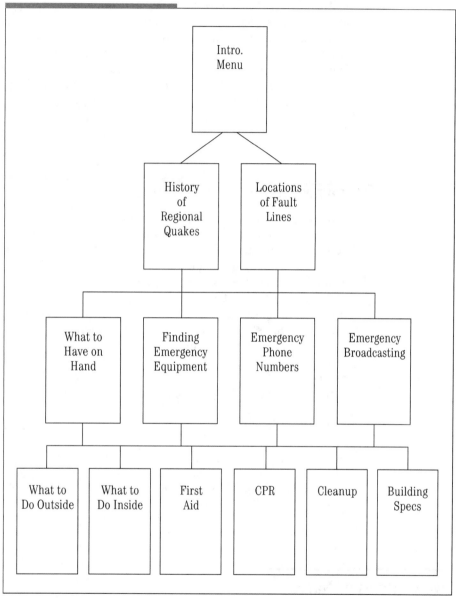

idea segment or otherwise determine how to proceed in the program. "These decision points are only available when [users have] completed a specific segment. Once they enter a pathway, they remain on that pathway until they either complete it, exit it via a return point, seek 'Help,' or crash the computer."[3] In simple terms, these decision points provide the user with a series of options. Based on the user's choice, the program goes off in a new direction.[4]

According to Carol Anderson and Mark Veljikov, decision points fall into four types:

Menu Driven: whereby users decide where to go in the program by selecting an item from an on-screen menu that, in turn, determines the chosen pathway

Test Driven: most specifically seen in educational or training programs whereby the user cannot continue through the program unless he or she has successfully completed a test based on earlier parts of the program

Exercise Driven: similar to test-driven points, whereby users cannot continue in a program until they have successfully completed an exercise based on material already presented within the program

Combination: obviously, some or all of the other elements combined[5]

BRANCHING STRUCTURES

The simplest multimedia program will consist of "a Title Screen, a Menu Screen, four linear topics, each with a Return, a Help tutorial, and an ending screen." There are, of course, different kinds of "branching structures" the writer can employ to create a multimedia program. To see how a flowchart for a simple multimedia program might look, see Figure 10-3.[6]

"The Branching Structure is less controversial when applied to non-fiction products (interactive reference titles, interactive travel guides, etc.). In non-fiction products, viewers welcome the element of choice, since it helps them efficiently track down the information they need."[7]

For something like *The Rebirth Project,* users might have any number of choices, but these choices are laid out in an easily discernible way. "Multiple pathways of access makes it possible for an audience to adjust their approach to information that is most compelling and satisfying to them."[8]

In dramatic multimedia programs, a story may have links or pathways that "loop" back to earlier scenes. "The hero of your story may have to keep exploring the lunar surface again and again, looping back in the story until they find enough fuel to depart for home. ... And a scene doesn't necessarily have to link to its nearest neighbors. It can have links to scenes anywhere in the story, [meeting] up with a scene on a distant branch."[9]

Twelve Rules of Navigation

For the writer, there are twelve basic rules for creating multimedia navigation:[10]

1. *Avoid simple page turners.* In other words, don't turn the product into the equivalent of an on-screen book. Remember, you are writing for a new genre, a new art form: Use the tools available to you as well as your imagination.

FIGURE 10-3 | *Flowchart for a simple multimedia program. Created by Chris James for his* Intro to Multimedia *class.*

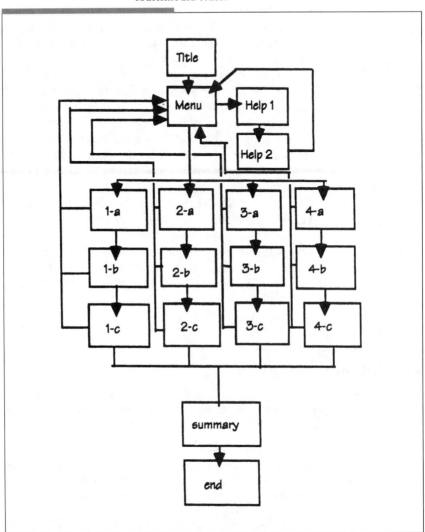

Created by Chris James for Intro to Multimedia class. Used by permission.

2. *Keep the written text simple.* Using a lot of text could bore a user. You can use video, sound, graphic images, and animation. Don't limit yourself or the program you're writing.
3. *Use the "50% Rule."* You can keep the text material simple if you "cut 50% of the words without changing the meaning."[11] People in the business suggest that you limit each screen to between twenty and thirty words. This can be done using video clips or stills, though with stills more text will be used than with clips.

4. *Communicate clearly and concisely.* Use simple phrases and verb structures.

5. *Use the active voice in your screen dialog.* In other words, talk directly to the user in concise, declarative sentences.

6. *Keep the process as visual as you can.* "Show, don't tell."

7. *Use consistent screen formats.* If your navigation screen uses a specific format, then use that format on all your navigation screens. "If you combine text and graphics, then place the text and graphics in a consistent format. If you use buttons for navigation, don't make the viewer search for them on the screen."[12] Consistency helps users feel comfortable.

8. *Provide feedback to users.* Should users need to answer a question, perform a task, or take a test, feedback allows them to stay connected with the program and still feel in control of it.

9. *Make sure users know what they have to do.* In other words, users have to understand what is expected of them and need clear directions and a way to review the material.

10. *Provide Help.* "Help" should be accessible from *any* point in the program.

11. *Keep users engaged by the program without frustrating them.* That is, follow rules one through nine.

12. *Make sure your content meets the goals and objectives of the program.* Avoid the mistake of using something because it's cool, even if it doesn't necessarily make sense to have it in your program.

Technological Constraints

According to Bruce Wolcott, who uses the metaphor of economics, everything in new digital media communications—text, graphics, sound, or motion video—is

paid for in bytes. Simple text is merely pocket change, while 24-bit images, high-quality sound, and motion video is paid for in big denominations. A CD-ROM disc in current technology can store 650 megabytes of information. That means that every digital message must be reviewed to see if it's necessary, or if it's too "expensive" in terms of available storage space.

Consideration must also be given to playback speed of systems for which a program is designed. High-resolution graphics, video, and sound will not play back as smoothly on machines with slower processors. New compression algorithms, high bandwidth transmission, and increasing processor speeds are alleviating some of these problems, but the demand for ever greater data put through for enhanced message output will continue, especially as interactive multimedia is introduced to online environments.

It's been said that putting a video signal through a modem is like trying to push an elephant through a straw. These limitations can actually be a benefit for CD-ROM developers, because ... designs must be simplified, and only the most important parts of the message are used. In the *Rebirth* project, it has meant that we will have to compromise some sound quality, scale down the number of colors in our images, and limit the amount of video used. It means we will have to make creative use of sound and video loops [which reuse the same information over and over again], and restrict the number of interactions and movement of video characters as they appear, and use stills instead of full-motion interaction in our 3D scenes. On the other hand, we are able to splurge for our most important sections, such as the introductory sequence to the virtual 3D world. Just make sure you don't end up blowing the entire budget up front by having very exciting visuals there but nowhere else. Try to structure your program so powerful images are seen throughout.

Writers who are working on interactive scripts must be aware of these constraints as they plan a project with a technical and design staff. Buckminster Fuller had stated the best approach when he described the process as "more with less," or simply, getting more bang for the megabyte.[13]

The next section provides templates of navigational charts for the following: a Homepage, a training program, an edutainment title, and an interactive game.

Navigational Templates

HOMEPAGES

Homepages provide one of the easiest navigational templates to understand. As an example, I've chosen the Bellevue Community College (BCC) homepage. Note Figures 10-4 through 10-11, which include an initial flowchart followed by charts of the content areas and various linked material.

Basically, the "map" of the homepage (Figure 10-4) categorizes content into seven areas: college programs, student services, continuing education, our campus, happenings, innovative programs, and international programs.

The homepage's content menu (Figure 10-5) opens with a quote about the college and where it is located. Next, some of the choices a student or user might choose are mapped out. For example, "College Programs" brings you to another menu page (Figure 10-6) that opens with some general information about the size of the college and enrollment. The user/student can then choose one of four paths to take: "Four Paths to Your Future" is subdivided into four areas the student might want to investigate (see Figure 10-7), and "Applying to BCC" is subdivided into three specific areas or paths and the current academic calendar (see Figure 10-8). Note that the bottom of each menu page presents additional areas that the student might explore. Those, in turn, subdivide into other paths (Figures 10-9 through 10-11).

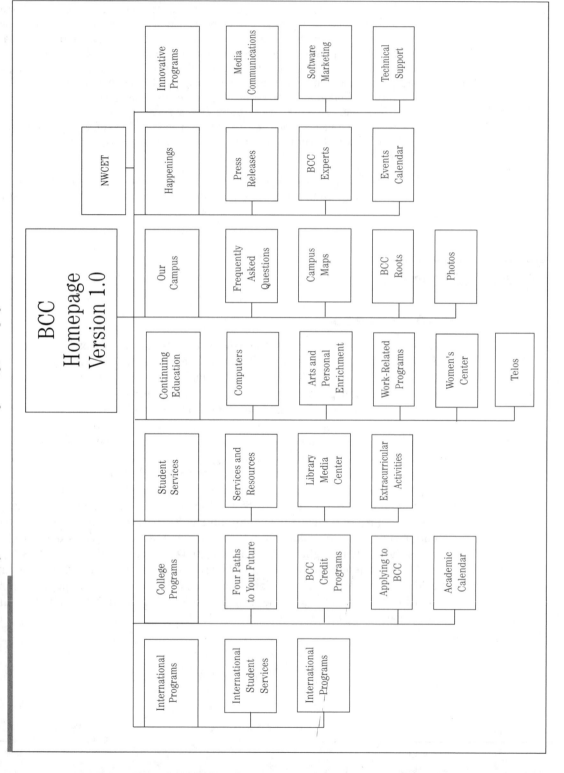

FIGURE 10-4 ▮ *Flowchart for the Bellevue Community College homepage.*

FIGURE 10-5 *Content menu of the BCC homepage.*

Large graphic including buttons to main content areas

College Programs	Continuing Education	Our Campus	Innovative Programs
Student Services	International Programs	Happenings	NWCET

Bellevue Community College is located in the beautiful and thriving Puget Sound region of Washington state. BCC, Washington's most comprehensive community college, is the third largest of the state's 48 public and private post-secondary institutions. The college serves approximately 16,000 students per quarter in over 70 areas of instruction. BCC is diverse, innovative and renowned for quality instruction.

FIGURE 10-6 *"College Programs" menu in the BCC homepage.*

graphic	**College Programs**

For over 27 years, Bellevue Community College has been educating Eastside residents and their families. Nearly 16,000 students attend classes each quarter, making BCC the third largest college or university in the state. Yet, BCC doesn't feel big or overwhelming. Our average class size is 25, allowing personalized learning with our talented faculty.

○ **Four Paths to Your Future**
Seeking a transfer degree, occupational education, general studies, or Continuing Education Courses?

○ **BCC Credit Programs**
From A to Z

○ **Applying to BCC**
Application ("downloadable"), eligibility, tuition information

○ **Academic Calendar**
Fall 1995

Home	College Programs	Student Services	Continuing Education	Our Campus	Happenings	NWCET	Innovative Programs	International Programs

FIGURE 10-7 | *"College Programs" subpage A for the BCC homepage.*

Four Paths to Your Future

BCC offers four main paths of study which you may take to reach your educational and personal goals:

O   **Path #1**
    Transfer Programs

O   **Path #2**
    Occupational Programs

O   **Path #3**
    General Studies

O   **Path #4**
    Continuing Education
    (link to Cont. Ed. main page)

Home	College Programs	Student Services	Continuing Education	Our Campus	Happenings	NWCET	Innovative Programs	International Programs

FIGURE 10-8 | *"College Programs" subpage B for the BCC homepage.*

Applying to BCC

Bellevue Community College admits high school graduates and adults 18 years of age or older. Currently enrolled high school students may take college courses with written approval from their school official. These requirements do not apply to students taking only **Continuing Education** non-credit classes.

The following information applies **ONLY** to students who are planning to earn an occupational or transfer degree. Enrollment information for non-degree or non-transfer students can be obtained by calling (206) 641-2222.

O   **Application**
    Download our application.

O   **Enrollment services hours**
    Come right in and visit us!

O   **How much does it cost?**
    BCC tuition

Home	College Programs	Student Services	Continuing Education	Our Campus	Happenings	NWCET	Innovative Programs	International Programs

FIGURE 10-9   ▎ *BCC homepage, "Our Campus."*

| graphic | **Our Campus** |

Want to get a glimpse of our campus and students? Need to find your way once you get here?

- ○ **Frequently Asked Questions!**
- ○ **Photos!**
- ○ **Campus Maps**
  Where to go when you hit our campus
- ○ **BCC Roots**
  Details, details!
  A dose of our history, mission and purpose

Home	College Programs	Student Services	Continuing Education	Our Campus	Happenings	NWCET	Innovative Programs	International Programs

FIGURE 10-10   ▎ *BCC homepage, "Happenings."*

| graphic | **Happenings** |

If you are from the media, or just want to see what is new and exciting on the BCC campus, this is the place!

- ○ **Press Releases**
  Our latest press releases plus a library of past releases can be found here.
- ○ **BCC Experts**
  Need a quote from a reliable source? Want to find a colleague with similar interests?
- ○ **Events Calendar**
  What's going on at BCC

Home	College Programs	Student Services	Continuing Education	Our Campus	Happenings	NWCET	Innovative Programs	International Programs

FIGURE 10-11 ▌ *BCC homepage, "Innovative Programs."*

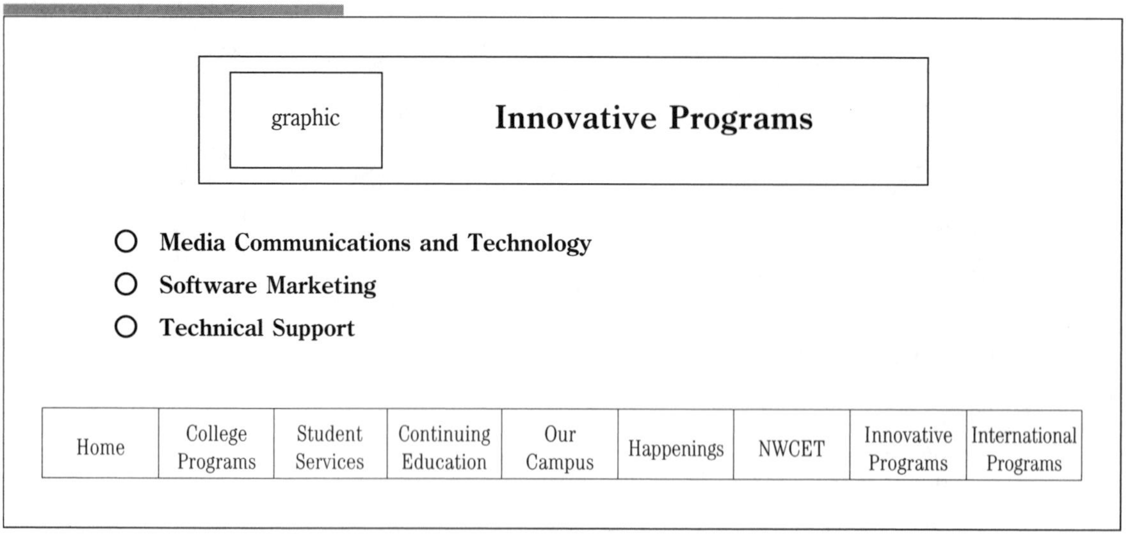

graphic	**Innovative Programs**

○ **Media Communications and Technology**
○ **Software Marketing**
○ **Technical Support**

Home	College Programs	Student Services	Continuing Education	Our Campus	Happenings	NWCET	Innovative Programs	International Programs

TRAINING PROGRAMS

Though considered a relatively straightforward multimedia piece, this home-page flowchart can easily serve as a template for other sorts of multimedia projects. For example, a training program must take more into account than a homepage. First of all, there will most likely be points where users will have to stop and either take a test or evaluate themselves in some way.

The RLC project   The Rehabilitation Learning Center (RLC) at Harborview Medical Center was discussed at some length in Chapter 4. One of the main components of the center will be a multimedia information system for people who have sustained spinal cord injury. The multimedia program will help prepare these users for new experiences as well as learning a whole new set of skills.

This particular program contains several interactive modules. Let's look at the flowchart and menus for one particular module: "Bed to Chair Transfer." This module will show the user how to get out of bed and into a wheelchair. After the introductory menu is seen and users have decided to check out this module, they basically have four options: immediately learn about the mechanics of the transfer, see what kinds of beds are available, see what preparation is needed "pretransfer," and learn about the variety of equipment available to aid users and/or therapists during the transfer (see Figure 10-12). Figures 10-13 and 10-14 show, respectively, the "Equipment" menu and the storyboard of what users see on-screen should they choose the "Equipment" pathway. When users complete the "Equipment" node, they go back to the "Preparation" screen and move on from there.

FIGURE 10-12 █ *RLC program flowchart.*

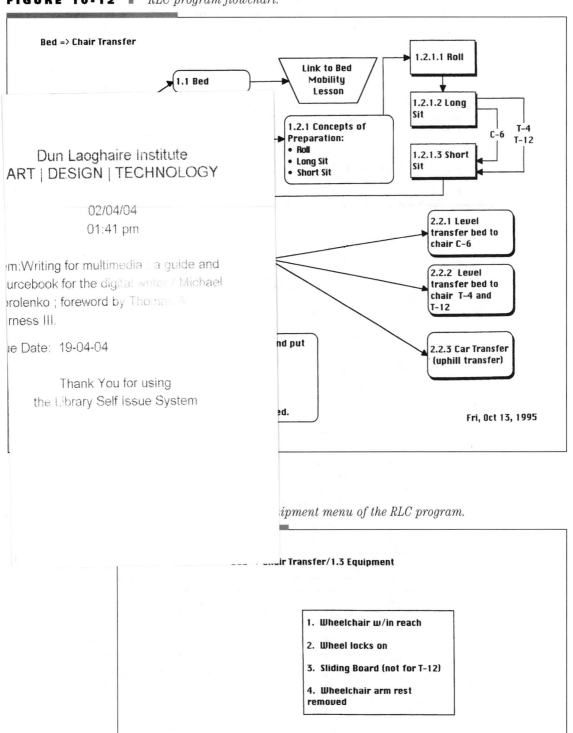

Bed => Chair Transfer

1.1 Bed

Link to Bed Mobility Lesson

1.2.1 Concepts of Preparation:
- Roll
- Long Sit
- Short Sit

1.2.1.1 Roll

1.2.1.2 Long Sit

1.2.1.3 Short Sit

C-6

T-4
T-12

2.2.1 Level transfer bed to chair C-6

2.2.2 Level transfer bed to chair T-4 and T-12

2.2.3 Car Transfer (uphill transfer)

Fri, Oct 13, 1995

ipment menu of the RLC program.

...air Transfer/1.3 Equipment

1. Wheelchair w/in reach

2. Wheel locks on

3. Sliding Board (not for T-12)

4. Wheelchair arm rest removed

Note the buttons on the bottom of the screen designed to take users backward, forward, or to the opening menu. Thus, clients can go backward to reevaluate, or forward if they feel competent enough to move on.

FIGURE 10-14 *Storyboard and screen for "Equipment," RLC program.*

1.3.1 Equipment

Mobility and Transportation

Screen No. ______
Next Screen ______

- ☐ Audio
  1. ______
  2. ______
  3. ______
- ☐ Animation
  1. ______
  2. ______
  3. ______
- ☐ Graphic
  1. ______
  2. ______
  3. ______
  4. ______
  5. ______
- ☐ Video
- ☒ Stills
- ☐ VR
- ☐ Other ______

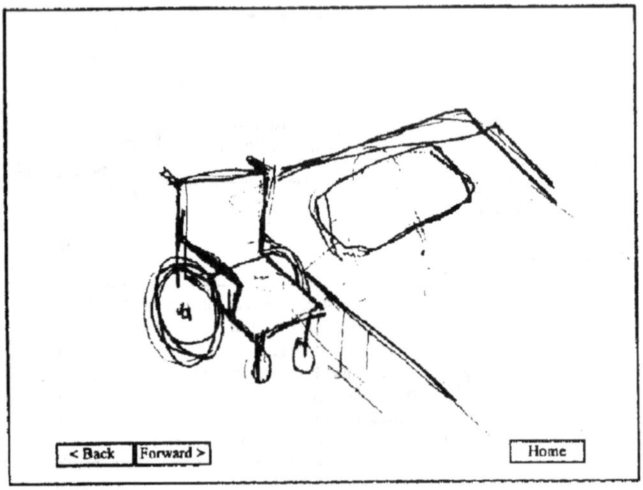

AUDIO/SCRIPT The wheelchair should be positioned next to the bed facing the foot of the bed.

VISUAL A still photo of the chair next to the bed—(maybe have a person in shot to show proximity/reach.

NOTES ______

FEED BACK ______

BRANCHING

Field 1 to:___	Field 4 to:___	Field 7 to:___	Field 10 to:___	Field 13 to:___
Field 2 to:___	Field 5 to:___	Field 8 to:___	Field 11 to:___	Field 14 to:___
Field 3 to:___	Field 6 to:___	Field 9 to:___	Field 12 to:___	Field 15 to:___

Should users choose to move ahead, they will likely have to answer correctly a short series of questions, with or without visuals, in order to move on. Feedback to questions is usually given in the form of both text and a digitized voice that might say, "Good job! Continue on." Sometimes, depending on both the budget of the program and the delivery system, a video of an actual person either tells users they did a good job or suggests what they need to learn or review.

Elsewhere in the program, users can access a dictionary, watch a short "linear" introduction to the hospital and staff, or play "edutainment" games. Though Harborview originated this particular program, many others are being designed throughout the country.

A Program about CBT   An excellent example of a computer-based education program is Jim Benton's program on how to create a computer-based training or education piece. Here are a series of screens in the "Design" path of Jim's program (Figures 10-15 through 10-29). These screens and graphics give an excellent overview of the creation of a CBT program. I advise that anyone wanting to write or design multimedia review these screens carefully. Figure 10-27 is a multiple-choice "pop quiz." If the user chooses any answer other than "Planning," the screen with the correct information, this time underlined, would appear (Figure 10-28).

FIGURE 10-15

Screen one of "Design" path of Jim Benton's CBT program. From this screen, the user can go to a number of other "Design" screens.

Design

Planning is at the heart of designing computer-based training. Some of the questions that must be answered are:

Who are our subject experts?

How will we aim our training at the educational level of our employees?

What formats (templates) will we use?

What hardware and software will we need?

What should our budget be at each step of the way?

FIGURE 10-16

*Screen two, "Design."
Note the icons on the
bottom of the screen, for
stopping program,
asking for help, or
moving backward or
forward to other screens.*

Design

Training should be designed to keep the learner's involvement in the training process at a high level. The learner's retention of the material is increased by increasing the learner's involvement in the training process.

Graphics and sound should be used in a manner so as to clearly convey the training. However, computer memory should also be conserved where possible to increase the speed the training can be delivered.

FIGURE 10-17

Screen three, "Design."

Design

Storyboarding is the process of designing screen displays so they present the material in a logical manner. The material should be reviewed by the subject experts, instructional designers and potential students to reveal any confusing, inaccurate or missing information.
Storyboarding is the final step in the planning process. It should be completed before the production process begins.

FIGURE 10-18

Screen four, "Design."

Design

Subject experts are familiar with the topic in great detail. The selection of subject experts is an essential step in the design of any computer-based training.

They bring their extensive experience and knowledge to the development process.

These individuals also provide structure for the organization and presentation of the information.

FIGURE 10-18

Screen four, "Design."

FIGURE 10-19

Screen five, "Design."

Design

The format of the training is a major decision which needs to be reached early in the development process.

The format should provide consistency as the learner moves from one screen to the next. This is usually accomplished through the use of templates. A template provides for the same general location of text, graphics and control buttons on each screen. The same font and background are also used on each screen.

The education level of the learners is a major consideration in designing the format. You may wish to consider keeping the vocabulary at the level of a person with a grammar school education or have the computer read the text.

FIGURE 10-20

Screen six, "Design."

Design

Navigation should be under the control of the learner. The learner should be able to:

Move forward.

Move backward.

Get help.

Quit.

Buttons should respond in some way by changing color or shading when the user clicks on them to give the user feedback.

FIGURE 10-21

Screen seven, "Design."

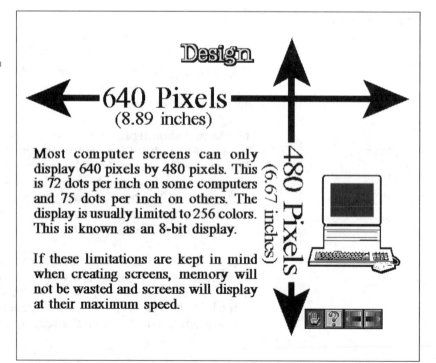

Design

←—— 640 Pixels ——→
(8.89 inches)

Most computer screens can only display 640 pixels by 480 pixels. This is 72 dots per inch on some computers and 75 dots per inch on others. The display is usually limited to 256 colors. This is known as an 8-bit display.

If these limitations are kept in mind when creating screens, memory will not be wasted and screens will display at their maximum speed.

480 Pixels
(6.67 inches)

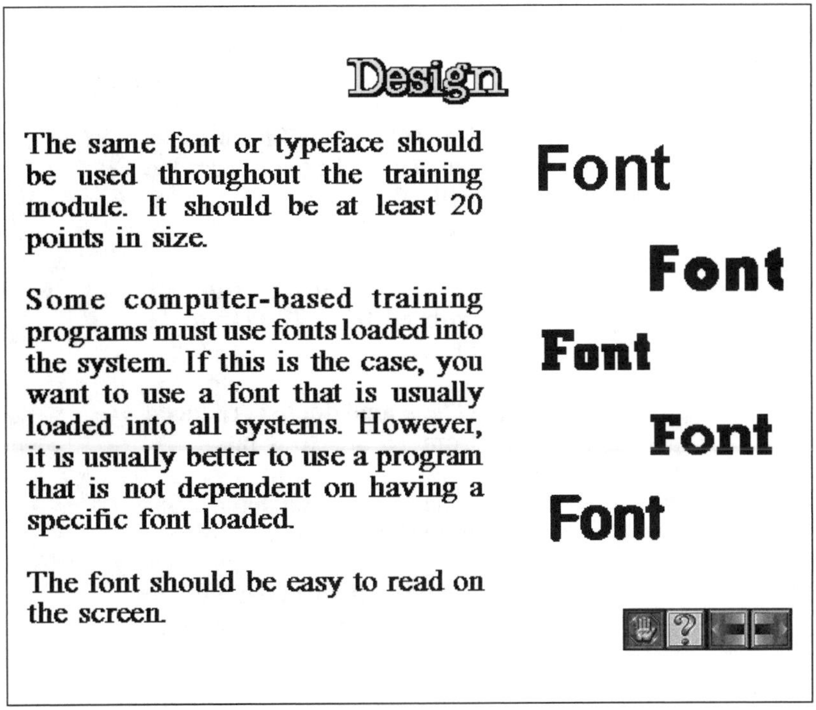

FIGURE 10-22

Screen eight, "Design."

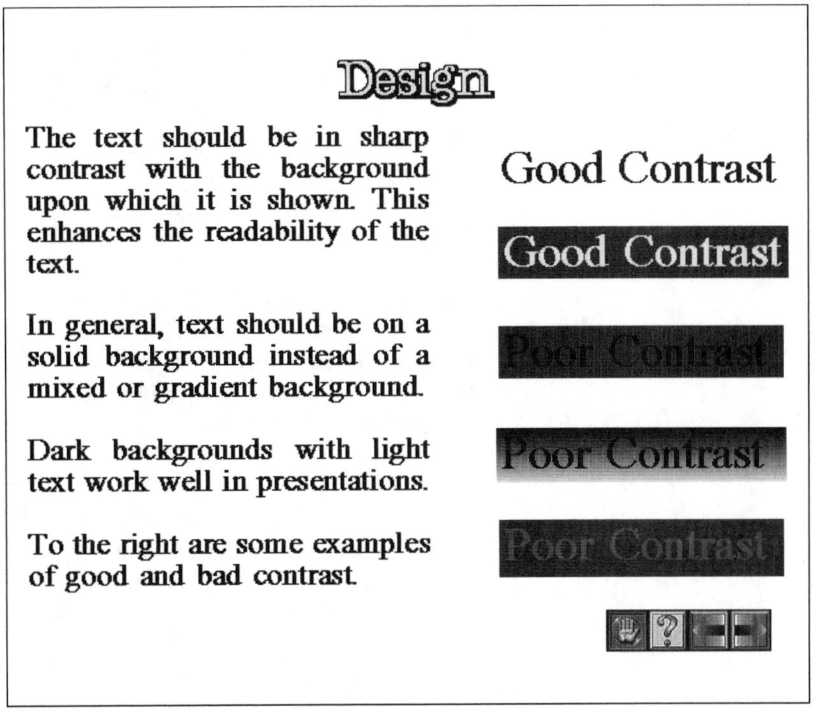

Design

The same font or typeface should be used throughout the training module. It should be at least 20 points in size.

Some computer-based training programs must use fonts loaded into the system. If this is the case, you want to use a font that is usually loaded into all systems. However, it is usually better to use a program that is not dependent on having a specific font loaded.

The font should be easy to read on the screen.

Font

Font

Font

Font

Font

FIGURE 10-23

Screen nine, "Design."

Design

The text should be in sharp contrast with the background upon which it is shown. This enhances the readability of the text.

In general, text should be on a solid background instead of a mixed or gradient background.

Dark backgrounds with light text work well in presentations.

To the right are some examples of good and bad contrast.

Good Contrast

Good Contrast

Poor Contrast

Poor Contrast

Poor Contrast

FIGURE 10-24

Screen ten, "Design."

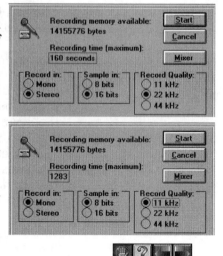

Notice that eight times as much sound can be recorded with the same amount of memory when:

•The sampling rate is reduced from 22 kHz to 11 kHz.

•The sound depth is reduced from 16 bits to 8 bits.

•The sound is changed from stereo to mono.

Sound will still be adequate for voice and most music.

FIGURE 10-25

Screen eleven, "Design."

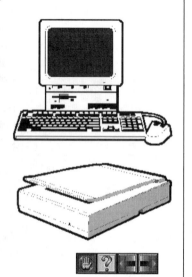

The hardware selected must be able to work with the software to create the files needed by the training software.

The computer must have enough memory available in RAM as well as on the hard disk for the timely creation of graphics, sound and video files.

Other hardware, such as scanners and sound boards, that will be used to acquire these files must be compatible with the computer and the software.

FIGURE 10-26

Screen twelve, "Design."

Design

Selection of the proper software is essential to the development of quality computer-based training.

The authoring software for any computer-based training is the software that pulls the graphics, text, sound, video and testing files together. This software needs to be powerful yet easy to use.

The graphics, text, sound and video software must all provide files in a format the training software can use.

FIGURE 10-27

"Pop quiz" for "Design" section. Should the user choose any answer but the correct one, the program takes the user to a "Correction" screen.

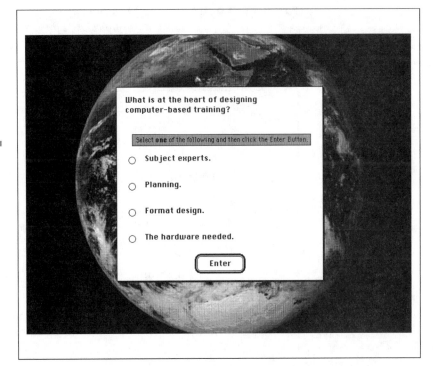

FIGURE 10-28

"Correction" screen giving feedback for wrong answer to quix.

Design

Planning is at the heart of designing computer-based training. Some of the questions that must be answered are:

Who are our subject experts?

How will we aim our training at the educational level of our employees?

What formats (templates) will we use?

What hardware and software will we need?

What should our budget be at each step of the way?

FIGURE 10-29

This is a copy of Jim Benton's initial flowcharts for his CBT program. Note: Jim drew this before any initial writing was done.

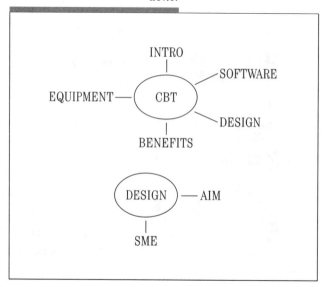

EDUTAINMENT

An edutainment product both teaches and entertains. Often, too much accent falls on the "entertainment" portion of edutainment. However, a few edutainment titles (such as *Just Grandma and Me*) point the way toward the perfect blend of education, investigation, and entertainment.

One of the best of these products is the award-winning *A Passion for Art.* Created by Corbis Publishing, an archive for multimedia material, *A Passion for Art* allows adult users to explore one of the greatest private art collections of the early twentieth century.

The core team members for this project were:

- Curtis Wong, Producer
- Pei Lin Nee, Designer/Art Director
- Eileen Monti, Assistant Producer
- Jim Gallant, Technical Lead/Developer

Gallant did all the coding as well as the development of the project. He is what is known as a "creative programmer"—someone who both knows the tools of programming and can creatively design a project.

On this particular project, the producer and the designers came first. Then developers joined to validate the choices and descriptions of the various art works.

A series of high-level meetings at Corbis determined the assets of the project (what images were attainable), how many paintings could be featured, and how much material could be fit onto one CD-ROM disc. Project developers also considered a variety of technical constraints, such as the size of the images and how well the paintings' colors would translate to a computer screen.

Finally, art scholars were hired to write about the paintings. Interestingly, because the paintings were all from a closed museum, no one had ever written about them before.

In its final form, the CD-ROM allows users to see and read about the paintings. They can also click on the featured paintings for zooming in. Users could zoom in so close, they could literally see the brush strokes.

Essentially, the group at Corbis created a virtual museum, with the gallery reproduced photographically. Users can rotate to see the entire area. Three hundred out of the fifteen hundred paintings in the collection are featured. That is, these paintings are in color, while the rest are in black and white, making the difference clear. After a while, users actually feel as if they are in the museum, something achieved through the constant use of the user's point of view (POV).

In terms of navigation, the program has a number of modules:

Archives (Figure 10-30)	Index
VR Gallery (Figure 10-31)	Slide Show
Paintings (Figure 10-32)	Timeline (Figure 10-33)
Artists	

FIGURE 10-30 ▌ *The "Archives" module of* A Passion for Art.

FIGURE 10-31 ▌ *The "VR Gallery" module of* A Passion for Art.

FIGURE 10-32 | *The "Paintings" module of* A Passion for Art.

FIGURE 10-33 | *The "Timeline" module of* A Passion for Art.

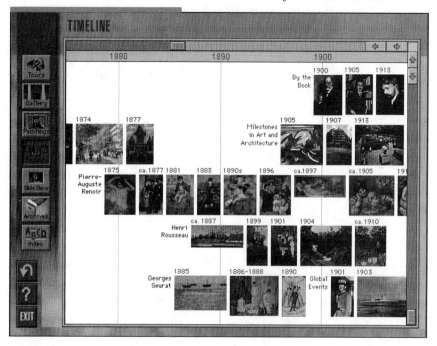

The "Paintings" and "Artists" modules are supplemented by scholarly writings. The "Slide Show" is similar to the "Roll Your Own Show" section of the Haight Ashbury program, in that users can put together their own slide show. This works wonderfully for teachers and lecturers.

A graphical presentation, the "Timeline" presents images of the paintings in the collection arranged chronologically. Thus, users can view the evolution of each artist's work while also having access to the historical events that affected the artists.

There are also four linear tours (see Figure 10-34) in the program, conducted by well-known art scholars:

The Development of the Giant Matisse Mural

The Theme of the Female Nude (Figure 10-35)

The Gallery Tour

The Life Story of Collector Dr. Albert Barnes

This last tour is presented like a newsreel, similar in some respects to the script for the first part of *Citizen Kane* (see Figure 10-36). Private papers and records document Barnes's controversial years of collecting. His personal relationships with the artists are also accessible.

The navigation structure looks something like Figure 10-37. Of course, there will also be pathways from, say, the "Gallery" to the "Timeline" or to the "Index" (see the dotted lines in Figure 10-37). Hence, users can get from the "Slideshow" to the "Timeline" or from the "Paintings" to the "Index" (and vice versa) whenever they want. The buttons that users can click on are always available (see Figures 10-34 through 10-36). This creates multilevel navigation, where users move from, say, a slideshow directly into the gallery, then click on a painting, and then decide to read about the artist.

This is a truly elegant program—multileveled, but easy to navigate. With the help of writers and experts, such as J. Carter Brown, the director of the National Gallery of Art in Washington, D.C., *A Passion for Art* provides an in-depth look at many of the paintings in one of the finest private collections of its kind, as well as chronicles artists, collectors, and artistic movements. It takes users to a place where, normally, they would never have the opportunity to go.

FIGURE 10-34   *From "Tours" of* A Passion for Art.

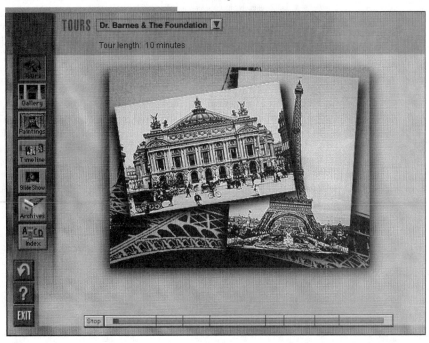

FIGURE 10-35   *The "Female Nude," a tour of* A Passion for Art.

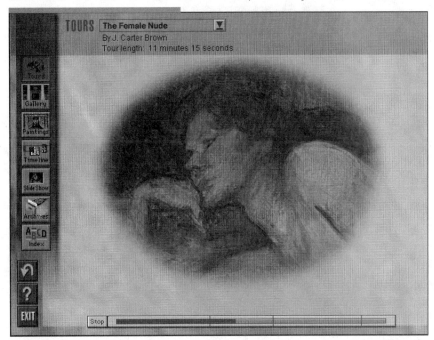

FIGURE 10-36 | *Screen from the tour about Dr. Albert Barnes.*

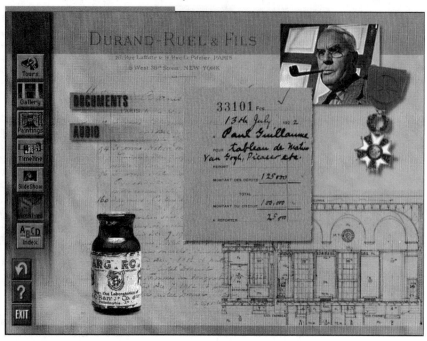

FIGURE 10-37 | *Navigation structure of* A Passion for Art.

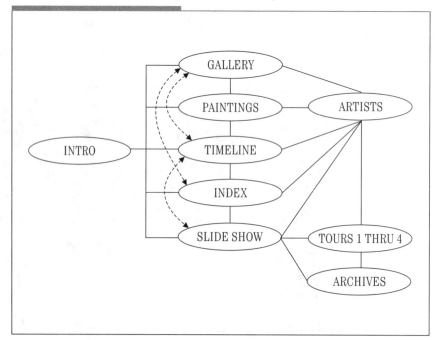

GAMES

The interactive game takes all I have discussed so far a step further. Flow-charts of homepages and even *A Passion for Art* basically show the sequence in which things occur—where a user can go to find a certain area of interest or information. In multimedia games, flowcharts become much more of a map showing how a user might discover clues, and important information. In games, the writer creates worlds, similar to the structure in *Rebirth,* and sometimes worlds within worlds, as in the game *Torin's Passage.*

In Capter 4, I discussed this game at some length. You will recall that *Torin's Passage* is a fantasy game in which the young Torin must rescue his parents from an evil sorceress's magic spell.

For this particular game, Al Lowe created five distinct Escher-like worlds within worlds. To maintain a strong plot, Lowe required Torin to journey through each world. Even so, because there are five worlds, users have many choices and paths toward reaching the ultimate goal.

For each world, Lowe and his team created a flowchart or map that defines its physicality. The writer also had to create a story, a series of scenes, that might take place in each location within each particular world.

Figure 10-38 shows how these five worlds can be connected figuratively. Then, Lowe's six-page flowchart, description, and content outline for the world of The Lands Above in *Torin's Passage* follow (Exhibit 10-1). See also Table 10-1 for the transition or interlude between The Lands Above and The Lands Below.

FIGURE 10-38 ▌ *Overview of the five "worlds" of* Torin's Passage.

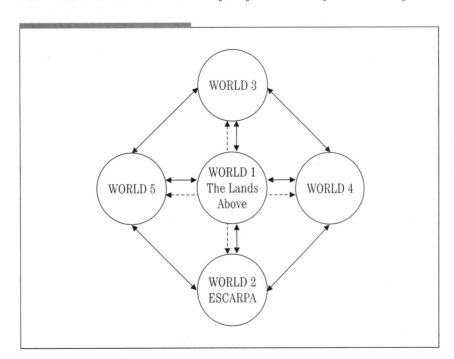

As an example, say Lowe decided to create a completely different game called *Torin's and Linda's Passage in the Lands Above,* concerning *two* characters, brother and sister, and their search to free their parents. This would probably be a much more linear game than *Torin's Passage,* though the user would have the opportunity to change perspectives during the course of the story from Torin to Linda. In this case, the writer would employ what Sawyer and Vourlis refer to as a "parallel structure," whereby the user can chart a somewhat conventional story from start to finish while switching between the perspectives of the two main characters.[14] A diagram for this parallel structure would look as follows:

Torin begins ↔ Torin uses sword ↔ Torin fights
Fahrman's House ↔ Razor Trees ↔ Guard's House
Linda begins ↔ Linda sings ↔ Linda uses wand

EXHIBIT 10-1 ▌ *Torin's Passage Design Document (Copyright 1995 by Al Lowe for Sierra On-Line, Inc.).*

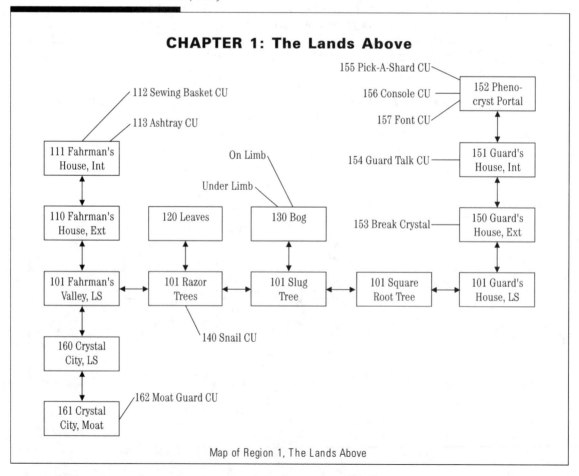

CHAPTER 1: The Lands Above

Map of Region 1, The Lands Above

EXHIBIT 10-1 ❚ *(continued)*

To find The Lands Below, you must explore the woods around your farm until you find Herman's house. Following the Guard's somewhat bizarre culinary demands, you fix dinner for him and he rewards you with access to the Phenocryst column chamber and thus to Escarpa, the next world down.

The 3-Screen Woods Scroller includes the pictures on either side, making it actually a 5-screen scroller.

Walk-thru

Go to the barn. Get the rope from the barn. Get the ax.

Enter the farmhouse. Get the pouch from the ashtray. Get the inchworm from the sewing basket.

Walk South to the opening scene, then go East. Get the chuckberries from the bush. Climb through the opening inside the razor blade vines. Walk North to the pile of leaves. Move the inchworm over the leaves until you find the "Yes" leaf. Try to take it. Then find it again. And again! Finally, the third time, you can actually get the leaf.

Return to the scroller. Walk East. Cross the bridge tree, then walk North to the bog. Climb the tree. Tie the rope to the tree. Tie the rope to yourself. Dive off the tree. Get the peat balls from the bog below you. Swing left & right until you can grab the branch at screen left. Swing to safety, just as the rope unties from your leg and the tree and plummets into the bog. Jump down from the lower branch. The rope is gone forever.

Walk South, then East. Get the square root.

Walk East to Herman's house. Click on his front door to read the sign. Use the ax to break the crystal in his front yard to wake him. Get the green shard. Talk to Herman. (Snails now appear on the bridge tree.) He's thirsty. Enter his house and fix him some chuckberry juice. Then he's hungry.

Return to the bridge tree. Talk to the snails. Give the leaf to the snails. Take the snails.

Walk to the moat. Put the snails in the moat. Receive the moat scum from the croctopus.

Return to the slug tree. Click the scum on the ground below the slugs. Click the Boogle interface icon to display all the available Boogle verbs in the Inventory area. Use the Boogle box on the scum on the ground. Boogle walks to the proper location and forms a box with his tongue as the prop. If you leave the area, Boogle remains in position until you solve this puzzle.

As you walk away from Boogle, the slugs work their way down the tree and eventually under the Boogle box to enjoy the moat scum. When they're all under there, Boogle falls on the slugs, Torin walks over, collects the slugs, and Boogle reforms to his old self.

Return to the Guard's house. Enter. Use the slugs & the peat balls on the kitchen cabinet. Make the square root pie.

Enter the phenocryst chamber with the guard. Play pick-a-shard with the guard.

Insert the shard into the console. Manipulate the crystal in the console until all four columns form a flat platform. (Blue-white-red is fast.)

Click the tobacco pouch on the risen font to get the eressdy powder. Stand on the platform. Use the eressdy powder on yourself to vanish to Level 2. Some fun, eh?

Fahrman's Valley L. S.

The Fahrman's farm spreads out across a small valley, with tidy fields of unknown crops, a pasture off to the left, multiple neatly-kept nondescript outbuildings and the small farmhouse with a front porch. A stream wends its way through the scene. Foreground bushes and trees take advantage of multiplane scrolling.

"New" from the File menu does a Restart Game to this scene.

Fahrman's Home, Exterior

Torin's parents are NOT visible on the porch of his home, despite what you may have heard.

EXHIBIT 10-1 ▍ *(continued)*

They're now trapped in their magic spell down in the Hall of Horrors at Lycentia's joint.

You can take the rope from the pulley on the side of the barn.

You can take the ax that's stuck in the chopping block near the woodpile.

A door on the front porch leads to Fahrman's Home, Interior, below.

Fahrman's Home, Interior

Very homey and plain, but with a comfortable chair for Mr. and Mrs., with an ashtray, pipes and empty tobacco pouch beside his, and a sewing basket beside hers. A fire burns in the stove.

If you click on the sewing basket, we go to the Sewing Basket C. U. below.

If you click on the ashtray, we go to the Ashtray C. U. Below.

Sewing Basket C. U.

You can take the inchworm from your mother's sewing basket. The rest of the basket is filled with interesting sewing stuff.

Ashtray C. U.

You can take the empty tobacco pouch from your father's ashtray. The old pipes and ashtray are clean, as Pop quit smoking years ago.

Crystal City L. S.

An extremely long, establishing shot of Palace City, stretching across a large valley (picture Monument Valley filled with crystal-capped mountains). A river runs through it, walls surround the city, and the largest, crystal-topped mountain dwarfs the city. It must look *very* far away from this point.

Crystal City Moat

A medium shot, from a fairly low angle looking up at the drawbridge and guard's post from the other side of the moat. The drawbridge is always up. Regardless of the names you call Zax, the guard, he refuses to lower the drawbridge

or let you in. The water level of the moat is far enough below eye level that we can't see it directly, nor the monsters swimming in it.

If you enter the moat, we see you fall over the edge and go behind a bush so we can see a splash and a water spout but no blood and gore. We hear you groan and a few crunching sounds. We see some sucker-covered tentacles whip around from the madly chewing croctopus. EndGame.

Place the snails (on their leaf) in the moat to receive the moat scum from the croctopus.

Woods Scroller Left

One particular bush here is covered with bright berries. Click on them and we see you take all of them from the bush. They're added to Inventory, where you have to look at them to learn they're called "chuckberries." Once you pick them, you can't pick more.

This scene hosts several examples of the "razor vine" plant, a thick vine whose stem is lined with razor-sharp blades. It has blades on the inner surfaces of its loops. If you click the vine's hot spot; we see ego gingerly reach over, touch the razor blades, comment on their sharpness and mention the need to be careful around them.

At the rear of this scene, behind the razor vine, is an opening in the brush. You carefully climb through the center of the loop to get past the razor vine and into that area. Enter that opening and go to the Pile of Leaves C. U. below.

A tree here has slugs crawling up and down its trunk. Their position is directly proportional to ego's distance from the base of the trunk, hopefully at a 1-pixel to 1-pixel ratio. As he approaches the tree, the slugs climb the trunk in unison. As he walks away from the tree, they climb back down in unison. There's no way he can reach them without help.

If you click on them before feeding them, you get a helpful message, whether you've talked to Herman or not.

If you click on them after feeding them, you only hear munching and crunching sounds.

EXHIBIT 10-1 | *(continued)*

If you click on them after they've finished eating, you overhear them say, "I'm ready for a long nap now" as they head up the tree to disappear.

If you place the moat scum on the ground at the base of the tree, they still behave the same, but this time, when you're across the scene, they eat your scum. But evidently you gave them so much scum that they can't ever get enough, because you can leave them there as long as you want before capturing them.

However, if you check out Boogle's verb collection by clicking on the Boogle icon in the interface, you notice one of his actions is Boogle-in-the-shape-of-a-box. The answer is then obvious: click the moat scum on the ground at the base of the tree, we see you place it there, then you select the box icon from Boogle's collection, and click it on Boogle. Boogle runs to where you placed the scum, forms himself into a box, forms his tongue into a stick, and places himself over the "delicious" moat scum. *Now,* when you walk far enough away, the slugs come down, attack the moat scum as before, but as soon as they're all below Boogle, he drops on top of them to prevent their escape. Boogle then remains here until you pick him up.

If Boogle is waiting for the slugs to reach him, and you click him, he just winks at you.

Once Boogle has trapped the slugs, you can then click him. We see Torin walk over to Boogle, reach under him, grab the slugs, and place them in his pouch. Add them to inventory. Score. Boogle then transforms back to himself.

Pile of Leaves C. U.

Here is a screenful of leaves, which all look approximately the same size. They're all in the shape of a hockey rink, with interesting vein markings for hockey.

There's no way you could tell which leaf is the largest without some measuring device. So you pass the inchworm around the screen over the leaves. Every time you pause, it says, "no" or "nope" or "17 smirgs" or "321 divirs" or one of twenty variants, until you are over the largest

leaf's feature, at which time it spouts an enthusiastic "yes!"

But the joke is on you. As you put away your inchworm, a gust of wind comes along and scatters the leaves again. Now you must find the largest leaf a second time. (Hint: it's near the middle of the scene.) When you do, as you put away your inchworm, the same thing happens again. Hunt for it a third time and you find it near the left edge of the screen. This time, before you can click to put away your inchworm, we see a big Torin foot come into the pic from the left and hold the leaves in place while a big Torin hand reaches down to pick it up. Add leaf to Inventory. Upon raising your foot, you see the inchworm, spread flat. "Boogle! Peel this off my foot?" He does, shakes the inchworm, who is none the worse, and then grants his freedom in the leaves. You then, also, "leave" this scene, never to return again.

Wood Scroller Center

There is a vague opening at the right rear of this scene to provide access to the Woods Bog, below.

Most of this pic is taken up by the "bridge tree," a large tree that is easy for ego cross, but every time he does we play a cute piece of animation showing him climbing under the roots, swinging and "surfing" down a rear root.

This is the home of the twin figure-sliming snails, Slim & Slime. To talk to them, climb only part-way up the bridge tree. If you then click on them, we go to the Snail Talk C. U. below.

Snail Talk C. U.

Slim & Slime will talk to you and tell you they want to go to the figure sliming contest at the Moat Olympics, but first they need a new figure sliming leaf. But not just any leaf, it must be the biggest leaf in the forest.

"I really enjoy bog scum," says one. Another responds, "Ahh, you can keep that bog scum. It's pond scum for me." A third says, "Perhaps. But I

EXHIBIT 10-1 ▌ *(continued)*

hear the greatest scum of all is ... moat scum!" There is a rumble of agreement.

If you click on them a second time before feeding them, they chat again among themselves. "You know, once you go moat, you'll never go back!"

We'll do a Dragnet dialogue, but with S words, including slug, snail, slime, sliming, scum, sliding, slipping, stolen, steal, snack, snag, snatch, sneeze, safely, sleuth, slick, slide, slip, slinky, sly, slob, slosh, slow, slush and ...

Woods Scroller Right

A tree here has a square root sticking up out of the ground, dead, drying. If you haven't taken it, you can. Score.

Woodsy Bog

The center of this scene is filled by an ancient peat bog. Peat moss is everywhere, but if you walk out onto it, you slowly sink in over your head. EndGame.

Nearby stands a large tree with reasonably-climbable branches extending out over the peat moss. If you click on it, you climb the tree. Score.

Once you're on the large tree limb that extends out over the bog, you have several more options. If you haven't tied the rope to yourself, you can click on the ground and climb down.

If you are up the tree and the rope is not tied to the tree and you click the rope on yourself, you tie the rope to your ankles and it dangles there.

If the rope is dangling from your ankles and you click on the "climb down" area, you untie the rope first, then climb down.

But, if the rope is dangling from your ankles and you click on the bog, you do a swan dive head-first into the peat, with the rope flailing above you, followed by a slow "sinking-into-quicksand" animation. EndGame. ('You seem to be "bogged down," Torin.')

If the rope is dangling from your ankles and you re-select the rope from Inventory, then click the rope on the branch, you tie the rope to the branch. You can also do this in reverse: tie the rope to the branch, re-select it from Inventory, then click the rope on yourself to tie it to your ankles.

If you are on the ground and click the rope on the limb, the limb is inactive.

If you are up the tree and the rope is tied to the tree and you click on the rope, we see you maneuver down onto the rope in a normal, right-side-up position. You can then maneuver up and down the rope. If you click on the peat moss, you maneuver to the bottom of the rope, try to reach it, but fail. Close, no cigar.

But, if the rope is tied to both the tree limb and yourself and you click on the bog, we see you dive off the branch, bounce down to the peat moss, automatically grab a handful, then slowly bounce to a full stop, hanging upside down from your "bungee." Add the peat to Inventory. Score.

Now you are hanging upside-down suspended by the ankles. If you click on the branch overhead, we see you struggle and twist trying to reach the rope, but fail to do so.

At this point, you must make Torin swing back and forth through judicious clicking near his body. Clicking in front of your body when your body is going that direction adds velocity. Clicking behind your body subtracts velocity. Think of swinging on a swing and "stretching or reaching" for power. (This code exists in *Freddy Pharkas, Frontier Pharmacist,* when Freddy's on the swing set in the schoolyard.)

At your farthest swing to the left, there are two cels when you can click the "lesser" branch conveniently placed nearby, and swing to safety, just as the rope unties from your leg and the tree and plummets into the bog. Score.

If you're swinging upside down and click the rope on yourself, you reach up, untie the rope from your feet and fall into the bog. (This animation always begins from the center cel and you only back and forth 3 cels. Therefore, if Torin is hanging still, start him swinging until

EXHIBIT 10-1   *(continued)*

he's moving 3 cels each way. If he's swinging more than 3 cels, slow him until he's moving 3 cels worth, then start the untie animation.)

If you are holding onto the lesser branch, you can then select the rope in Inventory and click it on yourself to untie it from your foot. The rope swings back under the upper branch as you swing to the ground and freedom.

If you do anything else while holding the lesser branch, you turn loose of the branch and return to swinging upside down by the rope.

Herman's House, Exterior

A curious old shack is built right near a tall cliff, directly in front of a palatial, but run-down, small building. The shack looks uninhabited, but isn't. There are many green crystal shards growing out of the ground here, ripe for the taking. To take one, you must have the ax from the barn to break it off.

If you click on a crystal, we show you try to break it off, but you can't.

You can ask Boogle to do it. He's able to form an ax. If you try him or the ax on any crystal, we go to the Crystal Breaking CU below.

The door to the guard's house is locked until you break off and take one of the green crystal shards.

If you break off a crystal in the CU below, we return to this shot to see the guard rush from his shack to confront you He's more than a little confused. (Picture Grandpa Simpson with a weapon.) Since he's never seen anyone come from town out to see him, he naturally assumes you came from The Lands Below. You argue back and forth a little, but soon you realize that's you way through: convince him you are from below and he'll have to send you "back" down there. You both enter his hut now.

Crystal Breaking C. U.

If you try the Boogle ax on a crystal, you get: "Boogle, can you make an ax?" you ask. Boogle promptly makes an X and looks at you proudly and expectantly. "Not an X, an ax!" you exclaim.

He makes the ax, you click him on the crystal, you swing him, he hits it and it hurts him! Little cartoon of Boogle hopping about in pain.

If you use the ax on the crystal, we see you swing the ax, break off a hunk of green crystal, and pocket it as Herman, awakened by your racket, comes out of the house holding his weapon—aimed right at you!

Herman's House, Interior

Herman is mentally confused. Sometimes he thinks you're from The Lands Above, sometime from The Lands Below. When you're from The Lands Above he insists you stay for dinner, implying "as my guest." Later you learn what that really means is "fix me my dinner!" But other times, when he thinks you really are from The Lands Below, he wants you to "just play along, okay?" Other times he's lucid. He even provides background on the phenocryst concept. (He's lonely.)

Clicking him before serving him gives, "I'm thirsty. Can you fix me some juice?"

You bring the chuckberries from the woods to his kitchen and use them on his kitchen cabinet berry smasher to squash them into juice (while duckwalking across the floor to a hot guitar solo), grab a glass, fill it, as you ask, "Say, what kind of berries are these?" As you serve him, he says, "Why, chuckberries, of course." (Drum fill.)

If you use the chuckberries on the kitchen before he asks for it, he suggests, "That looks good for later."

"Now I'm hungry. I'd love some 'Slugetti & Peatballs' like my mother used to make!" "Spaghetti & meatballs?" you ask. "What's that?" he responds. "Say…you sure you're from around here?" he asks suspiciously. "Slugetti and peatballs!"

You bring the slugs from the forest and the peat moss you grabbed from the bog to his kitchen cabinet and use them on his pots to prepare him "Slugetti & Peatballs." As you serve it to him, he says, "This is good, but I sure could

EXHIBIT 10-1 ▌ *(continued)*

use some dessert. A little root pie would sure hit the spot." ("Geez," you think, "no wonder nobody eats with this guy!")?

If you use the slugs or the peat on the kitchen before he asks for it, he suggests, "That looks good for later."

If you use the slugs or the peat on the kitchen when you don't have the other in Inventory, he suggests, "Peat is good, but not without slugs." And vice versa.

You bring the "square root" from the woods to the kitchen and use it on his kitchen cabinet to prepare a pie, then start it baking in his oven. "Mmmmm, smells delicious!" he says. "To me, there's nothing as satisfying as coming home to find 'square root pie!'" (Drum fill.)

If you use the root on the kitchen before he asks for it, he suggests, "That looks good for later."

In return for all of that, he tells you "While that's cooking, sonny, follow me. I've got something to show you." Then he insists upon sending you back down. He pulls the kitchen cabinet away from the wall, revealing a doorway. He leads you into it to find The Portal Down, below.

Guard Talk C. U.

Here's the gist of the conversations between Herman and Torin.

Conversation 1, Outside after breaking crystal

Herman: Hey, waddaya think you're doing there? Trying to sneak by me? I wasn't asleep, NO sir! I heard you come through!

Torin: Oh, no, sir. I wasn't trying to sneak anywhere. Truth is, I'm searching for Lycentia, the evil sorceress. From The Lands Below. Have you heard of her?

Herman: The Lands Below? That's where you're from? Well, you can't stay here. You have to go back down there. Right away. Yep. That's why I'm here. Nobody's come up from down there while I'm on duty. No, sir! Not in the last fifteen years, sonny!

Torin: NO, no. You misunderstood. I'm not *from* The Lands Below! I want to *go* there. Do you know how to get there?

Herman: Go there? No, no one goes there! That's no place for any self-respectin' citizen! Why them worlds is filled with nutso! Malcontents! Psycho! Politicians! No way will I send you down there!

Torin: You know how to get to The Lands Below?! Oh, please. Tell me. May I come inside? It's very important.

Herman: No. We can't. No, you can't. In fact, no one gets inside my guardhouse, except my replacement. Don't know where he is, either. Was supposed to be here 10, maybe 12 years ago! He's never been THIS late before! Gotta go. Don't come back. Ain't sending nobody to no Lands Below. Haven't in years. Won't either. Bye.

And he walks inside the house.

Conversation 2, after Torin knocks

Herman (through door): Halt! Who goes there?

Torin: It's me, Torin. (bluffing) Uh, I'm your replacement.

Herman: Well, it's about time. Where've ya been? You must be about 10 years late!

Torin: Heavy traffic.

Herman: Huh? Whatever. Hurry up and get inside here. I'm hungry.

Torin: Uh, okay. (He enters.)

Herman: (under breath) Can't say I care much for the new uniforms!

Conversation 3, inside guardhouse

Herman: Well? Get started.

Torin: Okay. (Pause) Started what?

Herman: Don't they teach you young'uns anything at Basic?

Torin: Well, maybe, but, uh, I wasn't at the top of my class you know ...

EXHIBIT 10-1 | *(continued)*

Herman: I can see that! Doesn't tradition mean anything anymore? What's this younger generation coming to? Where's your provisions?

Torin: Provisions? I, uh …

Herman: My meal, boy! The replacement guard *always* cooks the departing guard his last meal before taking over!

Torin: Why, uh, yeah. That's still taught to all of "us." What'll you have?

Herman: You mean you didn't bring anything with you? Well, you won't find no home fort comforts out here. Your problem, not mine. I know what I want.

Torin: So? What can I fix you for your last meal?

Herman: Last meal? I ain't dead yet! Who are you? What are you doing in here?

Torin: I'm your replacement. It's time for you to leave. Do you want a meal or not?

Herman: Course. Wouldn't have it any other way. For my appetizer this evening, I believe I'll begin light: just a small glass of berry juice, boy. You can use that juicer on the counter there.

Torin: Okay.

Hold at this state until user clicks berries on juicer.

Conversation 4: pre-berries on juicer

Torin: Berries? That's what you want?

Herman: What's the matter with you? Senile? Squeeze me some juice! I'm ready to go home. (If I can remember where home is!)

Conversation 5: berries on juicer

Torin: Here ya go, Sergeant. Berries. Just like you asked. Just let me squeeze them for you …

(Dances around floor to Chuck Berry music.)

Torin (giving juice to Herman): Say! What kind of berries are those?

Herman (drinks first, then): Why, *Chuck* berries, of course! (Pause.) But, now I'm hungry. I want slugetti and peatballs, just like ma ol' mammy used ta make.

Torin: Slugetti and peatballs? Don't you mean, *spaghetti and meatballs?*

Herman: Where you from, boy? You sure you're from around here? You're not from The Lands Below, are you? Course not! I want the real thing: slugetti and peatballs!

Conversation 6: pre-slugs & peat

Torin reconfirms meal.

Conversation 7: slugs & peat on pots

Torin bitches about how tough it was to get the peat moss from the bog. Herman orders dessert.

Conversation 8: pre-square root

Torin reconfirms meal.

Conversation 9: square root on pots

Torin hopes this is the end of his meal. Herman agrees, "And while it's in the oven, come on with me. I show you around the place." Leads them both to Phenocryst Chamber. Herman tells Torin "pick a shard." "Now I'm outta here, boy. My tour's over. I'm gonna take my pie and hit the road. You're on your own. Whatever you do, don't let anybody from The Lands Below in through that Phenocryst!"

The Portal Chamber

Behind the guardhouse is the formerly palatial Portal Chamber that can now only be entered through the guard's kitchen cabinet. It covers the very phenocryst where Lycentia was sent down to The Lands Below those many years ago. (Of course, since the player hasn't seen that flashback yet, this will all be news to him.)

The phenocryst column is a pale sandstone color, indicating the land where it concludes.

The room is circular, with the six-foot wide entrance carpet (tile pattern) leading directly to the hexagonal podium, which is also six feet per edge. At the rear of the room the walls end unevenly at the bare stone sandstone cliff. This cliff contains the actual phenocryst column, which is outlined with the hexagon shape. When you enter, the podium consists of four large sculptural

EXHIBIT 10-1 ▍ *(continued)*

rock columns rising out of the floor, effectively blocking much of the crystal. At the "two o'clock" position, a large stone console is located near the wall. This is the control panel for the podium's rock shafts. At ten o'clock, an elaborate tile pattern in the floor will open up as soon as you solve the crystal puzzle, so the "Eressdy Powder Font" can rise up.

There has to be an artificial lamp here, so Boogle can explore it, then add it to his Boogletory.

Once you have a shard, clicking it on the console takes you to the Crystal Console MS below.

The Guard waits around during all this, without saying a word. Perhaps he's asleep.

Once you have lowered all four stones to form the transmitting stage, the Eressdy Font is extended to its up position. Then if you click on it, we go to the Eressdy Font C. U. below.

Pick A Shard C. U.

When you enter, Herman opens a velvet-lined, form-fitting drawer filled with different crystals. "Pick a shard ... any shard!" he proclaims. "Hee hee!" he pops, "I've been waitin' fifteen years to use that line!" You can select any one, they're all the same. Score. You return from this C. U. to the main room scene, above.

Crystal Console M. S.

This shot shows a C. U. of the console in the foreground, the four-part podium of stone columns in the midground, and the phenocryst column in the background (not necessarily lined up).

The console has four holes, each a perfect fit for your shard. (The green shard you broke off out in his front yard does not fit.) Each hole emits colored light, namely from left to right: Red, Green, Blue, and White. When you insert your clear shard in the Red, Green, or Blue sockets, some of the rocks slowly and noisily change position (they lower if up, and vice versa) per the table below. When you insert the shard in the White socket (i.e., on mouseUp), the white socket becomes red and all the other colors shift left one

position. In addition, each hole's effect on the rocks is shifted left one position.

We begin with all four rocks in the Up position and the lights in Pattern A. See the chart on the right to find out what happens under each condition.

When all four columns finally reach the down position, we see the Eressdy Font rise up out of the floor to its full glory, then we automatically take you from this screen back to the full room shot above, never to return. The crystal shard the Guard gave you remains in the console.

Eressdy Font C. U.

The Eressdy Font is like a baptism or holy water font, except it contains a yellowish powder. If you have the tobacco pouch, you can click it on the font to receive enough powder to take you down and back on the ol' Eressdy highway.

Pattern A	Hole	Toggles stone #
	Red	1 2
	Green	1 3 4
	Blue	2 3
	White	changes to Pattern B below

Pattern B	Hole	Toggles stone #
	Green	2 3 4
	Blue	1 2
	White	changes to Pattern C below
	Red	1 4

Pattern C	Hole	Toggles stone #
	Blue	1 4
	White	changes to Pattern D below
	Red	3 4
	Green	1 2 3

Pattern D	Hole	Toggles stone #
	White	changes to Pattern A above
	Red	2 3
	Green	1 2 4
	Blue	3 4

TABLE 10-1 ▌ *Interlude 1–2*, Torin's Passage

Flashback: The Discovery

Time	Camera	Action
8	L. S. of grand royal hall	In a grandiose meeting room, men and women in robes stand by a long table. All are in turmoil, agitated, disarray. A soldier hurries in, walks to the Arch-Authority, Kurtzwell, the obvious authority figure.
3	2-shot	Soldier, quietly: "Sir, they were both there."
2		Room hushes. Kurtzwell: "And?"
3		Soldier, hushed: "They're gone."
2		Quiet room reaction
2	C. U. of Kurtzwell	Kurtzwell: "And the child?"
3		Soldier: "Missing."
3		Louder, although still subdued, reaction
5		Kurtzwell, forcefully: "The child must be found! Immediately!"
31	**Total Time**	*Fade to black*

Flashback: Capture!

Time	Camera	Action
5	POV of soldier	Soldiers search through woods. We see a small structure through leaves.
3	Cut to C. U. of Lycentia	Lycentia huddles inside barn, holding the baby. VO of soldiers growing closer.
3		VO of orders, sounds of soldiers searching
4	C. U. of Lycentia	Baby fusses. Lycentia, fearful, tries to quiet baby.
4		Door opens. Light from outside falls across Lycentia's body.
4		Her eyes grow wide with fear. She pulls the baby even closer.
23	**Total Time**	*Fade to black*

Time is in seconds.
Copyright 1995 by Al Lowe for Sierra On-Line, Inc.

A Preproduction Overview

Now I'll take a look at all the preproduction material put together. As a template I'll use a project I worked on a few years ago on a proposed interactive multimedia world's fair. The theme of the fair was to be "The Digital Future." I decided to include a variety of theme and exhibit centers based on actual world's expositions of the twentieth century. The treatment would read something like Table 10-2.

The content outline would be as follows:

OUTLINE: EXPLORING THE DIGITAL FUTURE—
An Interactive World's Fair

I. Introduction—Animation of the fair's theme (based on the 1939 New York Fair's Trylon and Perisphere)—to be used as metaphor for fair's Theme Center.
   A. Animation of Mr. Expo—a figure who can answer questions and guide users around the fair.
      1. "Welcome to the Interactive World's Fair."
II. How to Explore the Fair:
   (Animation sequence)
   A. Brief description of the fair and how it works
      1. Flowchart/map as menu device
      2. Click-on buttons
         a. take you to different sections & subsections
         b. click "end" to bring you back to fair logo/menu (can go to "Help" menus)
      3. Click on graphic images and/or photos from various fair sections
         a. takes you to pavilions you can enter by clicking on them.
         b. click "end" to bring you back to fair logo/menu and then flowchart/map.
   etc.

Following the treatment and the content outline, a script, storyboard, and flowchart would be created (see Figures 10-39, 10-40, and the following script):

Opening menu:

FADE IN:

As lines begin to form and slowly coalesce into geometric shapes: a triangular structure and a circle.

NARRATOR (V.O.)
Hello, and welcome to the
Interactive World's Fair of 1995 …

The structures become a Trylon and a Perisphere, the symbol of the 1939 World's Fair: "The World of Tomorrow."

TABLE 10-2 ▌ *Multimedia World's Fair Treatment—Exploring the Digital Future*

Program: This program will take the user on a tour of an interactive multimedia world's fair with the theme, "The Digital Future." There will be a map/flowchart of the fairgrounds, numerous pavilions that can be explored, animation, music, and quicktime movies to view.

Approach: The following content will be covered:

1. What digital technology is

2. Its effect on various areas of the world as well as on industry, education, communication, the home, space, medicine, and entertainment

3. A history of past world's fairs and their purposes

4. A variety of interactive games in the "Amusement" area of the fair

5. The possible futures for the development of digital technology

Graphics, animation and a series of in-depth interviews with New Media and technology experts will convey and clarify the concepts being discussed and taught in this program.

Design: After the title page, the first menu will concern the theme of the fair. There will be three "Help" menus that users can access now and at any time during the course of the "visit" to the fair.

From the fair's "Theme Center," the user can move to a variety of "Sections": "History/Services," " Worldviews," "Aspects of Life," and "Amusements/Entertainment." Each section is divided into numerous subsections that can be visited. For example: In "Worldviews," users can explore digital technology in North America, Asia, etc., or click into the next section ("Aspects") and concentrate on something like "Communication" or "Education" or "Medicine") that users can see by clicking directly into "Aspects."

etc.

Talent: A variety of experts in the fields of technology and New Media will be interviewed. Animated "guides" will also help users locate specific areas of sections. A variety of musical styles from around the world will be presented in "Entertainment" while bands that use digital technology will be highlighted in "Presentations."

etc.

NARRATOR (V.O.)
(continuing)
"Exploring The Digital Future!"

An animated swirl comes out of the symbol, and goes around it.

FIGURE 10-39 | *Storyboard for world's fair program.*

Campaign <u>Interactive World's Fair on Digital Technology</u>
Title <u>Exploring The Digital Future</u>
Length _____

VIDEO:
Lines form

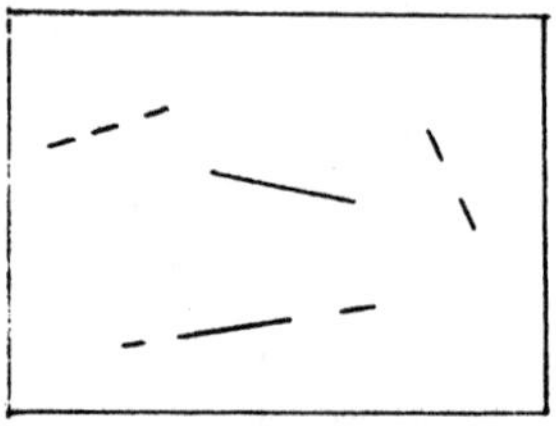

AUDIO:
"Hello, and
welcome ...

Lines begin to
form geometric
shapes

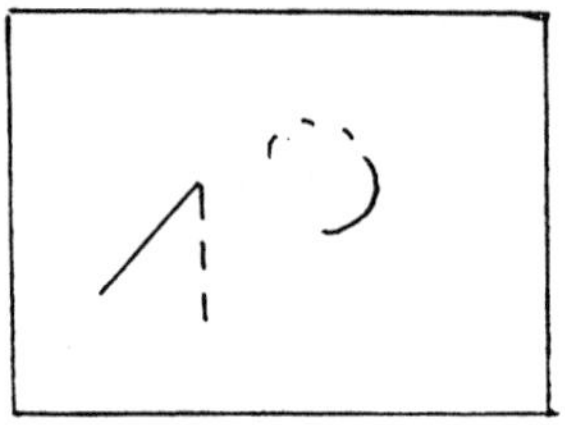

...to the Interactive
World's Fair of
1995 ...

Fair Theme Symbol/
Metaphor is formed

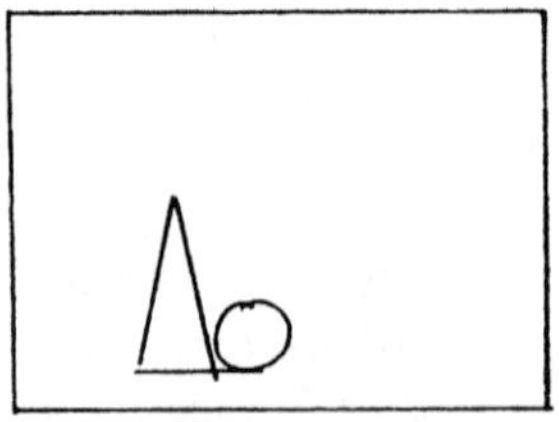

...Exploring the
Digital Future...

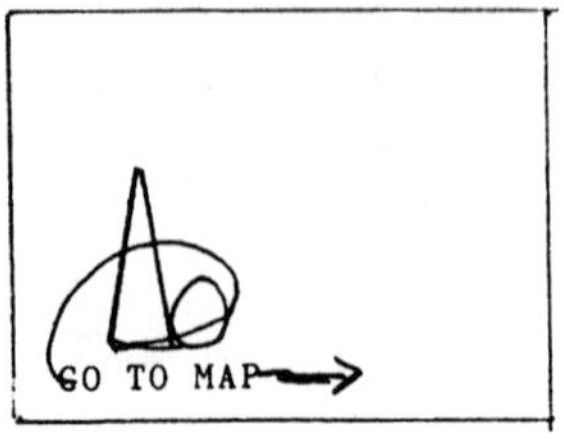

... Journey with us
around the world,
into cyberspace
and beyond the
infinite."

GO TO MAP

NARRATOR (V.O.)
(continuing)
Journey with us around the world, into cyberspace,
and beyond the infinite ...

The swirl points and the words "GO TO MAP" appear. At this point, the user can click on the arrow and move to the map/flowchart.

After all of the preproduction work is complete, the actual production of the interactive piece can begin, which you will see in the next chapter.

FIGURE 10-40   *Flowchart of world's fair program.*

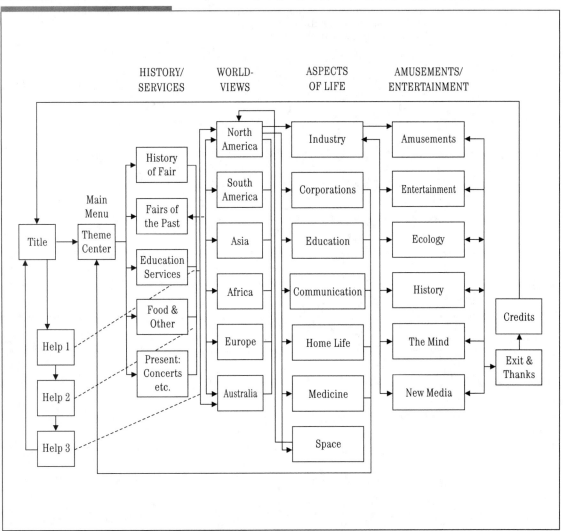

E N D N O T E S

1. Lorelei Shannon, interview with the author, July 1995.
2. Robert Aston and Joyce Schwartz, Eds., *Multimedia: Gateway to the Next Millennium* (Cambridge, MA: Academic Press, 1994), 266.
3. Chris James, "Navigation for Interactive Multimedia: An Introduction," January 1994, paper for Media Communication and Technology Department, Bellevue Community College.
4. Brian Sawyer and John Vourlis, "Screenwriting Structures for New Media," *Creative Screenwriting,* Summer 1995, 97.
5. Carol J. Anderson and Mark D. Veljikov, *Creating Interactive Multimedia: A Practical Guide* (Glenview, IL: Scott, Foresman, 1990), 149–150.
6. James, "Navigation for Interactive Multimedia," 2.
7. Sawyer and Vourlis, "Screenwriting Structures for New Media," 98.
8. Bruce Wolcott, interview with the author, August 1995.
9. Ibid.
10. Much of this material comes from Anderson and Veljikov, *Creating Interactive Multimedia* (pp. 150–151), one of the first and still one of the best texts dealing with producing, designing, and writing multimedia.
11. Wolcott, interview with the author.
12. Ibid.
13. Ibid.
14. Sawyer and Vourlis, "Screenwriting Structures for New Media," 98.

11

Production and Evaluation

The preplanning and planning steps and stages discussed in the previous chapters allow one to create a multimedia product efficiently, effectively, and within budget. After all the brainstorming, research, writing, and creation of prototypes, actual production begins.

The Production Process

Though the production process is sometimes called the "work phase" of a multimedia project, most writers and designers would probably take issue with that definition. A better way to describe the production process is the procedure by which the multimedia project is built and completed.

In production, the "author" begins work, along with videographers, editors, graphic designers, animators, and actors or narrators. In most cases, the writer remains involved with the project during this phase. Continual production meetings help keep the goals of the project clear. Writers normally attend production meetings, except perhaps those geared toward specific technical considerations.

As mentioned earlier, scripts for multimedia projects will often be changed during the course of both preproduction *and* the production process. As with film scripts, a number of drafts will be written (and rewritten). In multimedia, the first draft usually covers the entire project. Polishing grammar, checking spelling, and attending to technical concerns occur during the second draft. The final draft covers the entire project and includes all corrections, changes, and ideas. Most projects, linear or not, need more than three drafts.

Workers usually receive payment at each step. For example, a developer might be paid a third upon beginning the draft (up-front money), a third upon completion of the draft, and the final third for the polish. Complete rewrites, new drafts, treatments, and content outlines are paid separately, though a treatment can be considered part of the start of the project. Contract workers are also often paid by the hour.

The writer's role can become hazier as the project moves into its production phase. "A writer or editor might suggest type styles and formats but these are often the decisions of the graphic designer. This is an example where proper delineation of authority can reduce disagreements or 'turf wars.' "[1]

The tool of choice for the writer will be computer word-processing software (or any number of the scripting software mentioned in Appendix D). You might want a small, inexpensive tape recorder to use during meetings and interviews, or to record possible story ideas.

Production is also the period where videotaping or filming takes place. On dramatic projects, writers may well find themselves running from the office to a set where filming is taking place, then on to a story conference with designers and animators. Even while segments are being recorded, new dialog and/or narration may need to be written, or old material rewritten.

Once finished, all footage or animation must be combined and plugged in with everything else: text, graphics, audio material, still images, etc. This is known as *production integration*, a task performed by a computer programmer whose work is overseen by the project manager.

A marketer or marketing department designs the product's packaging. Occasionally, the writer will be asked to work with the marketing department on blurbs about the product or to write a short summary of the program for press releases. However, there is one final step before packaging and marketing a product—the product evaluation.

Using Evaluation Tools

Before the final product is shipped, the production staff needs to check the product completely for bugs, link problems, technical glitches, and anything else that doesn't work.

Anderson and Veljikov mention two phases of testing projects. **Alpha testing,** the first stage in testing a program, begins when the first prototype of a project is completed. It takes place on the production site and usually involves a small group under close observation. Employees with checklists note any unusual behavior by the individuals in the group doing the testing. The members of the group being tested also keep notes to record their experiences.

This is where pathways, choices, buttons, menu pages, and metaphors are checked: Does the user understand the program and how to reach different pathways? Are the buttons easy to understand? Do the metaphors make sense? Does the programming itself work without flaws? Alpha testing also gives developers a chance to correct technical problems and find more creative ways to design a program.

Beta testing has two additional phases. In *editing,* mistakes in grammar, spelling, content, and imagery are corrected. In *testing the design,* users in different geographical locations test a product beyond the prototype stage but not yet packaged.[2]

During this period, many companies try the product (or even a computer prototype) with an audience that represents the intended user group. Not only will this show if the product has lived up to certain goals and objectives, it will also make sure that the messages presented are actually getting across to the users and actively engaging them.

Developers might use many *evaluation tools* to find out if their goals and objectives have been met. Checklists, fact sheets, and written summaries are used. A good evaluation tool for an educational multimedia project or one aimed at training would be a test. In fact, each section of a particular program should probably have a quiz that the user must pass in order to continue.

Tests and quizzes only make sense for educational and training programs. Other evaluation methods for training and educational multimedia are long-term and include more efficient work habits, increased sales in a particular department, and fewer on-the-job accidents.

Other evaluation tools serve other kinds of products. Of course, having a user group that demographically matches the market one is aiming at is very helpful. Some companies put consumers who might be targeted for a specific product into **focus groups,** small groups in which a facilitator encourages the participants to discuss the product, its negative and positive aspects (for example, how user-friendly the product is, how engaged it keeps the user, if it reminds the user too much of a similar product), and why they liked or didn't like the product. Occasionally, advertisers or marketing personnel will use the exact statements of focus-group participants for ad copy.[3]

After all the testing and market research, a company finally presents its product to its intended audience. Because user testing and evaluation continues even after the product is put on the shelf for sale, companies often find themselves upgrading products. Sierra On-Line's *King's Quest* series is a perfect example of a multimedia product that is upgraded not only because of user reaction, but also because of improved technology. What started as a primitive-looking program now has complicated and attractive graphics, animation, voices, and music.

The Look of the Final Program

When writers first conceive a project, they have an idea of how they want it to look. Later, decisions on the look of a program are often based on the treatment as well as the main metaphor the writer developed. If the writer has done all the planning in a consistent manner, with the goals of the project continually kept in mind, then the look of the final program will usually excite and please him or her. This experience does not differ much from that of a screenwriter viewing a motion picture based on his or her script. There might be some disappointments: After all, no multimedia project has just one author or visionary.

In the end, the sense of accomplishment should feel pretty sweet. So, after smiling and telling themselves they knew all along the project would turn out well, each team member moves on to the next project.

E N D N O T E S

1. Randy Haykin, Ed., *Multimedia Demystified* (New York: Apple Computer, 1994), 177.
2. Carol J. Anderson and Mark D. Veljikov, *Creating Interactive Multimedia: A Practical Guide* (Glenview, IL: Scott, Foresman, 1990), 157–160.
3. Charles U. Larson, *Persuasion: Reception and Responsibility* (Belmont, CA: Wadsworth, 1992), 388.

The Digital Future

12

The Future of Multimedia

"I don't want more choices! I just want nicer things to choose from!"
— Edina on "Absolutely Fabulous"

"In a couple of years everybody will have access to the same multimedia technology. The profits will go to the people with the best raw material, the best stories."
— Paul Klebnikov, *Forbes* magazine,
February 27, 1995

"The real future for some of this stuff lies in having people trying on different faces. Masquerading electronically and trying on different characters. But you've got to define a journey through the electronic environment that's dramatic. Most people take a clichéd approach."
— Mike Backes, screenplay writer

The Effects of Multimedia

In their book *Multimedia: Gateway to the Next Millennium,* Robert Aston and Joyce Schwartz write, "A new multimedia aesthetic is taking shape and will increasingly define the market as the decade proceeds. It will be built on improved performance as higher processing and full-motion video is actively incorporated into the programs."[1] They then list a variety of media and genres that will be affected, including the following:

- *Movies* will be on CD-ROMs; that is, a complete motion picture will be contained on a single disc along with additional information.
- *Interactive movies*, unlike idiocies like *Mr. Payback*, will allow for multiple plot divergence as well as a variety of points of view.
- *Simulations* of everything from sports such as auto racing and mountain climbing to war games will have a higher degree of realism and will eventually become *immersive* VR programs.

- *Edutainment* or "learning-defined programming will be 'enhanced' with appealing entertainment elements to create popular learning titles along the lines of PBS shows for both adults and children."[2]
- *Infotainment* such as news and reference material will, in all probability, be "enlivened with an entertainment component to achieve greater popular usage."[3] In other words, stealth learning will be taken to the nth degree.
- *Interactive shows* such as game shows, soap operas, sit-coms, etc., will encourage user participation.

Already one of Aston and Schwartz's predictions has come true: In September of 1995, IBM, Sony, Philips Electronics, and Toshiba agreed to compromise and end the so-called videodisk format war. The **DVD,** or *digital video disc,* has a resolution three times that of a VHS player. Single-sided, this disc, the same size as a CD-ROM disc, can store a two-hour movie or "about seven times the computer information stored on a CD-ROM."[4] Eventually the discs will be double-sided with fourteen times the room of a conventional CD-ROM disc for narration, dialog, text, and other material—and that much more work and creative leeway for the writer. However, this is still an interim technology. The future of multimedia lies in other directions.

Interactive Television and the Internet

Broadcasting is a top-to-bottom system whereby radio and television programs are sent to the listener and viewer through the air. It has always been a system in which a handful of people decide what will air and when. Programmers and executives decide what the "dumb terminals," as audiences have often been referred to in the industry, watch. Now, a new system seems to be coming into play, one that Stewart Brand has dubbed **broadcatch.** In this system, the viewer becomes a "user" with much more control over what is seen. In Brand's words, it is a system of "content-specific selectivity and repackaging at the receiving end that computer technology is offering."[5]

If the information superhighway becomes the routine way to communicate, as many pundits predict, it could go one of two ways: a true democratization of arts and letters or a tightly controlled electronic surveillance system able to tell your buying habits, hobbies, extracurricular activities, political ideologies, economic status, and just about anything else about you someone might want to know.

Whichever direction online communication takes us, it is true that paper is becoming more and more expensive and the word is becoming increasingly electronic. Already the **electronic word** has created a new publishing frontier. Newspapers, magazines, scholarly journals, "preprint" archives (whereby "scholars in a particular field can preview upcoming articles without waiting for the print journal"[6]), and commercial references are all available online. In fact,

Omni is one of many magazines that began as a "hard copy" monthly magazine that is now available only online.

PROFIT ON THE NET

"For the future, we're definitely thinking of the Internet," says Steven Conrad.

> CD-ROMs are an interim solution—I thought we'd have to do online stuff in nine months or so, but the market changed and we got into it much more quickly. We have prototypes online now. The Net caught everybody, even Microsoft, by surprise—a lot of it is hype, but that's OK—hype drives the industry.
>
> If you develop your product right, developing it for the Net and CD-ROM, you can get two bangs for the buck—get two products—dealing with interface issues and how you structure the content of a program, which our philosophy on that changes. With the Net, you can provide technical training to anyone who wants to log on and take it—have to decide how you're going to charge for that, how you're going to track for that—all those things you have to worry about.
>
> We don't know how we're going to charge for this stuff, what form it will take—the only thing you can be sure of is that it will evolve.
>
> People perceive the Internet as being free, but that will change as well. Companies have to stay in business, someone has to provide this content—if it's of value, then people will pay for it. If it's not, then people won't. Parts of the Internet, like shareware today, will be free.[7]

In fact, one analogy that might provide some comfort is that, in the same way you have both bookstores and free libraries today, on the Net, there is information that is free as well as material that has a price. As Conrad states, "The utopian view is that information should be free. The practical reality is that authors, editors, and publishers expect to be compensated for their work. ... Increasingly, we can expect Internet publishers to sell access to their documents and databases on demand as new transaction systems (electronic cash, and so on) enable consumers to pay for wares as they need them."[8] Still, there is no denying that multimedia has already found a niche in online communications.

"Multimedia technology is another evolutionary step in communications," Tony Bove of Rockument says.

> The computer started to play a major role in the arts and publishing when the graphics arts community adopted desktop graphics and page-layout programs [such as *Adobe Illustrator, Adobe Photoshop,* and *Premiere*]. This community has moved on to using animation, video, sound, and Web-related tools to continue to find new ways to attract attention for advertising, to create new art forms, to publish titles, and to disseminate information. ... The leading creative people and artists are among the first to use the multimedia and Web-creation tools, which means their needs are the first to be heard by the vendors. Those vendors that listen and incorporate the feedback will survive to produce even better tools, and so on. The artists and creative types will benefit from a high demand for their services, plus a lot of skill needed to do interactive television, which will be the future delivery medium for multimedia content.[9]

Multimedia on the Internet

ONLINE FORUMS

Ruth Zaslow is the principal of R Z Communications, a Seattle-based consulting firm dedicated to helping people write with greater effectiveness, efficiency, and ease. The company carries out its mission through live seminars and presentations and, more recently, through the *Writing It Right Forum* on the Microsoft Network and their interactive multimedia training product, *Writing for Results.*

One of the most exciting things Zaslow is doing online is offering a whole new kind of help for business and technical writing. "Instead of waiting months to attend a scheduled in-house seminar, instead of wasting time wandering around the office searching for the answer to a writing question, people can pop into the forum. There, they can browse our Quick Tips, check out our Articles Library or post a question to one of the bulletin boards. They receive fast, expert advice about writing."[10]

Recently, R Z Communications began adding the same kind of help for people creating web pages. In fact, this area of the forum is currently the fastest growing one.

Another exciting online offering is R Z Communications's interactive multimedia writing product, *Writing for Results.* "Module-based for maximum convenience, *Writing for Results* lets people learn exactly what they need to know about writing—exactly when they need to know it."[11]

REAL TIME ON THE NET

One area that all creators of interactive multimedia hope to explore in the near future is the nature of "real time" online interactions on the Net. "I could see where you eventually could write code that stores data about the player's experiences and presents more or less or differences based on it," says Al Lowe. "So I could see how a program could evolve that way and online [might be the way to do it] should we speed up the delivery system. ... I mean, CD-ROM is too damn slow."[12]

The creators of *Rebirth* hope that, in the future, this "virtual Tibet" will become a social environment for the exchange of ideas and thoughts regarding Tibet, Tibetan Buddhism, cultural survival, art, Tibetan mind sciences, and role-playing adventures. As Bruce Wolcott notes, in this sense "the *Rebirth* story web is not just a series of pre-scripted events, but a legacy of human interaction taking place as a form of improvised theater within the context of the online site."[13]

ADVICE TO WRITERS

Andrew Anker is the President and CEO of HotWired Ventures LLC, a Web cyberstation featuring a suite of vertical content streams (or pages) about the digital revolution and the "Second Renaissance" with an integrated community space. HotWired is essentially *Wired* magazine's online forum.

"Online media, when done right, is wholly different from other media," he says. "The best advice any writer can get is to play with the media and build something unique in a personal web space. The best resumes we get include a **URL** which points to a writer's home page. We're much more interested in seeing something someone's done than hearing about the last ten jobs they had."[14]

Anker feels that with better integration between CD-ROMs and online communication, new forms of electronic literature will be created. "Eventually, the online bandwidth will get to the point that the local cache [CD-ROM] won't be as necessary."[15] He also feels that "online communications will make writers and designers much more directly accountable or answerable to the people they're writing for. ... This is a new [medium], and we haven't even begun to start to explore it. The Milton Berles and George and Gracies of the 90s are just starting to figure out how to use this. It's wide open territory and the fun is just beginning. I think it's a wonderful time to be a creative type. There are very few standard boxes to fit in. Thinking outside of the box is being rewarded and most creatives I know like that a lot."[16]

3D CHAT ROOMS

One company that's already created a real-time virtual environment by combining CD-ROM and online technology is Worlds Incorporated, which has taken virtual world technology out of a high-end computer workstation environment and made it available to the desktop. The company produces, publishes and markets shared virtual experiences. "In brief, Worlds Inc. is the leading producer of social computing applications. As a publisher of shared virtual environments, Worlds allows users to communicate and interact in fully navigable 3-D spaces with other real people. [Worlds Chat is] a radical leap from menu-driven, icon-based interfaces, users are represented in these shared environments by Digital Actors®, or avatars, allowing an unprecedented sense of community and individual identity."[17]

Worlds Chat "allows users to select or create their own online 'Digital Actors'®, (or 'avatars') that move through locally-rendered three dimensional spaces such as rooms, fields, game boards, or other private and public areas—and 'chat' with each other. (Ever read Snowcrash?)" Thus, it is the user who drives the content and thus brings to life new creations. "By connecting multiple users online, true interactivity is now possible: users no longer interact with their computers, but through their computers with other real people. That is the core of social computing: People."

Current Worlds Inc. sites online include the following:

- *Worlds Chat.* A space station with "conversation pods" where people from all over the planet, dressed as avatars, wander around and talk in a virtual space station.
- *Alpha World.* A virtual world in development, where avatars can "homestead" by building their own homes/building/meeting halls complete with

animated objects and dimensional sound. Alpha world publishes its own newspaper.

- *IBM World.* A virtual world constructed by Worlds Inc. for IBM, which includes a Renaissance library, complete with frescos and classic paintings. Here you can look for information in 3D space—a form of information architecture.
- *The Starbright Project.* This was set up with Stephen Spielberg to provide bedridden children in hospitals with a virtual world in which they could interact with other children as avatars who are in the same situation.

ONLINE THEME PARK

The technology Worlds Inc. is using points to the future. In fact, they have created an online theme park where users are invited to "Ride a jetpack© to a planetary launching pad. Learn how telescopes work© and then beam up to meet new friends in the Cyber Bar©. The IWF [Internet World's Fair, now part of a larger system called AlphaWorld] is like the ultimate theme park©, online … and you don't even have to park the car."

For this project, Worlds Inc. worked with Landmark Entertainment Group, one of the largest independent designers of "real" theme parks in the world. Worlds Chat and other Worlds Inc. projects are pretty amazing: After a little while on the Worlds Chat space station, "talking" with other avatars, you begin to really feel as if you are in a different place, a new and virtual environment.

VIRTUAL WORLDS

VRML Worlds Inc. is also bringing its leading edge multiuser technology to the Virtual Reality Modeling Language (VRML).

VRML is a standard way of describing three-dimensional models, and is to 3D what HTML is to 2D. While VRML was an important step beyond HTML, it lacked some critical functionality: You couldn't see or communicate with anyone else using a VRML space. VRML+ changes all of that, allowing multiple users to view and communicate with each other through the use of *avatars.*

> You can now not only explore VRML worlds, but view them and communicate with other people at the same time. Worlds Inc. is taking the static environments of VRML and bringing them to life with VRML+. With VRML+ your browser communicates with a World Server, letting it know where you are in the scene. The Server passes your position on to other browsers, which display your avatar. Your avatar can be any standard VRML object. With VRML+ you can send text messages to other people in a VRML+ environment, giving a chat capability far beyond conventional applications and previously only available in Worlds Chat.

Virtual Property Development Rob Schmults, the director of marketing for Worlds Inc., feels that, while some software companies are increasingly resembling movie companies (with producers, directors, writers, etc.), Worlds Inc.

is more of a virtual property developer. "Perhaps another way of looking at us is as the builders of the stages. We can set the theme, provide props and the like, but it is really the users who drive the drama."[18]

In fact, in AlphaWorld, each "citizen" who is a part of this virtual community, can build their own cybersite.

> Whether it is a house, a piazza, a garden, or a wooded glen, each user adds their own personal touch to AlphaWorld by actually building a part of it. Each cybersite is built by the user, either with prerendered objects or with objects they have created. This is their own private property which only they, or those they have given permission to, may alter. And because this is a shared environment, every user sees not only their own handiwork, but that of others as well. Because of this feature, AlphaWorld is not only constantly growing, but constantly changing as well. ... Virtual stages and sports bars, brought to life by real people, point to the future of entertainment. The ongoing convergence of the power of the telephone, television, and computer become much closer to being a reality in AlphaWorld.[19]

Digital theater   Particularly of interest to writers is what Worlds Inc. has planned for the future:

> *Dramatic pieces will very likely have the potential to be not only interactive but entirely Point Of View oriented.* You will, in a sense, be able to become detective Sam Spade or Captain Kirk or James Bond or whoever. With the potential of unlimited memory online communications has, you could see two major characters speaking to each other, notice two other people in the background, and zero in on them if you want, following their story for a while from either of the characters' POV. Creating such digital theater will be more challenging not only for the writer, but for the actors as well (that is, if human actors are used at all—companies may prefer to utilize entirely digitized people) [italics mine].[20]

As for what lies beyond the "digital theater":

> The gamer has a VR helmet, an SGI-quality graphics chip, and a high-speed hookup into a multiplayer Net service. So what's in it for the writer? Not much except an entire world to create. Sure, if the designer wants to give players guns and make them run around shooting at everybody, you can take a hike. But what if there are no guns? What if there are non-player characters (NPCs) rendered in 3D who can talk? What if they're complete with personalities, weaknesses, needs, jokes, whatever? Artificial intelligence sufficient to generate fully realized, realistically spontaneous people isn't really that far off if you define your characters to take very simplistic actions and have very simple responses.[21]

Impact on immersive VR   A few years ago, no one really thought that VRML (Virtual Reality Modeling Language) and the World Wide Web/Internet would affect **immersive VR** at all. Now, though, people are considering using the Web for this new form of communication.

> What does this brave new virtual world look like? What can you gain and lose out there? What are the central conflicts that drive this place? This is creative territory as well suited to a writer as a game designer. What are the dramatic possibilities when an onscreen player surrogate, or Avatar, meets and engages another? Is there

dialog? Action? Barter? Out of the primordial ooze of lifeless graphics explodes an endless self-generating society, and you get to design the Genesis Bomb that blasts it into being.[22]

Dr. Thomas Furness sees digital and communications technology merging in immersive VR. However, right now he foresees a problem with moving in this direction. The computational resources to make virtual worlds better and "faster," whereby everything will happen in real time, will take some time to develop. But develop they will, and when they do, the writer's job will once again take on new dimensions.

The Future of Writers in Multimedia

"We need to change the term *writer*," Furness says. "A writer is thought of as someone who manipulates symbols on a page. In this new age, we really need to call writers *creators*."[23]

"Predictions for the future of writers in a multimedia world [are varied]," Ruth Zaslow agrees.

> While writers and writing will always have their place, that place will increasingly be as a part of a multimedia team. Writers will become individual contributors to a project, rather than sole authors.
>
> If you're a writer in this new interactive multimedia world, I think you have two choices. First, you can hone the kind of writing skill that multimedia requires: scripting. Second, you can expand your skill set so that you can play more than one role on a multimedia team. Master programming tools as well as writing skills and you've more than doubled your value to a project. The same goes for adding skills as a project manager or even graphic designer.[24]

Zaslow feels that, in the near future, good writers who are experts in their fields will become more and more important to digital communications.

Furness also sees this era as a rebirth for writers. This new medium requires a writer's creativity:

> The first people involved in the creation of New Media were technologists who were generating tools and content. Creative people didn't care about the tools themselves; they were more concerned with ways of expressing themselves with these new mechanisms. And so, the writers began to generate content.
>
> The same thing happened with film and television writers. Yes, they generate dialog, but also content and environment and interactions. With new tools, you have new products. The key is the creative spark that writers use, that it will still be necessary, and it will still be there. We have a new medium that is growing, and yet we have few meaningful messages going into this new medium. The reason a CD-ROM like *Myst* was such a success was that it was thoughtful and really did create a world for you—an incredible and compelling world. I found myself, after solving it all, wanting to go back and revisit it. The journey itself was wonderful.
>
> There have been other creative games. The original *Zork* built an incredible virtual world and was all text based. It was in the imagination that the world was created (and it was the writers who created it).

The writer's role in digital media is going to be still giving the creative spark and building engaging worlds that are also not lonely worlds! There has to be intelligence in these worlds, and others we can interact with, other people, sparked by what the writers have created.[25]

And what will writers, or creators, need in order to express themselves well in this new medium?

A knowledge of theatrics, of story building and story telling. Also, with multimedia you must describe by pictures and storyboards and not just the written word. They will need to visualize as in movies, allowing the user to fill in the blanks. And then there is the element of interactivity: the consumer is passive in a movie, but if they're suddenly going to be part of it, there's a whole new set of things and no one is an expert on this at this point. You're trying to lead the user, but you're also leaving the user latitude, allowing them alternative pathways and endings.

Writers will need a venue for collaboration, working with artists and designers. There will need to be theater people and "stage managers" (for virtual places) who can say what works and what doesn't. And, they will all need a new lexicon in order to communicate with each other.[26]

Furness says one of the problems is that "consumers are terrified about being interactive. They don't know how to do it. Television has generated a civilization of passive observers, spectators. Remember, there was originally an aversion on the part of people to use a computer. We have an inertia we have to overcome. It's the kids who'll be involved [with the new medium] first."[27]

In fact, Furness believes it might take a generation before a true market, consumers for interactive multimedia and VR, develops.

However long it takes, a new medium, a new form of communication and language, and a new form of "literature" have already emerged. One big mistake people have made with technology, any technology, is always believing it will solve all their problems. What technology usually does is solve some problems while creating others. For the writer, new digital technology will open up whole new vistas to explore while very likely changing the entire concept of "the word" and just how important it will be to our culture and our civilization.

ENDNOTES

1. Robert Aston and Joyce Schwartz, *Multimedia: Gateway to the Next Millennium* (Cambridge, MA: Academic Press, 1994), 244.
2. Ibid.
3. Ibid.
4. Andrew Pollack, "After the Digital Videodisk War," *New York Times,* September 18, 1995, 219.
5. Stewart Brand, *The Media Lab: Inventing the Future at M.I.T.* (New York: Penguin Books, 1987), 42.
6. Richard Wiggins, "The Word Electric," *Internet World* magazine, September 1995, 31–33.
7. Steven Conrad, interview with the author, February 9, 1995.
8. Ibid.
9. Tony Bove, interview with the author, October 3, 1995.
10. Ruth Zaslow, e-mail to the author, February 26, 1996.
11. Ibid.

12. Al Lowe, interview with the author, August 1995.
13. Bruce Wolcott, "World Building and the Use of Metaphor," p. 10. Copyright 1995 Rebirth Development Project, All Rights Reserved, by permission of author.
14. Andrew Anker, interview with the author, August 6, 1995.
15. Ibid.
16. Ibid.
17. Worlds Incorporated online information material, here and in the next four quotes, from Worlds Inc. homepage.
18. Rob Schmults, interview with the author, August 29, 1995.
19. Ibid.
20. Worlds Incorporated online information material from Worlds Inc. homepage. Worlds Inc. Web site is: http://www.kaworlds.com; e-mail is: techsupport@kaworlds.com.
21. Robert Gelman and Kenneth Melville, "On the Trail of the Interactive Grail: A Roadmap for Would-be Script Writers," *Interactivity* magazine, January 1996, 59.
22. Ibid.
23. Furness, interview with the author.
24. Zaslow, e-mail to the author, February 24, 1996.
25. Furness, interview with the author.
26. Ibid.
27. Ibid.

Appendices

A

Getting into the Business

How should writers who are used to writing "linearly" prepare themselves to write for nonlinear digital media? Frank Catalano offers the following suggestion: "Visit Disneyland. Disneyland, in my mind, is an excellent example of nonlinear storytelling. It is a totally artificial ('virtual') environment, down to the nth detail, yet there is no 'correct' way to go through it. Within it are various smaller linear stories (attractions) that help one get a feel for the overall story of Disneyland. It's one of the few concrete examples of a good virtual world that exists in the real world."[1]

Immerse Yourself in the Technology

As stated before, the writers must also immerse themselves into the medium. Check out what's on the shelves at Egghead and other software retailers, buy a CD-ROM player if you don't already own one, play a variety of multimedia programs and note how they engage (or don't engage) the user, and network by talking to as many people in the business as you can.

"First, learn to use the tools," Tony Bove suggests, "and then you should be able to write your own ticket anywhere as a valuable asset to any multimedia operation."[2]

Bove also suggests finding a company or school with an internship program where students can earn course credit for working, giving them both a foot in the door and the real-world experience they need to gain a better job.

Paul Saffo feels that, although a writer should know how to use the tools at hand, the writer's understanding of the actual technology involved in interactive multimedia is much less important than people think.

For example, it is already a virtual waste of time to learn HTML because within the year we will have [new tools that allow us to do the programming much more easily]. [There was a time when] designers had to know Postscript in order to create cutting-edge effects. But once a new wave of design tools arrived, they could do these effects more rapidly and conveniently and without ever seeing a speck of Postscript code. So unless you are determined to be on the absolute bleeding edge of this revolution, don't worry about bits and bytes—focus instead on understanding the *experience* that users will want to have and how the technology might deliver it.[3]

Also, writers should understand both the capabilities and restrictions of the technology they're using.

Saffo emphasizes that multimedia writers should think in terms of experiences rather than mere stories. "Stories will still exist, but they will exist within larger experimental chunks sold to readers."[4]

Narrow Focus of Interest and Genre

Al Lowe of Sierra has another suggestion:

Rich parents? That's probably the best background. Let's take me for an example—I'm most familiar with my own instance here—I have a master's degree in music education, I was a high-school band director and orchestra teacher for years, a district school coordinator—always had a heavy interest in humanities and the arts—I used to chart half-time shows where I made little pixels move around on this hundred-yard-wide screen—so what in the world am I doing writing games? I've never had a class in computer programming, and yet I programmed the first products all by myself—I guess I had a lot of desire—and if you ask everyone along the way, I would guess every one of us had some unique background, I mean, none of us have parallel pasts or paths, so for me to say this is the way to go would be presumptuous.

I think, for me, what's more important than anything is to have the desire to excel. I think you have to want to do products—I think you have to look at other peoples' products and say, "God, how could they do that? That's so obvious, look at this, this is terrible ... " That's what I do all the time. Whenever I get something in I say, "Well how could they miss that? How could they—they should have done that." ... If there's any quality that ties all of this together I think it's that we look at things and say, "I could do better."

Now, having said that, if you're going to write, it seems to me you'd want a good background in English and a good background in writing—in all those things that I don't have—that I really would like to have (when's your class?). The only class in writing I had was in bonehead college English, I mean intro college English—normal freshman composition—but when I suddenly got interested in [interactive games] I had a story to tell and I wanted to tell it—and suddenly I was motivated and I keep going through and editing and editing and I read, I read a lot—it's a way to learn storytelling and writing—so I came in backwards—I don't think you could be successful in multimedia without understanding the media that we "multi." If you just know writing, you'll be lost—which is where the Hollywood guys [have had trouble] but part of the reason that I have been successful is that I know music, I know electronics, I was always an electronics tinker, I was a computer tinker, I read voraciously, and so I'm really involved in language and literature and I'm very aware of grammar, and I'm also an incurable proofreader, I find errors everywhere—that's what I do all day long—I look at my products and try to see how they can be better.[5]

Alex Shapiro feels that, at this point, it isn't necessary for would-be writers of multimedia to specialize. However, she adds that "people are going to be hired on the basis of their experience and background and titles. So for example, if you are a novelist—if you're William Gibson, then somebody might approach you and say, 'Hey let's do an interactive title based on *Johnny Mnemonic*.' If you are someone who's looking for work, who's gone through a course, then, ideally, you've narrowed your focus and genre based on your experience and interest."[6]

Lorelei Shannon of Sierra On-Line has always read speculative fiction, science fiction, fantasy, and horror.

[For students] I certainly wouldn't recommend my background—double degree in literature and fine arts, which actually is very beneficial to me in that I don't design things which the artists can't execute. My concepts are very possible—but ideally, now I'm a bit of an artifact at this point. The people [the industry] is looking for now I believe would have a background in at least some aspect of computer science, which can be fairly technical. You would definitely want some writing training. ... Getting into film and video studies is also a good idea because so many of the games are going towards real-time video. ... Actually, screen writing is a very, very good idea—screen-writing instructors frequently aren't as emotionally involved as creative-writing instructors—they'll give you more basic plot mechanisms and things, but the screenwriting model is pretty much what our scripts are based on (see illustration). Of course, what we create are much more interactive in branching than a screenwriting model.[7]

Intern

Robin Worley's advice is to intern.

Get your foot in the door somehow, even if it's not as a writer. Somehow get into a multimedia company and then prove to them that you can do the job as a writer. It seems like right now, at least, for writers, a lot of multimedia companies don't realize that they need writers, and they think the technical people can do all the writing. ... They think, we've got a great story idea—who needs to pay a writer for this? It seems it's a little bit tough right now to find a job as a writer in multimedia. I think it's going to get a lot easier though as [programs] flop when they have the engineers do the writing.[8]

Be Creative, Be Engaging

Janis Machala started out in the publishing industry, doing textbooks, marketing, and market research. The firm she worked for developed a software division for educational software, including the first computerized testing program.

Three years later, Machala became involved with high-technology industries, which she found much more exciting than publishing.

"Publishers can still be conservative about new media, investment-wise," Machala says, "and some still see New Media as threat to the core of their business."[9] She went to work for Wang and later for Sun Microsystems as well as Microsoft where she dealt with marketing for corporate accounts. She then got the opportunity to run a company focusing on both software and publishing. "What's happening in the industry is that the whole distinction between content and software is changing, the lines are blurring."

At Pinnacle, Janis began creating CD-ROM material. As she began to work on delivering content over online services, she left to start her own company in online services. "It's a lot like the gold rush," Machala states. "The people who made money in the gold rush sold Levis, picks, and shovels; not necessarily the people finding the gold."

Machala feels that the challenge of writing for new media lies in the presentation: People have a difficult time reading anything on a screen. Thus, the choice and layout of words become very important. Writers of new media have to be as concerned with user interface as with the content of their writing. This is as true for the documentation of interactive products as for the products themselves.

"Every writer in the interactive media world needs to take design or graphic art of some sort. In the area of interactive titles, you almost have to start out storyboarding and doing branch representations (flowcharts) of what you're writing. With all those alternate scenarios you'd better have all the paths well defined." Machala also feels that it takes more time to write interactive titles because they're more complex than linear pieces. Also, it takes a lot more work to write something that's simple. The adage, "If I had more time I would have written you a shorter letter," applies directly to multimedia writing.

At the same time, Machala also feels that it is an

incredibly rich time for both writers and editors. There's going to be a huge demand for that talent. There will soon be more balance between the creative side and the technical side. You will also see a lot of independents starting up. There is a great opportunity to create small businesses with new media. What you'll see are people creating independent organizations that bring story ideas to major studios. We're also going to see ... movies that then become interactive titles or electronic games. What you'll eventually find is an interactive story being written first, later to become a movie, then a CD-ROM title, and ultimately a game.

You will also see a repurposing of content. You're going to end up with content that's reusable in different [ways]—say, for example, a live-action sequence that you can use in both software and a CD. Right now, it's so expensive to develop original content in this software that it becomes cost prohibitive. The economics of the market aren't there to support a million-dollar project yet. We need to get a lot more PCs in the home. The American family watches 120 hours of TV a month, while the average family uses online services for 6 hours a month: a huge gap [from] the amount of attention the consumer is giving to online or CD-ROM titles, as they are to dominate the environment which could change when they become one and the same—when interactive television becomes a reality, though I'm not sure how much people want interactive TV.

Machala points out that there are a lot of bad CDs out there, and the boredom factor sets in quickly. One must spend a lot of time on how to engage and hold people's interest. In the end, it will be the creativity behind the technology that drives the market and opens up new job opportunities.

E N D N O T E S

1. Frank Catalano, interview with the author, September 2, 1995.
2. Tony Bove, interview with the author, October 3, 1995.
3. Ibid.
4. Paul Saffo, interview with the author, October 24, 1995.
5. Al Lowe, interview with the author, August 1995.
6. Alex Shapiro, interview with the author, June 29, 1995.
7. Lorelei Shannon, interview with the author, July 1995.
8. Robin Worley, interview with the author, July 1995.
9. Janis Machala, interview with the author, September 1995. Subsequent quotes from Machala.

Protecting
Your Work

Protecting work in this new digital age is becoming more and more difficult. With online services and the eventual information superhighway, completely protecting a work from being used by someone else in **cyberspace** may become downright impossible. Indeed, once programs online are altered by other users, the question of just who will own the altered program may be difficult to answer. Richard Lanham here states the inherent problems of intellectual copyright law in the digital age: "Who will 'own' an interactive novel after it has been repeatedly interacted with? The blurring of the creator/critic distinction here finds a direct legal and financial manifestation. Our ethics of quotation, and the stylistic formulas that embody it, is called into question by the electronic media. ... To litigate a copyright case you must have a 'final cut,' a fixed version, upon which to base your arguments. What if there isn't any?"[1]

As Lanham goes on to state, the main problem is that digital material by nature is not fixed. It essentially "exists *in potentia* as what it can become. ... How do we invest an intellectual property in an intellectual *potentiality?*"[2]

Fortunately, there are still some basic ways to protect the scripts written for interactive pieces. The easiest way to protect your work is to **copyright** it. Copyright protects "original works of authorship" that are fixed in a tangible or discernible form of expression, such as a printed screenplay, a phonograph record, or a CD.

Odds are that if you're doing a work-for-hire project, the program will be copyrighted by the company producing it. However, in many cases, the actual script for the program can be copyrighted under the name of the writer or writers, but you will need to check with whomever hired you before going ahead and doing this.

An independent piece, such as the *Rebirth* project, or even a documentary that uses many already copyrighted materials, can be copyrighted under your or your company's name. *Haight-Ashbury in the Sixties,* though containing footage from two linear documentaries, still has a copyright that reads, "Copyright © 1995 Rockument, Inc."

One thing you cannot copyright is an idea. You can't send a piece of paper into the copyright office that states "I have an idea for a great multimedia piece about dinosaurs." Sorry. Won't work. However, if you put the idea into a story or treatment format, you can copyright it.

And, of course, one of the first questions that comes to mind is what's it cost to copyright something? Actually, it doesn't have to cost anything. Copyright is secured automatically when a work is "created," or put into a fixed format, as in a script, videotape, audio cassette, etc. If the program you're writing evolves over time, the point at which it took on a fixed format, or became a first draft, is considered the copyright date, or date on which the program was "created."

When you create a work in a fixed format, the first thing you should do is type or print onto the work the following: The word "Copyright" followed by the copyright symbol (©), the date, and your name or your production company's name followed by the phrase "All Rights Reserved." This is called a statutory copyright or common-law copyright.

The next thing you probably want to do costs a little money. After putting a copyright notice on the work, mail it to yourself and, when you receive it, *don't open it!* The postmark on the unopened envelope can be construed as proof that the script, treatment, story, whatever, was created by you before the date on the postmark. This is true protection.

Interestingly enough, computer programs, scripts, or screenplays are registerable as "literary works." Actually registering your work gives it even more protection. It establishes a public record of the copyright. It also gives you the ability to file an infringement suit in court and to record the registration with the U.S. Customs Service, protecting the work against the importation of infringing copies.

To register a work, first send a self-addressed stamped envelope and a note to the Copyright Office requesting form PA (for a work of the Performing Arts, which interactive multimedia projects are considered to be). You send this material to

The U.S. Copyright Office
The Library of Congress
Washington, DC, 20559

When you receive the application form, return it to this address along with a filing fee (which through July 1995 was $20.00, but you should check on this) and a copy of the treatment and/or script for the program (this copy will not be returned to you but will be kept on file in Washington).

An added precaution might be to send a copy of your treatment, story, or script to the Writers Guild. This will protect your work for ten years from the date of registration. Again, if proof of authorship or the date a piece was created is ever needed, the Writers Guild of America will be able to supply the sealed envelope containing your work. Registration can be renewed after ten years.

Write to one of the following addresses in order to obtain a registration form and the current registration fee:

Writers Guild of America, West
8955 Beverly Boulevard
West Hollywood, CA 90048

Writers Guild of America, East
555 West 57th Street
New York, NY 10019

Remember to send your complete script unbound. In a few weeks, you will receive a WGA registration number, which you can print on your script's title page.

ENDNOTES

1. Richard A. Lanham, *The Electronic Word: Democracy, Technology, and the Arts* (Chicago: University of Chicago Press, 1993), 18–19.
2. Ibid., 19.

C

Intellectual Property Law

"Electronic information seems to resist ownership. To make sure that it does flow freely in the world of literary study, we will have to create a new marketplace based on a new conception of intellectual property and copyright protection, and make sure that the constitutional guarantees of free speech made good in the print world prevail here too. Such a readjustment will not come easily."

— Richard A. Lanham, *The Electronic Word*

Licensing and copyrights can be a sticky issue in multimedia. As Tony Bove of Rockument puts it,

> We believe that compelling titles require a lot of content. We also believe in the widest perspective, so we chose material from over one hundred contributors. The royalty database took a month to design, but the legal machinery took *more than three years* [italics mine] to complete the task of licensing everything.
>
> Licensing for multimedia is a tricky issue, and this project spanned a period in the history of CD-ROM in which the largest recording companies in the music industry were hesitant with regard to music licensing. ...
>
> Music licensing depends mostly on usage. If you are not synchronizing the music to one or more images, you might not need to obtain synchronization rights. However, for most multimedia use, you'll need the equivalent of a package deal that includes master rights for the recordings (if you use originals, as we did) from the record company, and synchronization rights for multimedia from the music publisher. Lyrics usage is yet another right from the music publisher. Some rights agencies are starting to offer such package deals as "multimedia rights," but it would be wise to check with a lawyer if your business depends on it.[1]

Bove goes on to say that there is no such thing as a standard contract. He suggests that multimedia producers send out a sample contract listing the terms and rights they are seeking. In almost every case, the producers will then receive contracts from the various audio and visual companies they have contacted.

Often, companies will insert what is known as a "favored nations" clause into the contract. That means that if a multimedia producer pays a higher royalty rate to anyone else, then he also has to pay the higher rate to those with a favored nation clause, even if the initial contract specifies a lower rate. This ensures that companies will receive top dollar for their content and, in Bove's words, it "makes them more comfortable about licensing material for a medium they don't yet understand."[2]

Here is a law primer important not only for writers in this new medium, but also for designers and producers of multimedia. It was made available to the textbook by J. Dianne Brinson and Mark F. Radcliffe.

An Intellectual Property Law Primer for Multimedia Developers*

LICENSE NOTICE: This article may be copied in its entirety for personal or educational use (the copy should include a License Notice at the beginning and at the end). It may be posted on gopher and FTP sites, but please provide notice of such posting to the authors at the addresses below. It may not be modified without the written permission of the authors. This primer is based on the Multimedia Law Handbook which is designed to provide accurate information on the legal issues in multimedia. The primer is provided with the understanding that the authors are not engaged in rendering legal services. If you have a legal problem, you should seek the advice of experienced counsel.

BIOGRAPHIES

J. Dianne Brinson has a Bachelor of Arts in Political Science and Russian, summa cum laude, from Duke University and a law degree from Yale Law School. She is the author of a number of articles in the intellectual property field and is a former member of the Executive Committee of the Intellectual Property Section of the State Bar of California. She has practiced law at firms in Los Angeles and Atlanta. She is a former tenured law professor at Georgia State University and has taught at Golden Gate Law School and Santa Clara School of Law. She is now in private practice as a consultant in Menlo Park, California. She may be reached at laderapres@aol.com.

Mark F. Radcliffe is a partner in the law firm of Gray Cary Ware & Freidenrich in Palo Alto (formerly Ware & Freidenrich). He has been practicing intellectual property law, with a special emphasis on computer law, for over ten years, and has been chairman of the Computer Law Section of the Bar Association of San Francisco and the Computer Industry Committee of the Licensing Executives Society. He is a member of the Multimedia Law Group at Gray Cary Ware & Freidenrich and represents many multimedia developers and publishers. He has spoken on multimedia legal issues at the AAP, National Association of Broadcasters annual convention, Game Developers Workshop, Seybold San

Francisco, and IEEE. He has a Bachelor of Science in Chemistry, magna cum laude, from the University of Michigan, and a law degree from Harvard Law School. He is the author of the chapter on legal issues in the National Association of Broadcasters book Multimedia 2000. He has been quoted in the New York Times, Wall Street Journal and the San Francisco Examiner on legal issues and multimedia. He can be reached at mradcliffe@gcwf.com.

An understanding of legal issues is essential to success in the multimedia industry. Mistakes can cost the multimedia developer tens or even hundreds of thousands of dollars in legal fees and damages. Delrina lost hundreds of thousands of dollars and had to recall all of the copies of its screen saver last fall when it lost a copyright suit. Delrina distributed a screen saver in which one of the 30 modules showed the comic book character Opus shooting down Berkeley Systems' "flying toasters" (made famous in Berkeley's "After Dark" screen saver program). Berkeley Systems sued Delrina for copyright and trademark infringement. The court ruled for Berkeley Systems, prohibiting further distribution of Delrina's product and requiring Delrina to recall all of the product not already sold.

Two leading multimedia developers, Michael Saenz and Joe Sparks have been in court since the fall of 1993 in a dispute about the ownership of the copyright in their successful game, *Spaceship Warlock*. The dispute focuses on whether Joe was an employee or independent contractor of Reactor, Inc. (Mike Saenz's company) when they developed the game. If Joe is right in claiming that he was an independent contractor, he is co-owner of the copyright and has a right to half of the profits from the game. These profits could be worth hundreds of thousands of dollars.

This primer will help you understand the legal issues in developing and distributing multimedia works. It is based on the Multimedia Law Handbook from Ladera Press, which has been endorsed by the Interactive Multimedia Association. This summary of the law should not be viewed as "answering" most questions (the Multimedia Law Handbook discusses these issues in more detail in 340 pages and includes eighteen sample agreements to show how these issues are dealt with in actual transactions; you can order the book by calling 800-523-3721). Legal matters in multimedia are frequently complex and you should not rely on the information in this primer alone. You should consult with experienced counsel before making any final decisions. Multimedia products require a knowledge of the four major forms of intellectual property as well as the laws governing rights of publicity, defamation and libel.

There are four major intellectual property laws in the United States that are important for multimedia developers:

- Copyright law—Protects original "works of authorship."
- Patent law—Protects new, useful, and "nonobvious" inventions and processes.
- Trademark law—Protects words, names, and symbols used by manufacturers and businesses to identify their goods and services.

- Trade secret law—Protects valuable information not generally known that has been kept secret by its owner. This primer will focus on U.S. copyright law because copyright law is the most important of these laws for most multimedia developers and publishers.

COPYRIGHT LAW

There are two reasons why it is important for you as a multimedia developer or publisher to be familiar with the basic principles of copyright law:

Multimedia works are created by combining "content"—music, text, graphics, illustrations, photographs, software—that is protected under copyright law. Developers and publishers must avoid infringing copyrights owned by others.

Original multimedia works are protected by copyright. The Copyright Act's exclusive rights provision gives developers and publishers the right to control unauthorized exploitation of their works.

Copyright law is a "federal" law and the law does not vary from state to state (although the interpretation of the law may be different in different courts).

Basic Principles   This section summarizes the basic principles of copyright law, including the types of works that are protected by copyright, how copyright protection is obtained, and the scope of the protection.

Works Protected   Copyright protection is available for "works of authorship." The Copyright Act states that works of authorship include the following types of works which are of interest to the multimedia developer:

Literary works
Novels, nonfiction prose, poetry, newspaper articles and newspapers, magazine articles and magazines, computer software, software manuals, training manuals, manuals, catalogs, brochures, ads (text), and compilations such as business directories.

Musical works
Songs, advertising jingles, and instrumentals.
Dramatic works. Plays, operas, and skits.
Pantomimes and choreographic works.
Ballets, modern dance, jazz dance, and mime works.

Pictorial, graphic, and sculptural works
Photographs, posters, maps, paintings, drawings, graphic art, display ads, cartoon strips and cartoon characters, stuffed animals, statues, paintings, and works of fine art.

Motion pictures and other audiovisual works
Movies, documentaries, travelogues, training films and videos, television shows, television ads, and interactive multimedia works.

Sound recordings

Recordings of music, sounds, or words.

Obtaining Copyright Protection   Copyright protection arises automatically when an "original" work of authorship is "fixed" in a tangible medium of expression. Registration with the Copyright Office is optional (but you have to register before you file an infringement suit, and registering early will make you eligible to receive attorney's fees and statutory damages in a future lawsuit).

Here's what "original" and "fixed" mean in copyright law:

- **Originality:** A work is original in the copyright sense if it owes its origin to the author and was not copied from some preexisting work.
- **Fixation:** A work is "fixed" when it is made "sufficiently permanent or stable to permit it to be perceived, reproduced, or otherwise communicated for a period of more than transitory duration." Even copying a computer program into RAM has been found to be of sufficient duration for it to be "fixed" (although some scholars and lawyers disagree with this conclusion).

Neither the "originality" requirement nor the "fixation" requirement is stringent. An author can "fix" words, for example, by writing them down, typing them on an old-fashioned typewriter, dictating them into a tape recorder, or entering them into a computer. A work can be original without being novel or unique.

> Example: Betsy's book How to Lose Weight is original in the copyright sense so long as Betsy did not create her book by copying existing material—even if it's the millionth book to be written on the subject of weight loss.

Only minimal creativity is required to meet the originality requirement. No artistic merit or beauty is required.

A work can incorporate preexisting material and still be original. When preexisting material is incorporated into a new work, the copyright on the new work covers only the original material contributed by the author.

> Example: Developer's multimedia work incorporates a number of photographs that were made by Photographer (who gave Developer permission to use the photographs in the multimedia work). The multimedia work as a whole owes its origin to Developer, but the photographs do not. The copyright on the multimedia work does not cover the photographs, just the material created by Developer.

Scope of Protection   Copyright protects against "copying" the "expression" in a work as opposed to the idea of the work. The difference between "idea" and "expression" is one of the most difficult concepts in copyright law. The most important point to understand is that the protection of the "expression" is not limited to exact copying either of the literal words of a novel or the shape of a stuffed bear. Copyright infringement extends to new works which are "substantially similar."

A copyright owner has five exclusive rights in the copyrighted work:

- Reproduction Right. The reproduction right is the right to copy, duplicate, transcribe, or imitate the work in fixed form.
- Modification Right. The modification right (also known as the derivative works right) is the right to modify the work to create a new work. A new work that is based on a preexisting work is known as a "derivative work."
- Distribution Right. The distribution right is the right to distribute copies of the work to the public by sale, rental, lease, or lending.
- Public Performance Right. The public performance right is the right to recite, play, dance, act, or show the work at public place or to transmit it to the public. In the case of a motion picture or other audiovisual work, showing the work's images in sequence is considered "performance." Some types of works, such as sound recordings, do not have a public performance right.
- Public Display Right. The public display right is the right to show a copy of the work directly or by means of a film, slide, or television image at a public place or to transmit it to the public. In the case of a motion picture or other audiovisual work, showing the work's images out of sequence is considered "display."

In addition, certain types of works of "visual art" also have "moral rights" which limit the modification of the work and the use of the author's name without permission from the original author.

Anyone who violates any of the exclusive rights of a copyright owner is an infringer.

> Example: Developer scanned Photographer's copyrighted photograph, altered the image by using digital editing software, and included the altered version of the photograph in a multimedia work that Developer sold to consumers. If Developer used Photographer's photograph without permission, Developer infringed Photographer's copyright by violating the reproduction right (scanning the photograph), the modification right (altering the photograph), and the distribution right (selling the altered photograph in his work). A copyright owner can recover actual or, in some cases, statutory damages (which can be as high as $100,000 in some cases) from an infringer. In addition, courts have the power to issue injunctions (orders) to prevent or restrain copyright infringement and to order the impoundment and destruction of infringing copies.

The term of copyright protection depends on three factors: who created the work, when the work was created, and when it was first distributed commercially. For copyrightable works created on and after January 1, 1978, the copyright term for those created by individuals is the life of the author plus 50 years. The copyright term for "works made for hire" (see below) is 75 years from the date of first "publication" (distribution of copies to the general public) or 100 years from the date of creation, whichever expires first.

Generally, the copyright is owned by the person (or persons) who create the work. However, if the work is created by an employee within the scope of his or her employment, the employer owns the copyright because it is a "work for hire." The copyright law also includes another form of "work for hire": it applies only to certain types of works which are specially commissioned works. These works include audiovisual works, which will include most multimedia projects. In order to qualify the work as a "specially commissioned" work for hire, the creator must sign a written agreement stating that it is a "work for hire" prior to commencing development of the product (please note that this primer deals only with United States law; most foreign jurisdictions do not recognize the "specially commissioned" work for hire, and you need an assignment to transfer rights in those countries).

Avoiding Copyright Infringement   Current technology makes it fairly easy to combine material created by others—film and television clips, music, graphics, photographs, and text—into a multimedia product. The technical ease of copying these works does not give you the legal right to do so. If you use copyrighted material owned by others without getting permission you can incur liability for hundreds of thousands or even millions of dollars in damages.

Most of the third-party material you will want to use in your multimedia product is protected by copyright. Using copyrighted material without getting permission—either by obtaining an "assignment" or a "license"—can have disastrous consequences. The owner of the copyright can prevent the distribution of your product and obtain damages from you for infringement, even if you did not intentionally include his or her material. An assignment is generally understood to transfer all of the intellectual property rights in a particular work, although an assignment can be more limited in scope. A license provides the right to use a work and is generally quite limited. A discussion of the terms of licenses and assignments is beyond the scope of this primer; it requires several entire chapters in the Multimedia Law Handbook. Consider the following example:

> Productions, Inc. created an interactive multimedia training work called You Can Do It. The script was written by a freelance writer. You Can Do It includes an excerpt from a recording of Julie Andrews singing Climb Every Mountain. It ends with a photograph of Lauren Bacall shown above the words, "Good luck." In this example, if the Productions staff did not obtain permission to use the recording of Climb Every Mountain or the photo of Lauren Bacall, You Can Do It infringes three copyrights: the copyright on the song, the copyright on the Julie Andrews recording of the song, and the copyright on the photograph. Productions is also infringing Lauren Bacall's right of publicity (which is separate from copyright) by the commercial use of her image. Furthermore, if Productions did not acquire ownership of the script from the freelance writer, Productions does not have clear title to Do It, and distribution of Do It may infringe the writer's copyright in the script. Any of the copyright owners whose copyrights are infringed may be able to get a court order preventing further distribution of this multimedia product.

There are a number of myths out there concerning the necessity of getting a license. Here are five. Don't make the mistake of believing them:

- **Myth #1:**   "The work I want to use doesn't have a copyright notice on it, so it's not copyrighted. I'm free to use it."

Most published works contain a copyright notice. However, for works published on or after March 1, 1989, the use of copyright notice is optional. The fact that a work doesn't have a copyright notice doesn't mean that the work is not protected by copyright.

- **Myth #2:** "I don't need a license because I'm using only a small amount of the copyrighted work."

    It is true that de minimis copying (copying a small amount) is not copyright infringement. Unfortunately, it is rarely possible to tell where de minimis copying ends and copyright infringement begins. There are no "bright line" rules.

    Copying a small amount of a copyrighted work is infringement if what is copied is a qualitatively substantial portion of the copied work. In one case, a magazine article that used 300 words from a 200,000-word autobiography written by President Gerald Ford was found to infringe the copyright on the autobiography. Even though the copied material was only a small part of the autobiography, the copied portions were among the most powerful passages in the autobiography. Copying any part of a copyrighted work is risky. If what you copy is truly a tiny and nonmemorable part of the work, you may get away with it (the work's owner may not be able to tell that your work incorporates an excerpt from the owner's work). However, you run the risk of having to defend your use in expensive litigation. If you are copying, it is better to get a permission or a license (unless fair use applies). You cannot escape liability for infringement by showing how much of the protected work you did not take.

- **Myth #3:** "Since I'm planning to give credit to all authors whose works I copy, I don't need to get licenses."

    If you give credit to a work's author, you are not a plagiarist (you are not pretending that you authored the copied work). However, attribution is not a defense to copyright infringement.

- **Myth #4:** "My multimedia work will be a wonderful showcase for the copyright owner's work, so I'm sure the owner will not object to my use of the work."

    Don't assume that a copyright owner will be happy to have you use his or her work. Even if the owner is willing to let you use the work, the owner will probably want to charge you a license fee. Content owners view multimedia as a new market for licensing their material.

In 1993, ten freelance writers sued the New York Times and other publishers over the unauthorized publication of their work through online computer services. And the Harry Fox Agency and other music publishers have sued CompuServe, an online computer service, over the distribution of their music on the service.

- **Myth #5:** "I don't need a license because I'm going to alter the work I copy."

Generally, you cannot escape liability for copyright infringement by altering or modifying the work you copy. If you copy and modify protected elements of a copyrighted work, you will be infringing the copyright owner's modification right as well as the copying right.

When You Don't Need a License You don't need a license to use a copyrighted work in three circumstances: (1) if your use is fair use; (2) if the work you use is in the public domain; or (3) if the material you use is factual or an idea.

Fair Use You don't need a license to use a copyrighted work if your use is "fair use." Unfortunately, it is difficult to tell whether a particular use of a work is fair or unfair. Determinations are made on a case-by-case basis by considering four factors:

- **Factor #1:** Purpose and character of use. The courts are most likely to find fair use where the use is for noncommercial purposes, such as a book review.
- **Factor #2:** Nature of the copyrighted work. The courts are most likely to find fair use where the copied work is a factual work rather than a creative one.
- **Factor #3:** Amount and substantiality of the portion used. The courts are most likely to find fair use where what is used is a tiny amount of the protected work. If what is used is small in amount but substantial in terms of importance—the heart of the copied work—a finding of fair use is unlikely.
- **Factor #4:** Effect on the potential market for or value of the protected work. The courts are most likely to find fair use where the new work is not a substitute for the copyrighted work.

If your multimedia work serves traditional "fair use" purposes—criticism, comment, news reporting, teaching, scholarship, and research—you have a better chance of falling within the bounds of fair use than you do if your work is sold to the public for entertainment purposes and for commercial gain.

Public Domain You don't need a license to use a public domain work. Public domain works—works not protected by copyright—can be used by anyone. Because these works are not protected by copyright, no one can claim the exclusive rights of copyright for such works. For example, the plays of Shakespeare are in the public domain. Works enter the public domain in several ways: the term of the copyright may have expired, the copyright owner may have failed to "renew" his copyright under the old Copyright Act of 1909, or the copyright owner may have failed to properly use copyright notice (of importance only for works created before March 1, 1989, at which time copyright notice became optional). The rules regarding what works are in the public domain are too complex for this primer, and they vary from country to country.

Ideas or Facts You don't need a license to copy facts from a protected work or to copy ideas from a protected work. The copyright on a work does not extend to the work's facts. This is because copyright protection is limited to original works of authorship, and no one can claim originality or authorship for facts. You are free to copy facts from a copyrighted work.

Creating Your Own Works   Naturally, you don't need a copyright license for material which you create yourself. However, you should be aware that the rules regarding ownership of copyright are complex. You should not assume that you own the copyright if you pay an independent contractor to create the work (or part of it). In fact, generally the copyright in a work is owned by the individual who creates the work, except for full-time employees working within the scope of their employment and copyrights which are assigned in writing.

PATENT LAW

While copyright law is the most important intellectual property law for protecting rights in multimedia works, a multimedia developer needs to know enough about patent, trademark, and trade secret law to avoid infringing intellectual property rights owned by others and to be able to take advantage of the protection these laws provide.

Works Protected   Patent law protects inventions and processes ("utility" patents) and ornamental designs ("design" patents). Inventions and processes protected by utility patents can be electrical, mechanical, or chemical in nature. Examples of works protected by utility patents are a microwave oven, genetically engineered bacteria for cleaning up oil spills, a computerized method of running cash management accounts, and a method for curing rubber. Examples of works protected by design patents are a design for the sole of running shoes, a design for sterling silver tableware, and a design for a water fountain.

Obtaining Patent Protection   There are strict requirements for the grant of utility patents and design patents. To qualify for a utility patent, an invention must be new, useful, and "nonobvious." To meet the novelty requirement, the invention must not have been known or used by others in this country before the applicant invented it, and it also must not have been patented or described in a printed publication in the U.S. or a foreign country before the applicant invented it. The policy behind the novelty requirement is that a patent is issued in exchange for the inventor's disclosure to the public of the details of his invention. If the inventor's work is not novel, the inventor is not adding to the public knowledge, so the inventor should not be granted a patent.

To meet the nonobvious requirement, the invention must be sufficiently different from existing technology and knowledge so that, at the time the invention was made, the invention as a whole would not have been obvious to a person having ordinary skill in that field. The policy behind this requirement is that patents should only be granted for real advances, not for mere technical tinkering or modifications of existing inventions.

It is difficult to obtain a utility patent. Even if the invention or process meets the requirements of novelty, utility, and nonobviousness, a patent will not be granted if the invention was patented or described in a printed publication in the U.S. or a foreign country more than one year before the application date, or if the invention was in public use or on sale in the U.S. for more than one year before the application date.

Scope of Protection   A patent owner has the right to exclude others from making, using, or selling the patented invention or design in the United States during the term of the patent. Anyone who makes, uses, or sells a patented invention or design within the United States during the term of the patent without permission from the patent owner is an infringer—even if he or she did not copy the patented invention or design or even know about it.

> Example: Developer's staff members, working on their own, developed a software program for manipulating images in Developer's multimedia works. Although Developer's staff didn't know it, Inventor has a patent on that method of image manipulation. Developer's use of the software program infringes Inventor's patent.

Utility patents are granted for a period of 17 years. Design patents are granted for a period of 14 years. Once the patent on an invention or design has expired, anyone is free to make, use, or sell the invention or design.

TRADEMARK LAW

Trademarks and service marks are words, names, symbols, or devices used by manufacturers of goods and providers of services to identify their goods and services, and to distinguish their goods and services from goods manufactured and sold by others.

> Example: The trademark WordPerfect is used by the WordPerfect Corporation to identify that company's word processing software and distinguish that software from other vendors' word processing software.

For trademarks used in commerce, federal trademark protection is available under the federal trademark statute, the Lanham Act. Many states have trademark registration statutes that resemble the Lanham Act, and all states protect unregistered trademarks under the common law (nonstatutory law) of trademarks.

Availability of Protection   Trademark protection is available for words, names, symbols, or devices that are capable of distinguishing the owner's goods or services from the goods or services of others. A trademark that merely describes a class of goods rather than distinguishing the trademark owner's goods from goods provided by others is not protectible.

> Example: The word "corn flakes" is not protectible as a trademark for cereal because that term describes a type of cereal that is sold by a number of cereal manufacturers rather than distinguishing one cereal manufacturer's goods.

A trademark that so resembles a trademark already in use in the U.S. as to be likely to cause confusion or mistake is not protectible. In addition, trademarks that are "descriptive" of the functions, quality or character of the goods or services have special requirements before they will be protected.

Obtaining Protection   The most effective trademark protection is obtained by filing a trademark registration application in the Patent and Trademark Office. Federal law also protects unregistered trademarks, but such protection is limited to the geographic area in which the mark is actually being used. State trademark protection under common law is obtained simply by adopting a trademark and using it in connection with goods or services. This protection is limited to the geographic area in which the trademark is actually being used. State statutory protection is obtained by filing an application with the state trademark office.

Scope of Protection   Trademark law in general, whether federal or state, protects a trademark owner's commercial identity (goodwill, reputation, and investment in advertising) by giving the trademark owner the exclusive right to use the trademark on the type of goods or services for which the owner is using the trademark. Any person who uses a trademark in connection with goods or services in a way that is likely to cause confusion is an infringer. Trademark owners can obtain injunctions against the confusing use of their trademarks by others, and they can collect damages for infringement.

> Example: Small Multimedia Co. is selling a line of interactive training works under the trademark Personal Tutor. If Giant Multimedia Co. starts selling interactive training works under the trademark Personal Tutor, purchasers may think that Giant's works come from the same source as Small Multimedia's works. Giant is infringing Small's trademark.

TRADE SECRET LAW

A trade secret is information of any sort that is valuable to its owner, not generally known, and that has been kept secret by the owner. Trade secrets are protected only under state law. The Uniform Trade Secrets Act, in effect in a number of states, defines trade secrets as "information, including a formula, pattern, compilation, program, device, method, technique, or process that derives independent economic value from not being generally known and not being readily ascertainable and is subject to reasonable efforts to maintain secrecy."

Works Protected   The following types of technical and business information are examples of material that can be protected by trade secret law: customer lists; instructional methods; manufacturing processes; and methods of developing software. Inventions and processes that are not patentable can be protected under trade secret law. Patent applicants generally rely on trade secret law to protect their inventions while the patent applications are pending.

Six factors are generally used to determine whether information is a trade secret:

- The extent to which the information is known outside the claimant's business.
- The extent to which the information is known by the claimant's employees.
- The extent of measures taken by the claimant to guard the secrecy of the information.
- The value of the information to the claimant and the claimant's competitors.
- The amount of effort or money expended by the claimant in developing the information.
- The ease with which the information could be acquired by others.

Information has value if it gives rise to actual or potential commercial advantage for the owner of the information. Although a trade secret need not be unique in the patent law sense, information that is generally known is not protected under trade secrets law.

Obtaining Protection   Trade secret protection attaches automatically when information of value to the owner is kept secret by the owner.

Scope of Protection   A trade secret owner has the right to keep others from misappropriating and using the trade secret. Sometimes the misappropriation is a result of industrial espionage. Many trade secret cases involve people who have taken their former employers' trade secrets for use in new businesses or for new employers. Trade secret owners have recourse only against misappropriation. Discovery of protected information through independent research or reverse engineering (taking a product apart to see how it works) is not misappropriation.

Trade secret protection endures so long as the requirements for protection—generally, value to the owner and secrecy—continue to be met. The protection is lost if the owner fails to take reasonable steps to keep the information secret.

> Example: After Sam discovered a new method for manipulating images in multimedia works, he demonstrated his new method to a number of other developers at a multimedia conference. Sam lost his trade secret protection for the image manipulation method because he failed to keep his method secret.

RIGHTS OF PUBLICITY, LIBEL AND OTHER LAWS

In addition to the intellectual property laws discussed above, you must also be familiar with the several other areas of law that deal with the right of the individual to control his image and reputation. The right of publicity gives the individual the right to control his name, face, image or voice for commercial purposes. For example, Ford's advertising agency tried to persuade Bette Midler to sing during a Ford television commercial. She refused. They hired her backup singer. The performance of the backup singer was so similar to Bette Midler that viewers thought Bette Midler was singing. On the basis of that confusion, she sued and won $400,000 in damages.

Libel and slander protect an individual against the dissemination of false-hoods about that individual. To be actionable, the falsehood must injure his or her reputation or subject them to hatred, contempt or ridicule. The individual can obtain monetary losses as well as damages for mental anguish.

If you intend to use pre-existing material from television or film, you may also have to deal with the rights of entertainment unions to "re-use" fees. These unions include the Writers Guild, the Directors Guild, the Screen Actors Guild, American Federation of Musicians and the American Federation of Television and Radio Artists. Under the union agreements with the film and television studios, members of these unions and guilds who worked on a film or television program have a right to payment if the work is re-used. Although you as the multi-media developer are not signatory to these agreements and may not be directly liable for these payments, the license from the film and television studio generally makes you responsible for them. These payments are generally modest. How-ever, if you are using many clips these payments can become quite expensive.

If you use professional actors, directors or writers in developing your product, you will also need to deal with these unions. Most of the unions have very com-plex contracts developed specifically for their traditional film and television work. They are still trying to understand how to deal with the multimedia in-dustry, although both SAG and AFTRA have developed a special contract for multimedia projects. You should be aware that if you use professional talent, you should be prepared for the additional complexity arising out of these union agreements.

HYPOTHETICAL MULTIMEDIA WORK

This section will apply these legal rules to the creation and distribution of a new multimedia work based on a retrospective of the Academy Awards. The work is being created by a new company, Hollywood Productions. Its intended market is individuals and film students. It will be distributed on a CD-ROM and laser disk. The work will consist of the following elements:

- Videoclips from the Academy Award ceremonies.
- Magazine articles about the winning movies.
- Excerpts from various books about the awards and the film industry, includ-ing Final Cut, Reel Power, and History of American Film.
- Software to permit access to the material in numerous ways.
- Still photographs.
- Film clips of news programs and excerpts from winning motion pictures.
- New video works created by Hollywood Productions to explain basic film industry concepts.
- Music, including some of the hit songs from the winning motion pictures.

A. TEXT WORKS AND COMPUTER SOFTWARE

The magazine articles, the excerpts from the pre-existing books and the com-puter software may be treated differently from a legal point of view. Hollywood

Productions is creating the new text and the computer software. As the creator, it will probably own the copyright in those elements, either through the work-for-hire doctrine or assignments.

On the other hand, Hollywood Productions must go to the owners of the copyrights, or licensees of the copyrights, in the magazine articles (or perhaps the authors of the articles) and books to obtain the rights to use these materials in its work.

B. PHOTOGRAPHS

Copyrights in photographs are initially owned by the photographer, although they may either be assigned to another party or transferred to the photographer's employer under the work-for-hire doctrine. The determination of who owns the appropriate rights in the photograph can be very difficult and time consuming because of fragmentation in this industry. For example, the fact that a photograph appeared in Forbes does not necessarily mean that Forbes owns the copyright in the photograph. Forbes may only have a license to use it once in its magazine. Common limitations in the licensing of photographs include the color of reproduction, the medium (i.e. newspapers, magazines, etc.), and attribution as well as those relating to numbers of copies.

The rights required for an interactive multimedia work would be quite different from those which are normally granted to use photographs. For example, the photograph may appear several times throughout the work and the number of its appearances could be controlled by the viewer. Such flexibility is quite different from the rights traditionally granted in the photography industry.

C. FILM CLIPS AND VIDEOS

Once again, Hollywood Productions must distinguish between video which it has created (for which, if the legal issues were properly structured, it will own the copyrights) and those for which it needs to obtain rights. The "authors" of a videotape may include the actors, directors, scriptwriters, music composers and the cameramen. To avoid the problems of joint ownership of copyright, Hollywood Productions should obtain the appropriate agreements from the individuals who are creating its videotapes. The use of the videoclips from the ceremony may require multiple clearances including clearing the music used in the videoclip, obtaining the license from the copyright owner, paying reuse fees to the entertainment unions such as SAG and Directors Guild, and clearing the rights of publicity of the participants. In addition, if Hollywood Productions uses the "scripted" performances, it will have to pay reuse fees to the writers if they are members of the Writers Guild.

D. NEWS PROGRAMS AND OTHER STOCK FILM

Stock footage is available from "stock houses" in many cities. Materials available from stock houses range from historical footage of various locations to commercials. Other institutions, such as television stations, may also license their newscasts. These institutions generally base their royalty on the type of use of the film. For example, different royalties are due for use on national television or regional television. Since the multimedia work would not fit easily into any of these categories, Hollywood Productions would probably have to negotiate a special license with these institutions.

E. FEATURE FILMS

The use of feature films can be particularly complex and expensive. Feature films are frequently based on a novel whose use is licensed to the studio. The film may also use music developed by a third party. Consequently, the owner of the copyright in the film may not have the necessary rights to the music or the underlying novel to permit their use in the multimedia work. This situation is further complicated by provisions of the various motion picture industry guild agreements (such as the Screen Actors Guild and the Directors Guild of America) which require payment of fees upon incorporation of parts or portions of the film into another work. Hollywood Productions may also have to obtain rights of publicity releases from the individual actors depending on their contract with the studio.

F. MUSIC

To use music in the new work, Hollywood Productions may require obtaining rights from several different parties. The rights necessary depend on whether or not Hollywood Production records the music itself or wishes to use the performance of a third party. Since the music will frequently be sound tracks from a particular motion picture, Hollywood Productions will need to clear the rights to particular performances of the music. Rights in music are quite complicated. The rights which Hollywood Productions must consider obtaining are described below:

Mechanical Rights   Mechanical rights are the basic right to use a musical composition. They do not include the right to publicly perform the music (see below). A mechanical license also does not permit the use of the music with still or moving images. Such use requires a "synchronization" license (see below). Although copyright law provides a compulsory license for mechanical rights, most licensees prefer to obtain these rights commercially through the Harry Fox Agency or other similar agencies. This preference is based on the very onerous payment and accounting requirements imposed on the "compulsory" license in the Copyright Act.

Synchronization License   If the music is to be synchronized with still or moving images on a screen, the licensee must obtain a "synchronization" license. Although these rights may also be handled by the Harry Fox Agency, in some cases Hollywood Productions may need to contact the musical publisher directly.

Public Performance Rights   Hollywood Productions will probably also need a license for public performance because its multimedia work will be shown to students and other audiences. Such a showing would be considered a public performance. A performance is considered public if it is "open to the public" or at any place where a substantial number of persons outside of the "normal circle of family and social acquaintances" gather. Most music publishers permit either ASCAP or BMI to license their public performance rights. These rights do not apply to a particular performance by a particular individual or group to use the particular recording of a performance of the musical composition. Thus, obtaining a mechanical license to "Yesterday" would not permit Hollywood Productions to use the Beatles' performance of the song.

Right to a Particular Performance or Recording   As described above, if Hollywood Productions desires the musical composition to be performed by a particular group or individual, it must also obtain the right of the copyright holder in that particular performance. The licenses described above are limited solely to the right to use the musical composition. Thus, unless Hollywood Productions is prepared to have new artists record the music, it must negotiate with the holder of the rights to the particular performance which it desires to use. These rights are generally held by record companies.

CONCLUSION

An understanding of legal issues is critical to success in the multimedia industry. These issues are complex because of the youth of the industry and the many industries upon which it draws to create its products. The Multimedia Law Handbook, which has been endorsed by the Interactive Multimedia Association, provides a guide to these issues.

License Notice

This article may be copied in its entirety for personal or educational use (the copy should include a License Notice at the beginning and at the end). It may be posted on gopher and FTP sites, but please provide notice of such posting to the authors at the addresses above. It may not be modified without the written permission of the authors. This primer is based on the Multimedia Law Handbook which is designed to provide accurate information on the legal issues in multimedia. The primer is provided with the understanding that the authors are not engaged in rendering legal services. If you have a legal problem, you should seek the advice of experienced counsel.[*]

ENDNOTES

1. Tony Bove, interview with the author, October 3, 1995.
2. Ibid.

---

[*] Copyright 1994 by J. Dianne Brimson and Mark F. Radcliffe.

D Software for the Writer and Developer

Of the many software programs available to help writers compose scripts, only one specifically addresses interactive multimedia writing. StoryVision®, available for both Macs and IBM-compatible PCs, gives writers the ability to create a flowchart of an interactive program by drawing a diagram of its scenes and attaching text and/or graphics to these scenes in any format. When completed, the writer will have a detailed yet alterable plan for an interactive program.

No knowledge of computer programming or authoring is needed. StoryVision essentially makes use of the mouse and pull-down menus, allowing the writer to visualize and navigate the complex tapestry of scenes that make up an interactive program. Writers can thus create a blueprint for an interactive product, a map of interconnected scenes and segments—the equivalent of a screenplay for a linear motion picture. The software allows one to go from an overview flowchart to a specific part or scene with just a click of the mouse.

StoryVision can be used for interactive screenplays, video games, and CD-ROM titles for education or entertainment, as well as homepages and training programs. Both the Mac and PC versions sell for about $200. For more information, call 310-392-5090 or e-mail StoryVision@aol.com

One of the best resources for writers, linear or "interactive," is The Writer's Computer Store. Way back in 1982, this store was founded specifically to sell customized software and hardware for the literary and film industries. The store has two locations: Los Angeles (phone 310-479-7774) and Sausalito, CA (phone 415-332-7005). Below is just a partial list from the store's catalog of software programs for the script writer:

- *Movie Master:* Easy-to-use program for feature-film, sitcom, and stage-play formats. Can add scene numbers, break dialog with MORE and (CONT'D), and mark revisions and omissions. IBM, $195.00.

- *Scriptware:* Excellent program that easily formats as the script is typed with automatic page breaks, character name capitalization, and margin changes. Includes spell checker. Also good at importing scripts from word processor or exporting them. IBM/DOS compatible, the software now works in Windows, making it one of the best scriptwriting software on the market. $265.00, or $195.00 for *Scriptware Light.* Upgrade to Windows, $50.00.
- *Final Draft:* Similar to Scriptware, but available only for the Mac. It also exports detailed breakdown information to *MacToolkie Scheduling.* $249.00.
- *Side by Side:* Allows the writer to compose a multicolumn script, a format often used for interactive multimedia. $79.95.
- *Collaborator:* An analysis tool for writers as well as producers and directors. Questions are arranged to produce a story outline with the necessary elements: characters, plots, crises, etc. $199.00.
- *3 x 5:* Writers can organize ideas for a linear or an interactive script. Developed by the makers of *Final Draft,* this program is only available for the Mac. It categorizes, sorts, and prints scenes, notes, and plot twists onto index cards or in an outline form. It will also import pictures. $99.00.
- *Storyboard Quick:* You can communicate your shot ideas by pointing and clicking to place built-in characters as well as locations and props in the frame. Turn characters' positions, zoom in or out to create different views, resize, add text notes, scan in pictures. Mac or IBM, $199.00.
- *Storyboard Artist:* Takes *Storyboard Quick* a step further to give you motion and 3-D capabilities as well as the other features described in *Storyboard Quick.* Mac or IBM, $449.00.
- *Mockingbird®CBT:* This is an authoring software package designed specifically for creating interactive multimedia document libraries, help systems, courses, tests, and commercial titles for stand-alone or network delivery. It is of great use for writers and consultants working in computer-based training. Mac or Windows. For information on Mockingbird and other CBT software, contact Warren-Forthought, Inc., 1212 North Velasco, Angleton, TX, 77515; phone 409-849-1239.

My thanks to The Writers' Computer Store, *StoryVision,* and Warren-Forthought, Inc. for the material contained in this Appendix.

Glossary

alpha testing The first stage in testing a multimedia program, usually begins when the first prototype is ready for presentation.

analog system Sound or images are replicated via transmitted signals. These wavelike transmissions exhibit continuous fluctuations and various intensities of voltage or current.

animatic In multimedia prototyping, a scene-by-scene video of the storyboard, with each panel being videotaped for the number of seconds the images sketched in the panel will be on screen—often shown with a rough soundtrack.

application A software program that performs a specific task, such as word processing or database management.

ASCII American Standard Code for Information Interchange. A universally supported way for encoding characters using 8-bit pieces of data.

authoring Generally done during the final stage in the production of an interactive multimedia program. The "author" is essentially a programmer who brings together the variety of media elements used in an interactive piece by using either authoring software or a programming language.

authoring programs Software used to create computer applications.

authoring tools Interchangeable with authoring programs; authoring tools allow you to write hypertext or multimedia applications, enabling you to create a final application merely by linking together objects. Examples include Toolbook and Director.

bandwidth The measurement that indicates the data transmission capacity of a particular system. The more bandwidth, the more information can be transmitted in real time.

beta testing A period near the end of software development when problems are worked out before the software is released to the general public.

bitraking Internet-based investigative reporting, where a journalist or other writers search the Internet for breaking stories, information, ideas, and gossip.

blue screen The blue screen process involves shooting in a studio against a large blue backdrop, allowing the background to be superimposed on the final image during postproduction. The actors literally have to imagine the setting they are in and be very aware of the limitations of movement.

branches   The pathways one can take within a multimedia program.

broadband   A network in which bandwidth can be shared by a number of simultaneous signals—for instance, both cable TV and telephone lines.

broadcasting   A top-to-bottom system whereby a small number of programmers decide what the viewers will watch and send programs to viewers over the air.

broadcatch   Phrase coined by Stewart Brand that means a new delivery system sends information and programming digitally to the viewer/user who then decides what to view—a system that offers much more control than broadcasting to users.

browser   A tool used to access and display files on the Internet.

bug   A problem in hardware or software. Sometimes caused by incompatibility of systems being used.

CD-I   Compact Disc Interactive—a format for storing different types of information (graphics, video, sound, text, etc.) on a compact disc compatible with a CD player that hooks directly into one's television set. Designed to be an "information terminal" rather than a workstation such as a computer.

CD-ROM   Compact Disc Read-Only Memory. CD-ROMs can today store about 650 MB of data digitally and CD-ROM drives are attached to or part of a computer.

close-up (CU)   A camera shot that closely examines and/or emphasizes some detail on either a person or an inanimate object.

content outline   A list of specifications of what will actually be included in the project. The production people will not necessarily know anything about the content until they read this outline.

copyright   The exclusive legal right to the representation, sale, or screening of a multimedia work.

cyberspace   Phrase coined by William Gibson and other writers of "cyberpunk" science fiction, which entails a digital world or alternate reality—a mass hallucinatory world or experience where millions "plug in" and get "connected" through everything from e-mail and the Internet to *immersive VR*, which makes people feel as if they are literally experiencing another place.

digital   Devices or circuits in which the signals are represented as a series of on/off impulses in bits that do not degrade.

digital audio   True digitized audio almost duplicates reality. A computer sends commands to a CD-ROM drive.

digitize   To convert or represent data (such as images, sounds, text) in digital form.

DVD (digital video disk)   A new compact-disc format with resolution three times that of a VHS player. The same size as a CD-ROM disc, the DVD can store a two-hour movie or about seven times the computer information stored on a conventional CD-ROM on just one side.

edutainment   Combining educational information with exciting and/or entertaining ways of presenting it.

electronic word   Online conversations, books, and/or information available online or on CD-ROM.

evaluation tools   The tools used to test a program within the company and with the public at large.

EXT. (Exterior)   Indicates that a scene takes place outside. Used in scene headings in a script, always abbreviated in capital letters with a period.

Fade In   Traditionally the first phrase in a motion-picture screenplay describing the opening image of a film, the transition from black screen to image.

flowchart   A map of steps to complete a task or find information within a multimedia program.

focus groups   Small groups in which a facilitator encourages the participants to discuss the product, its negative and positive aspects, and why someone liked or didn't like the product.

full-motion video boards   Boards that digitize and then compress multiple frames and store them in a PC. This allows for special effects.

graphics adapter   Allows a PC to display computer-generated text and graphics, scanned images, and animation—links PC to monitor.

hard disc   The device within the computer that contains the information and programs. Hard discs range in size from 20 megabytes to several gigabytes of information.

HTML   Hypertext Mark-up Language; a simple set of commands that describe how a document is structured. Includes the coding of screen documents for headers, objects, buttons, and hyperlinks to allow for the formation of documents to specific screen systems.

hyperfiction   Online text that any number of people can become involved with, either as participants, readers, or writers.

hyperlinking   Nonlinear navigation through information.

hypermedia   As with *hypertext,* the user can jump from point to point, moving from a written word to a graphic or a moving image and vice versa by use of a pointing device.

hypertext   A nonlinear system for information storage, management, and retrieval whereby links between associative information can be created and subsequently activated and (often) manipulated. The concept behind hypertext was extended in recent years to include images and audio material which, in turn, became known as *hypermedia.*

icon   A sign or other representation that stands for something by virtue of a resemblance or analogy to it.

immersive VR   Virtual reality in which people's senses make them feel as if in another place, a world inside a computer or in cyberspace.

information superhighway   The digital roadways through the Internet/Web and, ultimately, through all of cyberspace.

infotainment   Information that is clear and understandable while also being entertaining and exciting.

INT. (Interior)   Indicates that a particular scene will be shot inside. Used in scene headings, always abbreviated in capital letters with a period.

interactive video   Gives the user the ability to move and control the image on the video screen (or television screen, or monitor). An early example is *Pong.*

interface   The method by which the user will interact with the screen: objects the user will be able to click on to move around, etc.

Internet   A "network of networks," a decentralized global network linking computers for the exchange of news, data, and ideas.

menu   Allows you to select, either through pictures or words, where you want to move through the program.

metaphor   The application of a word or phrase to an object or concept that it does not literally denote, in order to suggest comparison with another object or concept, as in "a mighty fortress is our God."

MIDI   Musical Instrument Digital Interface, it has no intrinsic sound of its own. It is through the MIDI that electronic musical instruments can communicate with both the computer and each other. The MIDI will receive a string of computer commands and then create the sound from a group of preset sounds that are then played through speakers.

motherboard   The main circuit board for a computer, which contains the CPU, slots for expansion boards, and memory installation.

multimedia   The combination of audio, video, text, graphics, and/or animation; a new medium combining a number of older media.

Net   Abbreviation for the *Internet.*

New Hollywood   Entertainment-industry power shift from the traditional linear motion picture and television venue to the interactive multimedia arena.

nodes   Stopping points on a path, information screens, or segments.

nonlinear editing   Editing done from images stored digitally on a PC's hard drive that can be manipulated, making this process much easier than linear editing.

object orientation   Makes complicated operations accessible through pointing and clicking with a mouse or some other device.

O.C. or O.S. (Off Camera or Off Screen)   Sounds or dialog heard while the camera is on another subject. Off Camera is used in three-camera television or video productions.

pathways   Links from screen to screen within a multimedia program.

plot   One of the basic elements of good screenplay structure, the plan of action of a story. For example: the plot of *Frankenstein* is "a man creates life from nonlife." Plot often is the structure of a screenplay, particularly interactive screenplays.

The plot is made up of scenes, challenges, crises, etc., which move the story along.

plot point   An action taken or circumstance created that moves a story in a certain direction.

pop-ups   Visual or audio cues that appear at certain points during an interactive piece. With visual cues, the viewer/user usually can click on the image with a mouse or other pointing device to receive more information.

producer   Person in charge of the financing and coordination of all activities in connection with the production of a software or CD-ROM title.

production integration   When everything is shot or animated and edited, and the material is combined and plugged in with everything else: text, graphics, audio material, still images, etc.

program   Set of instructions written in a computer language that tells the computer how and when to manipulate data.

prototype   A model of what a final interactive multimedia program might look like and entail. Many potential designs and ideas can be explored during the prototype phase. Prototypes can be a simple storyboard, a flowchart, or a simple computer simulation of what the final program might look like.

quicktalk   Dialog as sound bites; the shortest number of words needed to get a point across; currently necessary for a lot of multimedia due to finite amount of space on a disc.

real time   The speed of the computer corresponds to the speed of the user; in other words, there is no delay in the response time of the computer, and the user has the impression of an instantaneous response.

screenplay format   A script format that conforms to what is generally accepted in Hollywood for feature films and one-hour television shows—one page equals approximately one minute of film or video.

split page format   Script format sometimes used for television and video production whereby the visual and audio portion of the script is divided into separate columns on the page.

sprocketware   Term for Hollywood taking a movie and attempting to repackage it as multimedia.

stealth education   A situation where your audience (usually children) might not necessarily realize they are being taught something by a program; *edutainment*.

story   The telling of an event, or what happens. The story of *Frankenstein* is "an undead being is created who longs for love and feels alone and hated, etc."

storyboard   Essentially an attempt to indicate the shots in a motion picture or a multimedia piece on paper in picture form.

symbol   An object used to represent something that doesn't necessarily resemble what it is representing. For example, an eagle symbolizes the United States.

teleplay or **video format**   Script format often used for television sitcoms, it presents much visual information about a scene; is usually in a split-page format.

terminal objective   What it is developers want a project to do, what they want it to tell the user, etc. For CBT programs, the terminal objective determines what the user will be able to do when the course is completed, what they walk away with from the program.

URL   Uniform resource locator, which is the global address of documents and other resources on the Internet.

VGA   Video graphics array, the standard for display.

videoactive   A program made for television that the audience can interact with; for interactive television.

video adapters   Adapters that accept input from a variety of video sources that use NTSC (National Television Standard Committee) standards—can convert analog video from a VCR to digital video, which then lets one display the image on a PC monitor.

video capture boards   These "frame grabbers" let one digitize a single frame from an NTSC source and store it on a hard disc.

waveform audio   Digital, waveform audio is stored in a form that a PC can understand and manipulate, allowing sound to be created by digitizing an analog audio waveform and then storing the digital sample on a disc.

working draft A working draft, according to Tony Bove, consists of callouts for images (using *PhotoCD* ID numbers and descriptive names), music loops (filenames with designations for different sampling rates), and tangents with either high-resolution images or digital video movies (filenames with indicators).

World Wide Web WWW, a global hypertext system that arranges Internet information as a series of menus or screens that allow the user to jump from one linked document to another.

Selected Bibliography

Books

Ambron, Susan, and Hooper, Kristina. *Interactive Multimedia: Visions of Multimedia for Developers, Educators, and Information Providers.* Redmond, WA: Microsoft Press, 1988.

Anderson, Carol J., and Veljikov, Mark D. *Creating Interactive Multimedia: A Practical Guide.* Glenville, IL: Scott, Foresman, 1990.

Apple Computer, Inc. *Multimedia Demystified.* Edited by Randy Haykin. New York: Random House/New Media, 1994.

Aristotle. *On Poetics.* Edited by Robert Maynard Hutchins. Chicago: Encyclopedia Britannica and University of Chicago, 1952.

Aston, Robert, and Schwartz, Joyce. *Multimedia: Gateway to the Next Millennium.* Cambridge, MA: Academic Press, 1994.

Blacker, Irwin R. *The Elements of Screenwriting: A Guide for Film and Television Writing.* New York: Macmillan, 1986.

Bolter, Jay David. *Writing Space: The Computer, Hypertext, and the History of Writing.* Hillsdale, NJ: Erlbaum, 1991.

Brand, Stewart. *The Media Lab: Inventing the Future at M.I.T.* New York: Penguin Books, 1987.

Brestoff, Richard. *The Camera Smart Actor.* Lyme, NH: Smith and Kraus, 1994.

Burr, Keith, and Gillis, Joseph. *The Screen Writer's Guide.* New York: New York Zoetrope Books, 1982.

Clute, John. *Science Fiction: The Illustrated Encyclopedia.* London: Dorling Kindersley, 1995.

Delany, Paul, and Landow, George P., eds. *Hypermedia and Literary Studies.* Cambridge, MA: The MIT Press, 1991.

Ellison, Harlan. *The Glass Teat.* New York: Pyramid Books, 1975.

Ellison, Harlan. "Introduction." In *Omni's Screen Flights/Screen Fantasies: The Future According to Science Fiction Cinema.* Edited by Danny Peary. New York: Doubleday, 1984.

Field, Syd. *Screenplay: The Foundations of Screenwriting.* New York: Dell, 1982.

Field, Syd. *The Screenwriter's Workbook.* New York: Dell, 1984.

Gilder, George. *Life After Television: The Coming Transformation of Media and American Life.* New York: Norton, 1992.

Goldman, William. *Hype & Glory.* New York: Villard Books, 1990.

Gross, Lynne S. *Telecommunications: An Introduction to Electronic Media.* Dubuque, IA: Brown, 1992.

Hahn, Harley, and Stout, Rick. *The Internet Complete Reference.* Berkeley, CA: Osborne McGraw-Hill, 1994.

Halpern, Paul. *Time Journeys: A Search for Cosmic Destiny and Meaning.* New York: McGraw-Hill, 1990.

Hofstetter, Fred T. *Multimedia Literacy.* New York: McGraw-Hill, 1995.

Holsinger, Erik. *How Multimedia Works.* Emeryville, CA: Ziff-Davis, 1994.

Huxley, Aldous. *Brave New World* and *Brave New World Revisited.* New York: Harper & Row, 1932, 1960.

Jacobson, Linda, ed. *Cyberarts: Exploring Arts and Technology.* San Francisco: Miller Freeman, 1992.

King, Stephen. *Stephen King's Danse Macabre.* New York: Berkley Books, 1981.

Lanham, Richard A. *The Electronic Word: Democracy, Technology, and the Arts.* Chicago: University of Chicago Press, 1993.

McKibben, Bill. *The Age of Missing Information.* New York: Penguin Books, 1992.

Melville, Herman. *Moby-Dick or, The Whale.* New York: Norton, 1976.

Mirabito, Michael. *The New Communications Technologies.* Newton, MA: Focal Press, 1994.

Negroponte, Nicholas. *being digital.* New York: Knopf, 1995.

Postman, Neil. *Amusing Ourselves to Death: Public Discourse in the Age of Show Business.* New York: Penguin Books, 1985.

Postman, Neil. *Technopoly: The Surrender of Culture to Technology.* New York: Vintage Books, 1992.

Rushkoff, Douglas. *Cyberia: Life in the Trenches of Hyperspace.* San Francisco: HarperCollins, 1995.

Simon, John. *Reverse Angle: A Decade of American Films.* New York: Potter, 1982.

Talbott, Stephen L. *The Future Does Not Compute: Transcending the Machines in Our Midst.* Sebastopol, CA: O'Reilly & Associates, 1995.

Periodicals

Barcott, Bruce. "Second Thoughts on the Virtual Life." *The Seattle Weekly,* July 19, 1995, 17.

Diller, Barry. "Don't Repackage—Redefine!" *Wired,* February 1995, 82–84.

Gelman, Robert, and Melville, Kenneth. "On the Trail of the Interactive Grail: A Road Map for Would-be Script Writers." *Interactivity* magazine, January 1996, 57–59.

Gussin, Lawrence. "CD-ROM Publishing, Education, and Boom Years Ahead." *CD-ROM Professional,* June 1995, 58–70.

Lombardi, Doug. "Enhanced CDs—The Sound of Things to Come?" *CD-ROM Today,* August 1995, 30–35.

Platt, Charles. "Interactive Entertainment: Who Writes It? Who Reads It? Who Needs It?" *Wired,* September 1995, 145–149, 195–197.

Sawyer, Brian and Vourlis, John. "Screenwriting Structures for New Media." *Creative Screenwriting,* Summer 1995, 95–103.

Snow, Richard F. "American Heritage On-Line." *American Heritage,* July–August 1995, 7.

Ulanoff, Lance. "The Top 100 CD-ROMs." *PC* magazine, June 27, 1995, 102–165.

Wiggins, Richard. "The Word Electric." *Internet World* magazine, September 1995, 31–34.

Williams, Roberta. "On Phantasmagoria." *Interaction,* Spring 1995, 30–37.

Unpublished or Internet Writings

Chris James, "Navigation for Interactive Multimedia: An Introduction," January 1994, paper for Media Communication and Technology Department, Bellevue Community College.

McDonald, Rand; Moore, Amanda; Wieczorek, John; and Wolcott, Bruce. "The Rebirth Project: Brief history of an independently developed interactive multimedia presentation." Created specifically for this text, 1995.

Rohrer, Tim. "A Brief Paper on Metaphor Generation," Internet, April 1995 (by permission of the author).

Interviews

Anker, Andrew. Personal interview. August 6, 1995.

Asimov, Isaac. Personal interview. April 1977.

Bakken, Theolene. Personal interview. September 1, 1995.

Benton, Jim. Personal interview. February 6, 1996.

Bove, Tony. Personal interview. October 3, 1995.

Bull, Emma. Personal interview. September 26, 1995.

Catalano, Frank. Personal interview. September 2, 1995.

Conrad, Steven. Personal interview. February 9, 1996.

Davis, Rhonda. Personal interview. October 8, 1995.

Furness, Thomas. Personal interview. October 1993.

_____. Personal interview. October 1995.

Gaiman, Neil. Personal interview. September 11, 1995.

Gottlieb, Lynn. Personal interview. July 1995.

Johnson-Evers, Leslie. Personal interview. September 12, 1995.

Lowe, Al. Personal interview. August 1995.

Machala, Janis. Personal interview. September 1995.

Miller, Drew. Personal interview. September 22, 1995.

Palwick, Susan. Personal interview. September 10, 1995.

Saffo, Paul. Personal interview. October 24, 1995.

Schmults, Rob. Personal interview. August 29, 1995.

Shannon, Lorelei. Personal interview. July 1995.

Shapiro, Alex. Personal interview. June 29, 1995.

Sherman, Delia. Personal interview. September 10, 1995.

Shetterly, William. Personal interview. September 13, 1995.

Shuman, James. Personal interview. September 18, 1995.

Waldman, Helayne. Personal interview. March 1994.

Weston, Terry. Personal interview. January 18, 1996.

Windling, Terri. Personal interview. October 5, 1995.

Wolcott, Bruce. Personal interview. August 1995.

Worley, Robin. Personal interview. July 1995.

Zaslow, Ruth. E-mail to the author. February 26, 1996.

INDEX